Gay
Cops

Gay Cops

STEPHEN LEINEN

RUTGERS
UNIVERSITY
PRESS

New Brunswick
New Jersey

Library of Congress Cataloging-in-Publication Data

Leinen, Stephen H.
Gay cops / Stephen Leinen.
p.   cm.
Includes bibliographical references and index.
ISBN 0-8135-2000-2
1. Gay police—United States—Social conditions.   2. Gay police—
United States—Attitudes.   3. Homosexuality—United States.
I. Title.

HV8138.L353   1993
363.2'08'664—dc20   93-9216
                                                            CIP

British Cataloging-in-Publication information available

Book design by Liz Schweber

Eleven years after Charlie Cochrane made his public declaration before City Hall spawning the Gay Officers Action League, the uphill battle for acceptance of gays on the police force was rewarded. On June 9, 1992, a GOAL monthly meeting was called to order with the mayor of New York City in attendance.

Contents

	Acknowledgments	ix
	Preface	xi
One	Introduction: "Gay and Proud of It"	1
Two	Recruiting Gay Cops	7
Three	Taking on a Doubly Deviant Identity	16
Four	What It Means to Be Gay and a Cop	32
Five	Staying in the Closet	46
Six	Coming Out Tentatively at Work	72
Seven	Coming Out Publicly at Work	97
Eight	The Off-Duty World of Gay Cops	122
Nine	Coming Out to Family	175
Ten	Summary: The Challenge of Coming Out	194
Appendixes	Entering the World of the Gay Officer	217
	Profile of Officers	231
	Notes	235
	Index	243

Acknowledgments

First and foremost, I would like to express my gratitude to Ed Schur for his suggestions, contributions, and support; to Dave Greenberg for his feedback and encouragement; to Dave Caplovitz for his constructive criticism; and especially to Pat Jenkins, who spent countless hours reviewing and commenting on earlier drafts of this work and to whom I turned for advice when I needed a precise word or phrase to explain my thoughts.

Special thanks are due to Bernard Cohen, who has been both mentor and friend to me over the past fifteen years. For this project, Dr. Cohen not only offered support, as he has done in the past, but provided critical insights into the deviance-defining process in the police world.

Finally, I owe a special debt of gratitude to the anonymous men and women who took time out of their personal lives to tell me what it was to be a homosexual police officer. This debt is extended personally to Sam Ciccone, who responded to the many questions that surfaced from the interviews. It was from Sam that I gained a political perspective on the process of coming out as a way of managing stigma.

Preface

Over the past two decades homosexuality has become a major social issue. The subject has triggered protests, counterprotests, and the formation of hundreds of activist groups across the country organized to liberate gays from the laws, public policies, and attitudes that have relegated them to a deviant status in U.S. society and subjected them to persecution and penal sanctions. Largely as a result of the activities of vocal homosexual groups, legal and social restrictions have eased and tolerance toward homosexuals has grown in some social circles. Nevertheless, many individuals of homosexual orientation continue to live and work in environments essentially hostile to them and their choice of life-style. This is especially true for those who work in occupations without a traditional link to homosexuality. The disclosure or even the suspicion of being gay in some circles can expose a person to a variety of negative sanctions and censure.

Of all the occupations seemingly antithetical to homosexuality perhaps none is more so than law enforcement, a profession that traditionally symbolizes the essence of manliness. Cops are expected to present an aura of toughness and aggressiveness. They are expected to demonstrate courage, bravery, and confidence. Above all, male cops are expected to avoid the appearance of femininity. The police also tend to see themselves as upholders of society's social and moral order and to view homosexuals as a serious threat to that order. Perhaps more importantly from a police occupational point of view, gay men are thought to possess traits (e.g., insecurity, effeminacy, and oversensitivity) that prevent them from carrying out police work and to lack the emotional requirements that cops have come to believe will protect them from the dangers inherent in policing, such as courage, bravery, and loyalty to their fellow officers. That gays are, or aspire to become, police officers is seen by many in the police profession as paradoxical. Yet despite this apparent incompatibility there is evidence that gays are entering the world of law enforcement in growing numbers.

In this book I look at the worlds of homosexual men and women who have chosen policing as a career. I examine the subjects of being gay, of being a cop, and of how one status affects the other. While

I will consider a number of substantive issues involving gays in law enforcement, my central aims are to explore the conflict experienced by people whose occupation appears at odds with their sexual orientation and life-style, to identify the social identities gay cops present to others at work and in their private lives, and to analyze how gay cops manage their identities to cope with conflict. Then I look at the implications of these strategies and decisions for the work and private lives of gay officers in New York and other metropolitan areas.

I hope that readers of this book will come to understand what it means to be both gay and a cop in today's society. Beyond that, I hope that this work enables gay men and women who have chosen policing as a career to make more informed choices about coming out of the closet at work.

Gay
Cops

One

Introduction: "Gay and Proud of It"

It's a big turn-on to people. They love it. They eat it up. The uniform, the authority, the image. You are on a very high pedestal as a rule. Guys like to say they went home and went to bed with a cop. That's hot. It's the fantasy thing to have a relationship, to have sex with a policeman.

It's my nightmare that something happens when I'm in a gay setting and either I lose the gun and the shield or something happens like I'm assaulted or robbed and I have to go inside and report it. It's not a comfortable situation, but it's something we have to deal with all the time. If you're going to be in the life-style and be a cop in the city, it's something you have to prepare yourself for. If you don't you're a fool.

n the course of this investigation, I would learn that gay cops live with both the thrills and the dangers of dual identity—the turn-ons and the nightmares. But the last thing on my mind on November 22, 1981, was the question of what problems face homosexual men and women who choose policing as a career. I got home from work that evening, kicked off my shoes, and settled down to watch the six o'clock news. That's when Charlie Cochrane came into my life, and that's when I first began to think of studying gay cops. Cochrane, a sergeant in the New York City Police Department, was testifying before a city council committee *in favor* of a gay rights bill. That, in itself, was enough to attract my attention. But after reading from a prepared text, Cochrane further surprised me and those in his audience by announcing that he himself was gay "and proud of it."[1] I recall my stunned reaction at hearing for the first time a member of the police department publicly expose this controversial facet of his personal life that would, no doubt, subject him to ridicule and harassment or even isolation from his fellow officers. I wondered, as Cochrane continued to speak, what prompted his startling disclosure. More importantly, what impact would this public sharing of his sexual orientation have on other gay NYPD cops who were still "closeted" at work? It was unrealistic to think that Cochrane was the only homosexual officer in the department, although, at that time, I had neither known nor heard about other gay cops in New York City. Would Cochrane's public and visibly proud declaration of his homosexuality provide other gay cops with the courage to "come out" as he had just done? Or, in spite of Cochrane's revelations, would these cops continue to remain in the closet, fearing the stigma and negative reactions disclosure might bring? Or would some of these gays choose to take a wait-and-see attitude?

The more I reflected on the possibility of a "homosexual element" in the NYPD, the more intrigued I became about the possibility of studying such a group. I was certain that those cops who would intentionally reveal their sexual preferences in the workplace, or who were discovered or just suspected of being homosexual, would confront rejection and discrimination similar to what blacks had experienced as newcomers to the police community in the early 1970s. The difference, however, is that sexual orientation cuts across gender, ethnic, and racial lines, and in the situation of gay cops, the bigots were as likely to be black as white. Of course, one crucial element was missing in the situation of the gay officer as an object of discrimination; homosexuals have the option of remaining anonymous. Because there is nothing inherently visible that sets them apart from their straight colleagues, homosexuals are not compelled to expose this potentially discrediting stigma to others. Given the history of irrational abuses blacks and other minorities suffered in policing and the stigma still attached to homosexuals in this society, disclosure at work seemed to me an unappealing choice for most gay men and women.

Such reflections prompted me to contact Sergeant Cochrane. He wasn't very encouraging at first, but later he introduced me to GOAL (Gay Officers Action League) which he had helped form and which he had served as president. That connection allowed me to meet many gay cops.

Although many heterosexual police officers believe that gay men project an effeminate demeanor—that they walk and talk like women—I found otherwise. Most gay men appear just as masculine as straight men, while most lesbians are no less feminine than heterosexual women.[2] My own direct observations—at GOAL meetings and associated gay social functions where I could observe many more gay officers beyond those interviewed—also contradict these myths. Not one of the men I interviewed or observed in public or private settings either spoke, dressed, or behaved in an effeminate or affected manner. These observations are partly supported by a reporter for a local newspaper who attended a recent GOAL Christmas party. "Though the room was full of swishy guys," she wrote, "they were all cops' dates or prospective dates, not members of the force themselves."[3] Many of the lesbians I interviewed appeared quite feminine. Also, in my own twenty-three years of service as a New York City police officer, I never saw an overtly effeminate male officer in any of the commands to which I was assigned (I have, however, observed a few masculine-looking female officers). The totally closeted gay police in New York City have, for the most part, succeeded in remaining invisible not only to their heterosexual colleagues but to many of their homosexual ones. As one of the men I interviewed said when he found out his partner was also gay:

I was deeply shocked when he told me. We had worked together for over three years and neither of us knew about the other. He said, "How the hell could we have worked together for so long and neither one of us knew it?"

Members of this extremely "inner-closeted" group have taken great pains to appear as conventional as possible and to behave on the job exactly like their straight brother and sister officers. This is especially so for the closeted gay men in the NYPD, who tend to adopt, as Charlie Cochrane once said, "a form of exaggerated machismo to hide what they are, to protect themselves."[4]

I was able to interview forty-one of the gay cops I met through GOAL—twenty-eight men and thirteen women. Of the forty-one, twenty-seven were white, seven were Hispanic, and seven were black. Gaining their trust was a long and difficult process, the details of which I describe in appendix 1, where I also discuss the advantages I had as a retired police lieutenant studying my former peers and the ethical dilemmas I faced as a heterosexual studying homosexuals, among them some early hostility I came up against, my concern about contracting AIDS, and the delicate diplomacy required in social situations.

For example, early in the project I gave some thought to how I would handle a sexual advance made by a member of GOAL. As there was no standard way of dealing with such an awkward situation I decided that should the occasion arise, I would try to reject the advance in a way that would not publicly embarrass the man who made it. The predicament arose at dinner party attended by GOAL members and their guests while I was in the kitchen helping with the cooking and serving. At one point I was putting spareribs into a microwave oven when I felt two arms reach around my waist in a friendly though uncomfortable manner. I glanced over my shoulder and saw that the arms belonged to a man in his early fifties whom I had met earlier that evening for the first time. He was neither a member of GOAL nor a police officer but had come as someone's guest. When we had been introduced, no one had mentioned my research or my sexual orientation. As I turned to face him, he released his hold on my waist, smiled, and commented that he preferred his ribs well done. From the expression on his face I assumed this response was meant to indicate his age preference in sexual partners. I stepped aside and matter-of-factly agreed to cook his portion of the ribs a little longer, pretending I did not understand the double entendre. My action did not seem to offend him, and he made no further advances toward me that evening.

Once I knew I could find and talk to gay cops, I decided to focus on their conflicting identities as police officers and as gay men and women. Do they conceal the stigma of homosexuality? We know that many gays try to conceal their sexual differentness from their work associates. One study, for example, reports that in a sample of almost five thousand homosexuals recruited as potential respondents from the Bay Area in San Francisco (an area known to be more accepting of homosexuals), more than half the men and about two-thirds of the women believed that their employers and co-workers *did not* know or suspect that they were homosexual. An earlier study that targeted male homosexuals found that 30 percent of the gays they looked at concealed their homosexuality from *all* straights and an additional 38 percent from *most* straights. Homosexuals looking to conceal their stigma at work may construct false biographies or present only selective aspects of themselves to others. For example, secret homosexuals may maintain staged relationships with members of the opposite sex, engage in stag talk with men at work, wear wedding bands, denounce gays at appropriate times, and cultivate speech patterns designed to misinform others about their true sexual preferences.[5]

I knew there were some gays who decided to "let on to a few" by selective disclosure or by leaving clues around that drew attention to their preference. Gays may pass discreditable information to "safe others" such as close friends, select work associates, and family members. To come out to a select group of others serves a number of functions for the gay cop. For some it is a form of therapy to share or diffuse the burden of feelings about their situation; for others it allows relationships to be tested in their early stages. Partial disclosure can also be less direct. The gay cop can, for example, choose not to tell the entire truth, leaving the suspicion intact or even strengthening it. Zoglin, the author of an article on homosexuality, quotes one gay man who assumes this stance: "If people ask me about girls, I just say that I don't date much, or I joke that I'm too old to get around anymore [he is thirty]. When I go to parties I'll often go alone."[6] If testing the waters with a select group brings only negative reactions, concealment begins to look safer. Other gays decide to disclose their homosexuality at opportune times while trying to change the way people think about this sexual orientation. A gay cop may simply announce his or her homosexuality, as Cochrane did. Or the cop may wear a symbol that draws attention to homosexuality, such as a lapel button supporting gay rights.

Once out in the open, gay cops no longer have to manage information about their homosexuality, but they do have to manage uncomfortable social situations. They may downplay the stereotypical features of homosexuality by avoiding promiscuous behavior and by using conventional speech habits and mannerisms.

As I studied the world of the gay police officer, I found all of these strategies. I have organized this book to follow gay officers through their police world, from the barriers they encountered when they decided on a career and dealt with recruitment policies to the ways they must manage and cope with their conflicting identities on the job and in their private lives. I also write about the sexual adventures of these gay cops, and how their identities as both gays and cops shape their socializing patterns, leisure time, and sexual relationships with other gays. Although I focus on their sexual identities and work identities, I also consider how these men and women present themselves to members of their families, given the prevailing stigma attached to homosexuality in larger society.

Although most of the gay cops I talked to worked in New York, the problems of gay police nationwide are similar.

A NOTE ON LIMITATIONS

I was faced with some limitations in this investigation. First, I reached out to only forty-one gay cops in varying degrees of openness. These men and women were drawn from a voluntary, not random, pool. I cannot, therefore, make any claim that the views and experiences of this sample represent those of the larger population of gay cops in New York City or anywhere else. Still, I am confident from the noting of repetitive problems and concerns in the interviews and other documented sources that tentative generalizations about the world of gay police can be reached.

Additionally, my information came mainly from interviews. Unlike Laud Humphreys, who *observed* sexual behavior in public restrooms, I was, except for a few visits to precincts, gay bars, and cruising areas, unable to observe firsthand the work and social worlds of the gay officer.[7]

Two

Recruiting
Gay Cops

All over the country they're [police departments] dead set against us coming on [the job]. A lot of departments don't want us because they see us as freaks.

Hate and mistrust for the police have become endemic to the ghettos of American cities. Most, if not all, of the racial unrest and riots that plagued our urban areas in the 1960s were triggered by the actions—or inactions—of the police in their dealings with minority citizens. Toward the end of the 1960s, city governments attempted to resolve this conflict and reduce mistrust of the police by instituting a number of community relations projects, including the recruiting and hiring of blacks for police service. A form of political cooptation long used by politicians to deal with disorder and open hostility, the hiring of blacks brought the hostile opposition into the police department in an effort to still the critics.[1]

Contempt for and distrust of the police have also become facts of life within gay communities across the country. As in the black community, these sentiments—which have brought the gay community in some cities to a near state of war with the police—stem in large part from years of oppressive treatment at the hands of homophobic cops. The police, who should have been at the forefront of the fight against bias-related crime directed against homosexuals, often engaged in, or at least condoned, verbal and physical attacks against gays.

In recent years the gay community has begun to fight back publicly, borrowing from mainstream civil rights tactics to mobilize support for its cause. In some instances gays have formed activist groups and coalitions, staging protests over discriminatory police tactics directed against homosexuals. In other instances, where members of the gay community have appealed directly to the police and failed to receive support, they have taken legal action.[2] The response of some city governments to their aggressive actions has been to introduce "sensitivity" programs in their police departments and to recruit and

7

hire police candidates from the gay community. This new pattern bears a striking resemblance to the reactive position some political leaders took in the early 1970s in their attempt to resolve racial conflicts between blacks and police. More than simply opening up jobs for homosexuals, the hiring of gays would create a new base of support for the police and legitimize the department and city government as a whole. But beyond that, some city governments saw the inclusion of gays as a necessary adjustment to the growing political power of and pressure from homophile groups who were demanding a greater say in the policies and operations of their police departments.

In their attempt to open law enforcement positions to homosexuals, government leaders along with members of the gay community have confronted a number of unique and, in some instances, unexpected problems that have not arisen with other minority groups entering policing. For one, there has been blatant vocal resistance to the recruiting of gay police candidates from within the wider police community itself. The prestigious International Association of Chiefs of Police (IACP), for example, had long decried the hiring of gays, stating that "every policeman should conduct his private life so that the public . . . regard(s) him as an example of stability, fidelity, and morality." The inference, of course, is that gays are not stable, trustworthy, or morally principled. In another published report, the spokesman for the IACP, Robert Angrissani, defended his organization's position against the hiring of gays, explaining "that until such time as homosexuality is accepted by the general public, the association is against such programs."[3] Support for the exclusion of gays from policing was also found in one of New York City's influential civil service newspapers. In a June 12, 1987, editorial, the *Chief-Leader* justified a position of "selective discrimination" by arguing that the NYPD should not publicly recognize immoral behavior by actively recruiting those who practice homosexuality.

Police union and fraternal organization leaders in some cities have also vociferously opposed hiring gay cops. In New York City in 1984, shortly after the police department embarked upon a program to hire gays, Phil Caruso, head of the powerful 25,000-member Patrolman's Benevolent Association (PBA), vowed to fight, in court if necessary, any effort on the part of the NYPD to recruit from the gay community. Caruso stated for public record that gays "could not hold the dignity and image of a police officer." He followed up with the strong implication that allowing gays to infiltrate the department in mass numbers would be very damaging, as they "would not serve the best interests of the community." He added, "It is a question of standards, of acceptability. We have historically been opposed to the hiring of gays." Caruso defended his position by pointing out that his office had been besieged with phone calls—presumably from other cops— protesting the department's proposed drive to recruit gays. He stated that "since the department is equated with military standards which ban gays from entering, so should the police." The PBA later backed off somewhat from its threat to sue the city to block the police depart- ment from hiring homosexuals. A spokesperson for the PBA said that officials of the organization would instead monitor *how actively* the department solicited gays before determining what legal steps they would take.[4]

There has also been fierce opposition to homosexual recruitment from most of the NYPD's influential religious-fraternal organizations. After the department's assistant commissioner for community affairs asked GOAL to assist in the recruiting of homosexuals, the president of the Jewish Shomrim Society said that his organization was against homosexuals in the police department and in the community as well. Echoing this sentiment, the head of the Irish Emerald Society bluntly stated, "We're against it, without a doubt. It's a shame we can't get moral people on the job." Further opposition to the proposed gay recruitment drive was expressed by an official of the Catholic Holy Name Society of the NYPD, who went on record stating that his or- ganization was also against the hiring of homosexuals. Claiming to speak for members of the society, he added that "cops do mind work- ing with homosexual officers." As recently as 1989, in a further at- tempt to deny gays their right to full membership in the NYPD family, a coalition of twenty-five New York City religious, fraternal, and ethnic police groups refused to acknowledge officially the exist- ence of GOAL. At a ceremony for newly appointed police recruits at which officers were invited to meet with representatives of these groups, it was discovered that a booklet prepared by the Community of Police Societies (COPS) had excluded any mention of GOAL from its listing. This clearly biased omission occurred under the pretext that it was sanctioned by the police commissioner, even though the mayor of New York City had, as far back as 1986, signed into law a bill that made it unlawful to discriminate against anyone in the area of employment on the basis of sexual orientation.[5]

A crucial question, of course, is why the PBA and other religious fraternal organizations have taken such a strong and decisive public posture against the recruitment and hiring of gays for police service. One explanation may be that individual union leaders and fraternal officials are simply engaging in pressure politics or moral crusades that spring from their personal disdain and contempt for gays. Or they may believe that when they publicly voice antigay sentiments, they are speaking for the rank-and-file membership.

Leaders of powerful religious groups outside the police department have also demonstrated resistance to the recruitment of gays. Representatives of the Archdiocese of New York, the Central Rabbinical Congress and the Knights of Columbus, for example, have continuously urged the defeat on both moral and religious grounds of many gay rights bills coming before New York City legislators. As Rabbi Hillel Handler of the Union of Orthodox Rabbis openly put it, "This law [a proposed amendment to the city's administrative code that would forbid discrimination because of sexual orientation—such as the hiring of gay cops] attacks the moral foundations of this city."[6]

Programs that encourage hiring homosexuals for police positions have also come under attack by individual high-ranking police officials in direct opposition to their department's official policies. One chief, remarking on the need among law enforcement officers for mutual trust and confidence, stated that homosexuals were "sick persons" and as such were unreliable. In an obvious attempt to justify the exclusion of gays from police careers, this same official expressed the opinion that "few officers would be willing to work with homosexuals, and the effect on morale would be disastrous." In Houston, a project that was to include the hiring of two homosexual civilians to fill teaching positions at the police academy triggered strong homophobic responses from two high-ranking police officials. Here, too, these negative reactions were in direct opposition to Houston's official departmental hiring policies. One deputy police chief went so far as to liken the idea of gays teaching police recruits to "thieves, prostitutes, and narcotic addicts teaching classes on their activities."[7]

Yet these views and public statements are hardly surprising. Although the U.S. public's perception of homosexuality has changed since the 1950s, its deep-rooted biases continue to extend beyond simple moral disapproval. In a survey conducted by the Institute for Sex Research in 1970, for example, a substantial majority of the people sampled nationwide agreed that gays should be denied access to positions of *influence* and *authority*, particularly when the profession involved moral leadership. The reasons offered for denouncing gays centered on lack of trust, fear, and moral repugnance of same-gender sex as a life-style.[8] No doubt some police beliefs about the recruitment and hiring of people thought to be sick and morally unfit to wear the police uniform reflect the more conservative and traditional aspects of thinking in our society.

A more formidable barrier to homosexuals' obtaining police positions has been the absence of antibias legislation in some cities and the persistent reluctance in other cities of government leaders to actively seek qualified gay police candidates. In Dallas, for example, until early 1993 the police department had systematically refused to hire gays under the pretext of the state's penal law, which criminalizes certain homosexual conduct. Texas is one of twenty-four other states that criminalize consensual or anal intercourse or both with others of the same sex, even in the privacy of their homes. In Chicago, as of 1991, there were no publicly out gay cops in the 12,000-member force. Additionally, there was no liaison between the gay community and the police department and no targeted recruitment of gays and lesbians. In New Jersey, not only is there no policy to recruit gays into police service, but up until 1989 homosexual cops could be dismissed simply because they were homosexual. More recently, the governor of New Jersey signed into law an amendment to the state constitution that prohibits discrimination based on sexual orientation, making New Jersey only the fifth state to legislate such a measure.[9]

In a New York *Daily News* article in 1981, Ed Koch, then mayor of New York, listed thirty-nine U.S. cities with gay rights legislation already in place. But, in reality, few police departments in these cities had policies that encouraged the recruitment of homosexual police candidates. And, not surprisingly, still fewer actively reached out into the gay community for recruits. According to several recent reports and accounts, as of 1992 only ten police departments in the entire country had made any direct attempts to recruit gays: Boston, Minneapolis, Madison, Seattle, Portland, Atlanta, Philadelphia, San Francisco, Los Angeles, and New York City. Other cities such as Washington, D.C., while going so far as to forbid discrimination in employment on the basis of sexual orientation, still do not attempt to recruit gay police candidates.[10]

In contrast, Boston began its recruiting in 1987 in response to pressure from local gay activist groups. These groups had documented and, at one hearing, testified to 135 cases of verbal and physical attacks on gays in 1986 alone, including five allegedly committed by police officers. Support for this recruitment drive also came from Boston's mayor after members of New York City's Gay Officers Action League testified at this same public hearing. GOAL's presence was in response to a request from the Boston Lesbian and Gay Political Alliance, which asked for help for the city's gay community in its efforts to push through a plan to recruit gay officers. GOAL's testimony generated extremely heavy media coverage and added to the success of the hearing, which resulted in the mayor of Boston's issuing an antidiscrimination policy statement and, for the first time in that city's history, a move by the Boston Police Department to actively recruit from the gay community. At the time of this hearing, according to both the police and the gay activists, the department had *no* officers who admitted to being gay.[11]

Despite a 1986 U.S. Supreme Court ruling that upheld a Georgia statute outlawing consensual homosexual sodomy among adults, the Atlanta Police Bureau began its recruitment campaign that same year by placing advertisements in local gay newspapers. Until then, a person could not be accepted into the police department, according to the Atlanta public safety commissioner, if a background check indicated homosexuality. In Philadelphia, it was nearly ten years after police commissioner Mort Solomon put forth an order in 1980 outlawing discrimination within his department before the police began to actively recruit gay candidates. According to a statement issued from the recruitment unit, the recent Philadelphia campaign, though geared toward all segments of Philadelphia's minority population, centered on homosexuals. Similarly, it was not until 1991, after a meeting between the city's police chief and members of the Gay and Lesbian Police Advisory Task Force, that the Los Angeles Police Department began to recruit from the gay community. This drive began on the day of the annual Gay and Lesbian Pride Festival and involved openly gay officers, dressed in full uniform, staffing the recruitment booth. By contrast, the San Francisco Police Department began actively seeking gay recruits as far back as 1979, not surprising in view of the considerable economic and political strength of San Francisco's gay community, its unequaled voting power (20 percent to 25 percent of voters in San Francisco are homosexual), and the belief that homosexuality does not in itself deprive a person of "stability, fidelity and morality."[12]

The New York City Police Department didn't begin to address the question of gay recruitment until 1984. By this time Mayor Koch had already issued Executive Order #50, which *legally* barred discrimination against homosexuals. Since then the official position of the NYPD toward gays has been unmistakably clear, as reflected in policy statements issued by the commanding officer of the department's Equal Employment Opportunity Unit ("If you can do the job, that's all we ask") and by the assistant commissioner for community affairs ("We're sending a message to the gay community—we're not discriminating against them. They're welcome"). It is, however, only since 1987 that the NYPD has actually gone out of its way to seek candidates from the city's gay minority communities. In May of that year, at the persistent urging of GOAL, the department began a concerted effort along with GOAL members to enlist qualified gay candidates. Also, for the first time, high-ranking police officials in New York City met with GOAL leaders to discuss recruitment strategies for upcoming police exams as well as career opportunities for gays already in the department. Since that historic meeting GOAL and activist groups within the city's gay community have continued a dialogue with the department and have provided support staff and recruitment materials aimed specifically at attracting gays. The NYPD has also put into effect a policy that directly forbids discrimination against gays in the workplace. The current position of the NYPD regarding gay recruitment was summed up by a former president of GOAL as "one of complete cooperation and support."[13]

To what extent recent efforts by GOAL and the NYPD have paid off in terms of attracting qualified gay police candidates cannot be known for certain, for all applicants, heterosexual as well as homosexual, fill out the same form, which neither asks nor requires them to state their sexual orientation. The success of earlier gay recruitment drives can loosely be judged, however, by the fact that a former president of GOAL said back in 1984 that he had personally received over a thousand calls from individuals requesting applications. He later estimated that up to a thousand gays, mostly men, had applied for police positions as the direct result of this recruitment drive.[14]

An equally serious and certainly more frustrating problem faced by members of the gay community seeking more direct participation in the policies and operations of their police departments is the guise of invisibility gays can choose to clothe themselves in once they have entered law enforcement. Unlike blacks, Asians, and even Hispanics, whose minority status is usually apparent, an individual's sexual preference is usually revealed at the discretion of that person. Though the precise number of homosexuals currently employed in New York City police agencies is unknown, it is clear from my own observations and information garnered through interviews that the overwhelming majority have chosen a cloak of invisibility. My interviews, specifically, have provided some current estimates of gay police officers that range from 10 percent to upwards of 30 percent of the NYPD population. Making the conservative assumption that the lower estimate is the more accurate (though I personally believe it falls somewhat short of the actual figure) would mean that there are approximately three thousand homosexual men and woman employed by city police agencies. In my sample of forty-one gay police, only twelve were publicly out of the closet at the time of the interviews.

Being out does indeed place gay police officers in the unique position of being able to tackle head-on instances of discrimination against gays that they observe or hear about. The simple fact of their presence in the street or station house warns the homophobic cop that assaults and verbal attacks against gays will not be tolerated. The officer who is out and known about in the gay community can serve as a source of reliable information for victims of homophobic police attacks seeking redress. Yet it is precisely because so few gay officers have actually unbolted the closet door at work that most areas of the city populated by gays remain virtually unprotected from the homophobic cop. The usual reaction of closeted gay officers to most overt instances of discrimination against gays in the community is to remain passive. These men and women, out of fear that intervention on their part might arouse suspicions of or even expose their true sexual identities, choose not to say or do anything. This is not my observation but that of the great majority of closeted cops in New York City, who fear above all else being exposed as homosexuals. The following comments from two of these "invisible" officers are typical:

It's happened I can't deny that. The way I handle it is, for example, when one guy n the precinct said, "Look at those two faggots over there, they're probably dicking each other up the ass," [in a voice loud enough to be heard by the two men] I just looked the other way and said to him, "Yeah." I just left it at that. There's nothing I can do to change that person's attitude right now.

I totally mind my own business. . . . If an incident occurs, I wouldn't do anything to encourage it and I wouldn't necessarily stop it either.

Thus, if one of the critical objectives of gay activist groups in drawing homosexuals into police service is to resolve conflict between the police and the gay community, then they have fallen far short of their desired goal. By taking no action when an assault is committed upon or a degrading comment is made to a gay by another cop, the closeted gay officer fails by default to protect the interests of the larger gay community. Nonintervention also does nothing to help eliminate negative stereotypes held by the police and members of the gay community about one another, and it does nothing to encourage the mutual respect that is sorely lacking between police and gays. What it does accomplish for members of the gay community is to help sustain existing feelings of mistrust and fear of the police and city government as a whole. It is only when individual gay officers choose to take deliberate and decisive steps against police homophobia that any real progress can be made toward establishing support for the police. But this cannot occur until a more significant sector of the gay police population decides to come out of the closet. Only when this group becomes more visible and vocal to both their heterosexual coworkers and members of their community can progress occur. Coming out in greater numbers could create, over time, a climate in which trust and respect for the police could finally develop within the gay community.

It is precisely this indecisiveness about coming out that has sparked one of the most intense controversies among members of GOAL.[15] Those urging complete and unequivocal openness claim, among other things, that some of the hard-won gains by gays are being watered down by the persistent reluctance of most gay cops to step forward, be counted, and then be *heard*.

Three
Taking
on a
Doubly
Deviant
Identity

I'd always known I was gay, although I didn't know the name for it. When I was four I had a crush on another boy. I thought all people felt that way. When I grew older, I saw my peers start to have an interest in women, girls at the time, but I didn't. I thought I was just a late bloomer, "Okay, next year you'll be interested in girls." But I waited, and I was still interested in boys.[1]

The question of when an individual discovers his or her true sexual orientation is complex.[2] The responses from this study suggest that there are at least two distinct phases in the social process of coming to grips with one's own sexual identity: (1) when the person first experiences an interest in or physical attraction to a member of the same sex; and (2) when the person comes out *to himself or herself* and admits that he or she is gay. These two stages in the development of one's sexual identity are often separated by a number of years. The "interest in" phase generally occurs before the "self-admission" phase.[3]

When asked when they first began to experience same-sex physical attractions, twenty-four of the officers in this study stated that it occurred between the ages of twelve and seventeen. Eleven acknowledged this interest as early as between five and ten years of age, while six said that they started to experience an interest in same-sex sex after they reached the age of nineteen. All, however, reported that some time passed (on the average, ten years) before they actually came to identify this interest as homosexual. The following comments are typical:

I can't put my finger on when I put the word *gay* together with what I was feeling. I've had affectional feelings [for men] for a long time, actually since I was in grammar school. . . . I finally admitted I was gay in my senior year of high school.

At thirteen I started having homosexual feelings and experiences. I didn't tell myself what I was until I was nineteen, in college.

I knew I was gay at sixteen. I preferred boys over girls sexually when I was eight
or nine years old.

A number of men and women claimed they always felt there was
something "different" about their sexual interests but could not (or
did not want to) account for this difference until later on in their adult
lives. One man, for example, said, "By the time I was five I was attracted to guys." Charlie Cochran said, "I always knew I was gay,
although I didn't know the name for it. When I was four I had a crush
on another boy."[4] And a woman stated, "As a child I had crushes on
little girls, when I was in grammar school. But I didn't connect these
feelings to sexuality until I was a freshman in high school. It was then
I understood what these crushes meant."

Many of the homosexual men in this study said that their first
sexual encounters—which began for all of them very early in life—
involved nothing more than engaging in mutual masturbation with a
consenting youthful partner. But in some instances they reported
that their first partner was an older male adult, often one who occupied a position of trust in the boy's community. As a veteran detective
stated, "I started looking at guys when I was 12. My first encounter
was with a pastor in high school. . . . We masturbated each other."

Mutual masturbation between same-sex individuals at a youthful
age appears to be a typical initial entry into the world of homosexuality and one that is followed a few years later by more traditional
forms of same-sex sexual behavior. One man reported, "This [mutual
masturbation] I kept doing and nothing else for about five years
when I finally met this older guy. He taught me about sucking cock
and butt fucking. He really opened my eyes." Another said, "Jerking
each other off, that's all we did when we were young . . . at seventeen
I had my first real experience and started doing other things."

For some men and women, the social process of coming out to
oneself only occurred after years of alternating between same-sex
and cross-sex dating. During this uncertain and often stressful phase,
heterosexual relationships were maintained as covers in order to
pass as straight among heterosexual friends or family. However, as
the individual came to realize that cross-sex dating was sexually un-
satisfying and increasingly frustrating, it was eventually abandoned
for secretive, same-sex dating and sexual encounters. It was during

this period in their lives that, for many, the ultimate self-admission of homosexuality ensued. The following quote is typical.

Looking back when I was fourteen, I was starting to have feelings about guys. . . . My first experience was in high school with my best friend when I was fifteen. He sucked my dick. That was a turning point for me. I then started dating this married guy and I continued to go out with women until I was twenty-one, even though I gradually lost interest in them sexually. I was just doing it so my friends wouldn't question me. But I realized I found what I was looking for so I stopped dating women because they did nothing for me. I could never go back with women. I knew I was gay, and I finally admitted it to myself.

One officer, now a sergeant with the NYPD, claimed that his gay tendencies began as far back as he could remember—when he was five years old. At fourteen he began to fantasize strongly about men and by sixteen began to engage in sporadic homosexual activities. He too continued to date women as a front until he reached the age of twenty-four, when "I finally said the words, 'I'm gay.' Then I stopped dating women."

For some of the men and women, cross-sex dating continued well into their late teens or early twenties not because they saw their real sexual inclinations as a transient stage in their social careers, or as a cover or front for their homosexuality, but because they truly enjoyed the emotional companionship and sexual experiences that dating members of the opposite sex provided. For others it was the result of the combination of parental and peer pressure to conform to heterosexual life-styles. However, for all of these men and women, once they grew older, entered policing, and assumed the role of adult, these pressures diminished, allowing them to more fully explore and commit themselves to alternate life-styles. For most, their emancipation from the parental home upon becoming police officers provided the impetus. As they became more involved in homosexual encounters and more committed to a homosexual life-style, they lost interest in members of the opposite sex as dating or sexual partners. As one male officer explained the process as he experienced it:

I dated women occasionally until I moved out of my mom's apartment. It was right after I joined the department. I guess I always preferred men to women and I was beginning to realize that. But at the same time I felt my hands were somewhat tied because I was living at home. When I joined, the salary was good enough so I could live on my own. That's when I began spending more time with my gay friends and lovers. I guess you could say it was then that I made a final break with women. . . . As I look back now I realize that a woman never really made me feel as good [sexually] as a guy.

A female officer's description of her sexual development was quite unique. Until she was seventeen her sexual experiences were exclusively heterosexual, but at that point she began to want to date women. This vacillating pattern continued for several years. Then, for a period of time, for unexplained reasons, she resumed exclusively heterosexual relationships. At the time of the interview she was having a relationship with a man and had just broken off an engagement with another man. She freely admitted, though, that should the right woman come along, she could and would resume a homosexual relationship.

The comments in this section suggest that for both men and women sexual experiences with same-sex persons led to self-awareness (and for many, self-acceptance) as a homosexual. For the great majority this self-awareness also preceded their entry into law enforcement and into the established homosexual community.

CHOOSING A POLICE CAREER

The images, attitudes, and expectations we have of the police and of police work are shaped in large part by what we see in the street, on TV, and in the movies, by the experiences of friends, neighbors, and family, by what we read in the newspapers and other printed sources, and by the meanings we attach to our own contacts with the police. These bits and pieces of information help us form an overall impression of the police and decide how we will react in encounters with them. To a large degree these impressions also help shape our consideration of the world of policing in terms of a career. Indeed, it was precisely the negative images of and attitudes toward the police that pervaded the black community in New York City in the late 1960s that steered many qualified blacks away from careers in law enforcement.[5] Career decisions, however, do not invariably and absolutely hinge on images of police and policing. There is also the question of individual needs and interests—that is, motives.

The Need for Security

The primary reason given by close to half the officers interviewed for selecting police work as a career was simply that it provided them with benefits not found elsewhere: a relatively high income, opportunities for advancement, substantial fringe benefits, and a pension system that offers the option of retirement at half pay after twenty years of service.

For a number of these men and women this combination of benefits proved irresistible and often resulted in their choosing to give up potentially rewarding careers in other professions to become police officers. As two who left teaching jobs put it:

I was teaching at Lehman College. A student told me about the [police] exam. She got me an application. . . . The final decision was about money. I noticed the salary. That was the deciding factor.

I joined the NYPD in 1984. In 1983 I was teaching high school for seven years. The pay was not that good. . . . They publicized the exam. It was the higher pay, and my family felt good about it. They also saw job security.

For others as well, there was no intrinsic value attached to becoming a police officer, that is, no particular commitment or dedication to the ideals of policing or to the image of public service.

I decided to take the [police] test along with other civil service tests. The salary was the best. It was the most important thing. I was making little money and this was more money. So when the appointment came I took it. . . .

Strictly financial. I was working in a bank—senior operations officer. I felt I was underpaid for the job I was doing. . . . So I took the police test and passed.

Another man, now a transit cop (the Transit Police Department and NYPD are separate entities), similarly reflects on the absence, for him, of alternative careers that were as well paying and secure as police work. "When I first got here from Puerto Rico I had some pretty shitty jobs. I had a high school diploma and that's all. . . . It was actually the job that paid the most, the benefits. So it came up. I wanted to get a good secure job. It just came up."

For some of the cops in this security-motivated group, secondary factors added to the appeal of economic protection that precipitated their entry into law enforcement. "It was job security, money, the whole package. But I also have to admit I enjoy helping people."

A few officers indicated that the economic benefits of a civil service job and the colorful and exciting elements of policing were equally important reasons for their joining the department. One woman went so far as to describe policing as a "romantic" occupation. "I did it for the money. I wasn't making much where I was. Besides, it seemed interesting, almost like an adventure. . . . First, it was for the money, then there were the romantic aspects to it."

Another woman, now assigned to the Transit Police Department, had yearned to escape from the monotonous routine of a nine-to-five job. She felt "trapped" in traditional job settings. Police work provided both the opportunity to free herself from a desk job and broaden her life experiences in a dramatic way and the economic security she needed to live comfortably. "I never intended to be a cop. I took the exam because of the salary, benefits. . . . Where I had been, it was like the same routine every day. . . . I figured being a cop you would see a lot of things, handle every situation you could think of."

A detective with the NYPD similarly reflected on the need to escape from the tedium of routine as a secondary factor prompting his entry into law enforcement. "I was working at CBS and the pay was excruciatingly poor. . . . It was largely for me a financial point. So I decided to join the PD on a trial basis. I didn't want to get stuck in another job from 9 to 5."

One man who listed salary and benefits as primary motivators in his decision to join the NYPD mentioned that another incentive for him was the importance of dispelling false myths about homosexuals in police work. "Most important reason, a career with good pay, pension, and a future. Also, proving that gays could be part of the PD, that we weren't subjected to being only hairdressers or clothing designers."

An essential element of policing is the authority to enforce criminal laws through the mandate of the state penal code. To back up that authority the police officer is provided with weapons and other occupational tools. This equipment also affords officers a degree of personal protection when off duty should they have to act in self-defense or to protect another person from victimization. In this context, as a secondary reason for joining the department, several women pointed to the growing number of violent crimes committed against women in New York City. As one explained, "I had been the victim of a burglary and robbery and the city presented itself as being unsafe for women and [joining the NYPD] gave me an ability to make myself safer."

Another woman spoke of the resistance she encountered from her immediate family when she first informed them of her decision to become a police officer and of her need to be free to pursue a lesbian life-style.

I thought it would enhance my life, both personally and materially. It would teach me to protect myself at a time when there was a lot of crime against females. . . . I was persuaded against it by my family. It wasn't something a woman [did], the kind of woman they wanted me to be, a feminine, fancy, and sophisticated lady. . . . It also provided me with the chance to leave home, leave my family, and establish myself as a single lesbian.

For other women, the knowing that they would never have the economic security of a conventional marriage with a husband to rely on, coupled with the combination of a good salary and pension system, played a dominant role in their decision to enter police work. "I had no idealistic reasons for joining. . . . Salary, pension, benefits for a single woman—knowing that I wasn't going to have a man supporting me or living off somebody else's benefits."

It is important to bear in mind that, by the time many of these men and women made their career choices, city laws had already been passed outlawing discrimination in the workplace based upon sexual orientation. Virtually all of them were aware of the existence of these laws or believed them to exist. It is perhaps this added assurance of *job* security attached to a civil service career in New York City that helped steer these homosexuals into policing rather than into other occupations in which tenure and job security were *not* assured after a given number of years.

Looking Beyond Oneself: Community Service

For nine of the police officers interviewed, community service in one form or another provided the primary incentive for choosing law enforcement as a career. Here, too, other occupational inducements often strengthened their motivation. One man's image of community service was largely confined to the prevention of crime. Implicit in his comment was a powerful need to see that certain criminal offenders were arrested and prosecuted, something he had no formal authority to control as a civilian. "I came to New York, rode the subway from time to time, and there were different incidents where I had to intervene on behalf of some woman who was being hassled. I joined because I couldn't deal with this shit as a civilian."

For others in this group, joining the department fulfilled an altruistic calling to help others in need. Salary and other job benefits were listed as unimportant or inconsequential by these more idealistic individuals.

I was working in computers for the government. I didn't join because of the salary.
It was the influence of some good cops I grew up with who were always
helping someone. . . . The job looked interesting. The opportunity to help people.
It's part of my character when I went to Catholic school. I really wanted to go
into the seminary.

Salary was not important because I had a degree in accounting and probably could
have made more money had I stayed in accounting. I just wanted to help
people, so I took the job.

It was not pension benefits, the uniform, or anything like that. It was because of
the incidents on the subway. I was always the type of person who wanted to help
crime victims and others in trouble.

Having family members in civil service jobs, especially in policing, provided the additional incentive for some to enter law enforcement. It is common knowledge in the police world that family members on the job can provide the necessary connections or contacts to get ahead and can offer invaluable insider advice on career paths within the network of the police department. However, interestingly enough, for those who did come from police or other civil service families, the overriding motivation was an idealistic dedication to serve the community. As a police lieutenant in this group remarked:

It was one of those long-held childhood things. I always looked up to cops. I came
from a civil service family. And civil service was the accepted thing to do. Plus,
I had this kinda late 1960s, early '70s liberal feeling that somehow I could go in

there and do some good in the police department. I was going to antiwar demonstrations and everybody was screaming about the pigs.

For two men, the desire to make some positive contribution to
society was combined with the practical need for economic rewards
and security. As one put it, "Since I was a kid, I always wanted to
become a policeman. Mostly, I wanted to help people, reach out to
them. . . . The real reason, to make some kind of difference in their
lives, everyone, men, women, children. Also, security, growth in the
department, the possibility of advancement."

A powerful motivating factor for one officer was the need to deal in
a positive and consequential way with his long-term frustrations over
being treated (along with other members of the gay community) as a
social pariah. "Before I came on the job I noticed the way cops
treated gay people, their complaints and everything. It's like they
didn't give a shit, they didn't care a fuck about us. We were treated as
if we had three heads. . . . That's why I joined, to make a difference."

From the point of view of the men and women in this community
service–oriented group, entering a career in law enforcement was
not just getting a job; it was getting a job in which they could be of
some help not only to the gay community but to the public at large.
Police work would provide them with tangible rewards from community service and would become the vehicle through which they
hoped to reshape prevailing definitions of policing as punitive, insen-
sitive, and discriminatory.

The Lure of Action

A third group of subjects chose to become police officers chiefly because of the promise of adventure in what they envisioned as an
unpredictable and potentially dangerous job. It was a career that
would afford them not only action and excitement, but prestige and a
true sense of power and authority over others. Coincidentally, a number of these men and women admitted that the mass media's portrayal of police work, usually highlighting the exciting and more
dangerous aspects of the job, influenced them in their decision to
become cops. As with many of the others in this study, salary and job
benefits were added attractions. As on officer explained, "I always
wanted to be a cop. I guess it was the TV shows and whatnot. The

thrill and excitement of police work. . . . The salary was very good, but the most important reason was the thrill and excitement."

A woman, noting the element of danger inherent in the job as an initial attraction, went on to include the importance of performing community service in her decision to become a police officer.

It was a challenge. Before I came on the job I was living dangerously in the sense that I was somewhat self-destructive. I didn't care very much about anything. Actually, I was looking for a dangerous job. If I got hurt, so what. . . . I [also] like helping people. People were mistreating gays and lesbians, abusing them. I figured I could be one cop who would be fair to them. So it was a combination of all these things.

One cop candidly admitted that helping people in trouble had little or nothing to do with his decision to join the department. What enticed this individual into policing was solely his fascination with and attraction to the more exciting and dramatic aspects of the job—racing through traffic with sirens screaming; investigating crimes; dealing from a controlling position with both victims and criminals; and ultimately, solving crimes.

I was a business major [in college]. I was working part-time in a shoe store. Then I took a job with cars. In 1981 they were recruiting. I always wondered what it would be like being a cop. It was the thought of all the excitement, nothing to do with helping people. It was the excitement of going up to a person who had just got shot and dealing with it.

Others in this group, similarly rejecting any notions of community service as a motivating factor, offered additional reasons for becoming police officers. For these gays the uniform itself, with its accoutrements and the image of manliness projected by its military look, proved crucial in their decision. One man explained it like this: "My cousin was a cop. I was very impressed with his ankle holster. . . . It's very manly. Besides, it was a good career, exciting, even dangerous work."

The police officer's authority to command and control and to elicit respect from the public can be an equally powerful motivating force for joining. This may be especially true for individuals who grew up in an environment in which they felt, for various reasons, intimidated, helpless, and even, at times, inferior to others. A recently appointed sergeant in the NYPD reflected on his insecure childhood experiences.

> I always felt inferior as a child. I didn't play sports like other guys. I was always getting beat up. I was pretty small and girls always beat up on me. . . . A cop has courage, respect. . . . A friend of mine was an auxiliary cop. So I joined the auxiliary. That made me familiar with the job. From there I took the exam and passed [in 1984]. I felt it would help me develop courage.

The action-oriented, idealized image of police work that many of these officers held before joining the department departs substantially from the day-to-day realities of the job. There are, of course, times when the work is exciting and adventurous, and the officer does experience exhilaration—as when cops get the dramatic and potentially dangerous call to respond to "a man with a gun," or when they find themselves involved in high-speed car chases. More often than not, however, police work is boring and stressful. The bulk of a patrol officer's time is spent performing repetitive, mundane, routine activities such as dealing with minor infractions of the law, tending to the sick, injured, and aged, responding to natural deaths, interviewing complainants and crime victims after the fact, directing traffic, issuing summonses, and doing his or her share of station house duty, which often involves preparing lengthy reports. These more tedious aspects of police work may not be apparent to most individuals considering policing as a career and do not come to light until the individual actually becomes a cop and spends time on patrol. It is only then that the new officer comes to realize that the image of constant action and excitement portrayed in the media bears little resemblance to the realities of the job of policing.[6]

The Influence of Family Tradition

A few men in this study chose a police career because of urging and pressure from a family member. They joined the department simply to carry on a family tradition in policing. As the son of a police officer put it, "My father steered me in the direction. He's been a cop for twenty-nine years. . . . To please him I took the test, and I scored extremely well on it. And that just fueled the fire for him to encourage me to become a cop. He felt I would do well on the civil service exams. I figured, why not." Another officer from a police family said, "The most important factor was my family. They pushed me. I'm the second generation. My father is a captain and my cousin is a sergeant."

CONCERNS ABOUT BEING GAY AND BECOMING A COP

A number of officers in this study chose to leave "safer" environments such as college or potentially promising careers in other professions to enter policing, an occupation fraught with danger and overshadowed by a reputation for homophobic discrimination. It is unlikely that they were not aware of police homophobia, as the media have consistently reported the gay community's loud protests against police persecution for the past few decades. If they were aware of these conditions, did they feel that as police officers they would be treated differently? Were they simply not concerned? Or did they feel confident they could avoid any problems by passing as heterosexuals when they joined?

When asked whether they thought that being gay would present problems once they became police officers, most of these men and women said they had been aware of the potential for trouble should their sexual orientation become known at work. Fourteen voiced strong concerns about the possibility of being victimized by homophobic co-workers and bosses. Their deepest fear was of unwanted exposure and being branded with the label of "fag" or "dyke." Most worried that such labels, if made public, would set them apart from their fellow officers, who would then treat them as social pariahs. Once isolated from the police family, they could find themselves abandoned when they most needed help (for example, if they called for a backup in a potentially life-and-death situation) or harassed in the precinct.

One officer who expressed such concerns added that his greatest single worry was that someone in the precinct would leak the knowledge of his homosexuality to an unsuspecting member of his family. "Oh, yeah, sure [I was] very, very paranoid. I was concerned about the reactions of cops who might find out. No doubt in my mind I would be ostracized. Would anyone want to work with me? Most important was my family finding out."

Two officers voiced the fear that should their true sexual identities be discovered they could be dismissed from the force. Both continued to worry about this even though they knew that New York City already had a law specifically prohibiting termination based upon sexual orientation. As one of these men put it, "At first, I thought if they found out [I was gay] they would somehow terminate me, get rid of me. This was always in the back of my mind."

A female officer expressed concern about being discovered because she feared the change in her straight co-workers' perception of her. "I feared it because I didn't want to be labeled, quote-unquote, 'macho.' I didn't want to be perceived as a man, because I am a woman."

Fearing the social stigma of being labeled a deviant and subsequently treated as such, most officers decided the safest and most practical course of action to protect themselves from discrimination was outright deception. Consequently, upon joining the force, they concealed their sexual orientation from other cops.

A few simply put off joining the department for a while.

The fear of being found out initially stopped me in my tracks. It sent me in other directions. I went to John Jay [College] for five years. . . . My fear of discovery diminished because I was older, more mature, more able to defend any problems I might encounter. There was still some fear but now I was more willing to take a chance. So when I was twenty-five I took every police test, State Trooper, Corrections. I eventually got called by Corrections in 1978.

In sharp contrast to the above group, sixteen gay officers expressed few if any concerns about combining the seemingly discordant worlds of homosexuality and law enforcement. These men and women claimed that their sexual orientation did not have any significant impact one way or another on their decision to become police officers. Because they felt a strong need to enter policing, they defended their right to do so. Moreover, they felt neither that their homosexuality should be an issue nor that it would affect their ability to serve the department in as professional a manner as anyone else.

Although they felt strongly that a person's sexual preference was nobody's business and should not become a factor in the choice of *any* career, there was, even among most of the men and women in this group, a strong inclination toward self-protection through the time-proven strategy of remaining closeted at work.

I had a conversation with Louie [a gay cop]. At that point I decided to join. He kinda assured me that my life was my life. . . . I decided that there was going to be a line drawn between the job and my personal life, meaning I would not tell anyone [about my homosexuality].

I wasn't concerned at all. I would play the straight life. I didn't want people to know. It was simply none of their business.

Before I joined I wasn't out to anybody. So I wasn't concerned. I was living a double life anyway. I was in the closet, so I was willing to live in the closet again.

A few officers did find solace in the existence of New York City's antibias legislation. They sincerely believed it would protect them from discovery while they were candidates for the job, as questions about one's sexual orientation could not be raised during the department's initial background investigation.[7] As one put it, "I was very well aware of my legal rights. I was quite prepared to bring up Mayor Koch's legal order. . . . That would have put them on the defensive if they asked me." Another stated confidently, "No concerns. They couldn't ask specific questions about my sexual preferences. I knew that." And a third added, "I know they had no right to ask. . . . It wouldn't matter regardless because of the mayor's [directive against discrimination based upon sexual orientation]."

Still others in this group did not even think about making an effort to conceal their sexual identities. Policing and one's private life were simply to be kept separate. These officers were surprisingly matter-of-fact in vocalizing their feelings about discovery, stating that if the department should ever find out about their homosexuality, so be it. Yet they also made it clear that they too had no intentions of advertising their sexual orientation.

I didn't have any concerns about that. I just didn't think it mattered one way or another. I was going to do a job and I didn't think my sexual life had anything to do with it. And I wasn't going to parade it around.

I figured it was just another job. I promised myself it would be just like working on Wall Street. . . . I felt being a cop was no different. What's the big deal that I'm gay.

I'm very conservative in my life-style. I don't advertise it. The job has nothing to do with your sexual preferences. That's nobody's concern.

As a rationale for joining the department, one man pointed to his earlier military career. He believed that the experience he had gained in this traditionally conservative, antigay setting had prepared him for the worst should he accidentally be discovered by his police co-workers or eventually choose to share his secret with them. "As far as coping with my gayness I had already done that in the military. When it was found out that I was gay, I had to deal only with my peers, which I did successfully. I was not concerned, at that time, about what some cops might think."

Knowledge of the presence of police homophobia, conveyed by other gay officers, prepared several of the officers for the problems an openly gay person might encounter upon joining the force. For example, "I already knew I would have to deal with homophobia but it didn't scare me. Some of my friends were gay who were on the job, and they told me what to expect, the remarks and all. I wasn't afraid of it. I knew it was there and I would just have to deal with it."

Three of the officers I talked to had either not as yet fully acknowledged or accepted their homosexuality before entering policing and thus had no reason to be concerned about being discovered.

At the time, believe it or not, I really didn't consider myself gay. I really hadn't accepted my own gayness. I was still dating women.

I was not gay then. I was still married.

I didn't know I was gay at the time or rather I didn't admit it to myself.

In summary, the decision to enter law enforcement came about largely from the individual's images of police and police work and varying needs, interests, and expectations about the job. For most of the officers, the question of their homosexuality did raise concerns both about how they would be treated on the job and how they would handle the anticipated police homophobia. The most common reaction to these potential problems was to keep their homosexuality a well-guarded secret from their co-workers. Some, however, while acknowledging the strong potential for homophobic discrimination on the job, did assume the matter-of-fact position that their sexual orientation was not linked in any way to their job performance and, therefore, would not become a factor in their decision. Yet many of these

same gay men and women admitted that upon becoming police officers they too would keep their sexual preference a secret at work.
Only a handful claimed that at the time they decided to enter policing
they felt secure and comfortable enough with their homosexuality to
be unconcerned about the possibility of discovery and potential discrimination in the workplace.

Four

What

It Means

to Be Gay

and a Cop

From the locker room to the toilets, there's faggot this and faggot that. Up your ass here and all that other stuff. And they really mean it.

There's a lot of hate toward gay people, really.

ay cops violate the expectations of two worlds, as one of the officers in this study explains.

It's not a gay thing to be a cop. It's acceptable for a gay person to be an artist, a singer, instrumentalist. It's tolerated if you're a gay lawyer, banker, stockbroker. People in these professions aren't under the peer pressure as much as a cop. To be a cop is very hard. To be a homosexual and a cop, it's harder.

Besides the sources of status conflict that emanate from within the police ranks, such as the PBA's vow to fight, in court, the hiring of gay police candidates, are other potential sources of strain, some of which are linked more directly to the gay officer's immediate work environment.

Status conflict, in the sense that I will be using it in the pages that follow, is a sense or feeling of detachment, nonbelonging, or alienation that persons experience from possessing simultaneously two statuses that appear contradictory or at odds with each other. The world of policing provides the setting for just such feelings for the male homosexual officer.[1] For it is here that a contradiction exists between his moral worth as a person and his professional worth as a cop. How gays are thought to behave sexually—that is, their moral worth—is related to beliefs about how they will perform professionally. In the police world, as in other occupations (for example, the military), both the moral and the professional statuses are bound together, each acting upon and acted upon by the other. Thus, the perceived deviant aspects of the gay officer's private life (his moral worth as judged by his fellow officers) can shape, to a large degree, these others' expectations of him (his professional worth) in the world of policing. What I explored in this study was how information concerning the existence of status conflict is conveyed to and received by gays in law enforcement.

There are studies that identify sources of status conflict in a general way and in specific cases of policing, but none that deal with the situation of the gay cop.[2] Schneider and Conrad discuss briefly how those with a secret stigma (epilepsy) discover how their condition impacts on their social relationships and especially on their prospects for successful employment if it comes to be known. Through individual accounts of epileptics they conclude that both messages and actions, "even those intended to have the opposite impact, can convey an image of epilepsy as something stigmatizing, undesirable, even terrible. To the extent that [their] respondents learned of such meanings, their earlier ignorance gave way to apprehension about how others would see them and treat them."[3]

For homosexuals in certain occupations, the problem of status conflict rests firmly in their often fatalistic anticipation of the negative reactions they will get if their secret is discovered. This perception has a number of origins. First, the depiction of gays in the news media and scientific publications suggests that disclosure will be accompanied by rejection, ridicule, censure, imputations of mental illness or criminality, and even violence. Second, their own experiences or tales of the experiences of other gays often provide evidence that overdramatizes or exaggerates negative reactions to disclosure in spite of the fact that in specific situations reactions to homosexuals in the workplace are quite varied.[4] In their police world (as well as in their social lives) gays, interacting with others, constantly pick up and process information that provides them with a special sense of who they are and how they should manage their discreditable identity. In this and the following three chapters I will identify some of these key information sources, describe their nature and content, and suggest how gay cops construct their self-concepts and self-presentations around such accounts.

SOURCES OF STATUS CONFLICT

Media Accounts

Important sources of information about self as a member of a social category are the news media. Journalistic accounts of people and situations involving gay issues, including published interviews with police officers and civilians (both gay and straight) serve to provide homosexual cops with indicators or clues as to how individuals as well as groups view them and the risks and dangers facing them should they choose disclosure over secrecy. These often negative impressions are, in turn, passed along to other gay officers through informal networking channels. An example of such a key indicator is the first vice president of the PBA's speech before a televised session of a city council committee hearing in 1981, in which he was loath to admit even the existence of homosexuals within the police ranks. This statement was followed by the PBA president's strong condemnation of and determination to fight in court any city proposal to hire gays because homosexual officers could not, in his words, meet the conventional "character" requirements of a police officer.[5] I cannot emphasize too strongly that these inauspicious statements were not expressed in the privacy of a precinct locker room, nor were they simply the bravado of two homophobic cops. Rather, both statements were made at a public televised hearing by powerful and influential members of the largest police union in the country.

In a more recent article, an ex-New York City cop exposed his angry homophobic feelings about gays to a local reporter. His comments, directed specifically at homosexuals who marched in the 1989 Gay Pride Parade, were "Fry them all. . . . Hell, I'll strangle them with the flag." And in another recent article, a sergeant with the NYPD told a reporter that although he "personally didn't have anything against gays," he did object to working with them. When asked about GOAL, another member of the NYPD described the organization to this same reporter in two words—"those fags."[6]

While the majority of homosexual cops may seldom, if ever, come across articles containing such inflammatory and dehumanizing comments, the ego-damaging messages contained in these statements do find their way to them through a variety of secondary channels. GOAL meetings and informal gay social events are two such conduits. At a social gathering of gay cops I overheard one of the officers in this study speaking about a recent article he had read concerning a male homosexual officer who, having been called a "queer" by a straight cop in his command (outside New York City), became so upset that he immediately took his remaining vacation and sick time in order to recover.[7] Put more generally, gay officers themselves either intentionally or inadvertently become sources of vicious and sometimes exaggerated stories as to how others in their work world view them and, consequently, what they can expect should they choose to expose themselves as homosexuals to other cops.

A second source of information that chronicles the linkage between the perceived moral and professional worth of gay cops is the *GOAL Gazette*. This monthly publication, which first appeared in 1982, frequently reprints articles and stories concerning the work experiences of the gay police officer. While the *Gazette* is mailed only to dues-paying members of GOAL, its contents are accessible to, and often read by, gay cops who are not members. In a fairly recent issue, for example, an article appeared that graphically detailed the situation of a gay Los Angeles officer who claims he quit the force because of continual harassment from homophobic co-workers. In his account, the officer included, as illustrations, the following instances of harassment: first, someone sent him a package at work labeled "AIDS Survival Kit." After that, on several occasions officers refused to provide him with backup when requested during life-threatening situations. Every day, something was written or posted on his locker, and every time he walked down the halls, he heard someone whisper, "That guy's a faggot." He found warnings written on the station house bathroom walls as well as cartoons and photos attached to his locker—including one of the gay actor Rock Hudson, that someone had inscribed, "To Mitch—Love, Rock Baby."[8] There was also an incident in which the word *Beware* was written on his personal car while it was parked in a police parking lot. According to a lawsuit later filed by the officer, neither high-ranking police officials nor the mayor took any action to put a stop to these incidents.[9]

In another of the many *Gazette* articles that dramatize the imputed marginal status of gay cops not only in New York City but across the country, an openly gay officer reported an unusually disturbing experience. A member of the Detroit Police Department, he claimed he was targeted by two fellow officers because he objected to their brutal beating of a gay, effeminate friend of his. He described the incident as follows: "I came up and asked what was going on and they [the officers] told me 'mind your own business faggot.' I told them I was a police officer and they had no right to call me a faggot. Meanwhile [my] friend was screaming as police were putting handcuffs on him. I told them I'd follow them, and they turned around and slammed me up against a car, dragged me over to the police car, and dragged us both into the precinct."[10] In addition to these antigay horror stories, the *Gazette* frequently reprints articles citing occasions on which gay civilians have been subjected to abusive treatment by the police. Also reported are instances in which the police refused to take seriously or act upon bias-related crimes directed against gays.

Other, more widely read gay publications such as the *Advocate* similarly publish stories of the experiences of gay cops. In a recent edition of this magazine, a Miami Beach lesbian police officer was reported to have found her name scrawled over photos of women engaged in homosexual acts that were posted in the station house. She also said that fellow officers put vibrators, sanitary napkins, and used condoms in her mailbox. The department, in response, played down the incidents, claiming they were merely "horseplay," while the mayor was reported to have said of the officer "I'd like to give her a key to my apartment." In the same issue of the *Advocate* a closeted police sergeant assigned to a Southern California department expressed his fears about talking to a reporter about his homosexuality even under the cloak of anonymity. He said, "I'm taking risks just talking with you. There are Neanderthal thinkers that I have to deal with here. If they [my superiors] find out, it's just . . . I could lose my job." This officer like so many other closeted gay cops across the country remains a "good old boy—a macho, backslapping, fast-talking cop."[11]

Farther north, in Los Angeles, a closeted officer reported on how he was "outed" by a member of the sheriff's department in West Hollywood after being stopped in the street while talking to another man. The sheriff asked the officer if the two were lovers. From the officer's identification the sheriff found out he was a cop and called his command. Soon afterward it was announced during roll call that he was a "fruit," and from then on no one would talk with him. Even in San Francisco, one of the most progressive cities with regard to gay rights, homosexual cops experience harassment ranging from antigay slurs to personal property damage from their fellow officers.

One female cop explained, for example, that when she first joined the San Francisco Police Department she received "all kinds of interesting things in [her] mailbox: dildos and used condoms among them." She added that the harassment stopped only when she reported the incidents to her captain. In Chicago, similar problems plague gay cops. Even with a human rights ordinance in place in the city, gays are reluctant to, as one reporter put it, "put their asses on the line [by coming out]. There's peer harassment . . . verbal threats, and the refusal to work with gays and lesbians."[12]

Not all media accounts of police impressions of or reactions to gay civilians and gay cops, however, portray heterosexual cops in an unfavorable light. On a few occasions, articles have appeared in which straight cops have openly defied conventional objections to gays. For example, a heterosexual officer assigned to a Manhattan precinct, when asked about his opinion of GOAL, flatly stated, "This is America—more power to them." Another heterosexual cop interviewed by the same reporter pointed out that gay cops reflect the fact that the police department is made up of all types of people and added that he personally could work with anybody as long as that person did his job.[13] Yet, in analyzing the content of over fifty published articles concerning homosexuals across the country, I have uncovered fewer than a dozen statements made by heterosexual officers that could be interpreted as either favorable to or supportive of gay police. Most statements expressed views that condemned homosexual cops and their reputedly deviant life-styles.

Police Reactions to the Homosexual Community

Second to the media and perhaps equally as powerful a source of status conflict in the gay police world is the closeted officer's personal observations and passed-along assessments of how the police, on the whole, treat members of the wider homosexual community. I have documented no fewer than one hundred individually observed incidents, reported by the officers in this study, in which gay civilians have been intentionally victimized by homophobic cops simply because they were—or were thought to be—homosexuals. They range broadly from verbal intimidations and denial of police services to outright criminal violations committed by the police themselves. This prevalent and unmistakable victimization of gay people serves as yet another indicator to the largely closeted population of gay cops as to how the police feel about people like them.

Degrading comments and innuendos

Oh God, I've seen that a lot. I work in the Village. The cops are so abusive. They make fun of them and they curse at them because they are gay. They whistle, taunt them. It's open season on gays. . . . A sergeant had these two gay guys locked up. They're in the cell and he says out loud, "This AIDS thing is really doing a great job. All we have to do is just sit around and wait." They bring in people, drag queens, and ask, "What's that?"

Police cars would ride by and [the cops inside] would say [to gay men], "Hello, girls," on the car speaker.

A gay couple went into the precinct to complain about an assault on one of them. Someone said, "If you didn't live that life-style, you wouldn't have to worry."

Two gay victims were in my radio car and another car pulls up alongside us. My partner referred to them as "these fags," we have to take a report from them.

I locked up this guy one time and he had this tube of KY [Jelly] in his shirt pocket. And so when I had to search him, I had to take this out and a couple of officers made some comments, you know, "Is this your toothpaste," and stuff like that. They do as much as they can get away with . . . a lot of sick humor, off-handed remarks.

Outright harassment

So they go into the bathroom [in the subway station], catch the people who are having sex. They humiliate those people, really scare them, you know, like, "We are going to call your wife." They cause a lot of stress, anxiety. The guy doesn't know that they won't call his wife.

Cops used to single out gay bars to give them summonses, tag cars parked around the bars. Incidents like this have declined, but they will never end.

Front of a gay bar in Queens. Summons all the cars—wheels not to the curb, shit like that. Just the gay bars. Straight bars up the block, no summonses. The idea was to bang them, bang them, bang them.

The captain in [one] precinct was having his cops issue summonses to guys who were carrying open beer cans from [one gay bar] to [another].

Denial of police services

This may sound like vulgar police jargon but there's a temptation not to take the complaint [from a gay person] but to give him a stroke job and throw the report away once he's left [the precinct].

I've seen officers on a lot of occasions say to another cop, "I had to take a report from this fag," as if the person didn't count for nothing.

I was in the _____ Precinct on patrol. I had a foot post and a gay person had been mugged. I called for a car for assistance. The car responded and berated the gay for being a faggot. They cursed him, kicked him out of the car, and then lectured me about not calling them to this kind of bullshit.

Physical assaults and shakedowns

I was riding in the backseat of a radio car when the driver approached a male who was obviously gay, near the piers on the west side. The male was taking a piss and the driver got out of the car and ordered him to stop. The guy didn't stop soon enough so the cop shoved him into the bushes and came back to the car and said something like, "Fuck that goddamn faggot, teach him a lesson."

They were always shaking down gays. They'd catch two guys in a car and it was "shakedown time."

Police Reactions to Gay Cops

From conversations with the men and women in this study it would appear that the most compelling source of information affirming the discredited status of gays in law enforcement is personal, that is, on-the-job observations of homophobic co-workers' reactions to cops who have come out as well as to those who are only suspected of being gay. Virtually every officer I have spoken to, especially those not yet out of the closet, have related incidents in which other known, but mostly suspected, gay cops have been covertly victimized by some of their co-workers. The ease and apparent glibness with which these verbal attacks against gay police in general and their reputed deviant life-style took place suggests that these cops were totally unaware that they were in the proximity of, or even speaking directly to, another homosexual officer. The most probable explanation for this unabashedly open behavior among these officers was that if a male cop was not limp-wristed or exhibiting effeminate mannerisms, then he must also be straight and, thus, accepting of these discriminatory judgments and actions. The incidents to which I refer occurred primarily in the gay officers' workplace, although some took place at social events such as the Gay Pride Parade.

Among the varied messages gay cops receive that convince many that the police world views them as social pariahs, perhaps the most powerful—and certainly the most prevalent—take the form of gay slurs and antigay humor surreptitiously scrawled on precinct lockers and bathroom walls. Even though recent New York City legislation bars discrimination against homosexuals in the workplace, the relative privacy of the bathroom and locker room insures that those anonymous messages will be seen only by other cops, who, whether gay or straight, are generally reluctant to make any waves by reporting them to higher police officials. As one officer reluctantly put it, "It's a fucking disgrace, these comments and all. But, if you're in the closet you really can't bring it to the attention of anyone else unless you want to be out of the closet. So you close your eyes and tolerate the shit."

The following comments illustrate the types of slanderous and potentially ego-damaging statements cops either attach to or scrawl on precinct lockers and bathroom walls. Most, not surprisingly, are of a sexually explicit nature graphically depicting or suggesting men having sex with other men.

Things like, "He's a faggot, we saw him with other men. He sucks dick, gets fucked in the ass; time to suck cock; fucking queer," a condom stuck on someone's locker, those kinds of things.

From the locker rooms to the toilets, there's faggot this and faggot that. Up your ass here and all that other stuff. And they really mean it. There's a lot of hate toward gay people, really.

They're real cruel. They write things all over the locker, all over the bathroom walls. They put _____'s name all over the bathroom walls and this other guy, that _____'s the "catcher" and _____'s the "pitcher." And drawings of intercourse and things like that. And they slander the other person's reputation.

They put pictures of cutouts of guy's genitals on lockers, drawings, pretty good drawings too, of men having sex with statements like, "Fuck me with your big dick." They had a full spread on one guy's locker.

Occasionally, these messages find their way out of the private areas of the bathroom and locker room and into the more public areas of the station house where they are visible to both male and female cops as well as civilians who come into the precinct. In some instances the specific targets of these attacks had not as yet come out to anyone in the precinct. Mere suspicion that they were homosexual (based upon, for example, simply having been seen in an area of the city frequented by gays) was sufficient to provoke a negative reaction. This is pointedly demonstrated in the following comment.

I had a problem once and they put down "_____ is a homo" in large print on the bulletin board because I was spotted going into a restaurant in the West Village. Now, the restaurant is not a gay restaurant, but a straight restaurant. Somebody saw me there.

Other actions condemning homosexuals and their purportedly deviant life-styles assume the form of direct covert harassment. An example is when a gay cop, or one who is only suspected of being gay, like the officer quoted above, discovers that his locker has been turned upside down or otherwise disrupted so that when it is opened his personal effects come flying out. Another form of harassment, presumably based upon the mythical notion that gay males actively engage in seducing children for sexual purposes, is for a gay cop to find unsolicited brochures or correspondence from known pedophile organizations in his mail.[14] " _____ called me the other day and said he got mail addressed to him at the station house which was brochures for joining NAMBLA [a national pedophile group]."

Just as the drug addict is perceived to possess other undesirable qualities, to many straights homosexuality is linked to personal failings. One trait thought to be characteristic of the homosexual is, as noted earlier, untrustworthiness. The belief that gays cannot be trusted provides both the momentum and justification for some straight officers to resist having to work with an openly gay or even only suspected gay cop. One officer I interviewed, who, because of this anticipated treatment, kept his own sexual identity a secret at work for many years, stated, "I was assigned to the _____ Unit and worked with two girls who were gay. I was questioned about working with them. They told me never to trust them because they were lesbians."

A further reason to refuse to work with a suspected or openly gay colleague derives, I am told, from another longstanding myth about homosexuals—that they make persistent advances to *any* member of the same sex. As a female cop put it, "If two men are working, one is straight, one is gay, the straight might say, 'Wait a minute, we're gonna be in a radio car, he might try and put his hand where he's not supposed to.' And he would be very leery about working with him." She continued with this example: "One guy in the precinct was thought to be gay. The guys refused to work with him. The poor guy ended up on foot posts four days out of the week. You heard them say, 'That faggot, no-no. He's gonna touch me the wrong way or he's gonna get too close to my face and I'm gonna have to knock him on his ass.' That's the guys' reactions."

In addition, there have been reported incidents of homophobic cops violating the privacy of known gay officers. A sergeant who was still in the closet when the following incident occurred reports on a particularly embarrassing breach of privacy directed against two female officers. "There were two girls in this command. They were lovers. One night one of them was home and the other girl called her at home. The T.S. [switchboard] cop put the phone call on the monitor so the whole command could hear it. The girls didn't know everyone could hear their conversation."

Occasionally, I am told, discriminatory and provocative comments are uttered in the presence of an openly gay cop. The reaction of one officer who found herself in precisely this situation reflects the way closeted gay cops usually react in similar situations. "I've gone on jobs with three other cops and coming out of the apartment a couple of guys would be ranting and raving about faggots. Then they realize I'm there and they smile and I laugh."

While discrimination against lesbian officers is clearly not the main focus of this study, it should be mentioned that this group may experience additional problems in the workplace that stem from the conflict between gender norms and their chosen occupation.[15] That is, they may face harassment and isolation as *women* from male officers (homosexual as well as heterosexual). As we shall see, some lesbian officers do indeed experience harassment at work, some of which clearly springs from their known-about or suspected sexual orientation. However, in my extensive informal conversations and interviews with gay male cops as well as with lesbian officers, I have uncovered no evidence and certainly no pattern of discrimination against these women on the part of gay male cops. In fact, the solidarity and support demonstrated between these two groups of cops at GOAL meetings and social get-togethers is strikingly similar to what I have observed over the years as a member of the department between black male and black female officers. The crucial variable linking these men and women is their common marginalized status in society as blacks or as gays.

There is, however, one crucial factor that complicates any understanding of discrimination against lesbians in the police world: the inability of these women, in many instances of presumed discrimination, to clearly identify which supposedly inappropriate status—their gender or their sexual orientation (or, in the case of black lesbians, their race)—is being targeted by male cops or supervisors. It may be one or a combination of all three discreditable statuses that are seen as inappropriate for policing and thus the cause of discrimination in the workplace.[16]

Observations of public events at which both gay and straight cops are present, such as the Gay Pride Parade in which GOAL members march with other homophile groups, can reveal much about how homosexual cops are viewed by their heterosexual colleagues. My attendance as a spectator at three Gay Pride Parades afforded me the opportunity to observe a wide spectrum of reactions on the part of those officers assigned to patrol the parade route. The reactions of these on-duty officers as off-duty GOAL members marched by ranged from displays of intense contempt and disgust to turning away to just plain curiosity. At points along the parade route some GOAL members and some still-closeted gay cops who chose for personal reasons not to march also overheard the responses or observed the reactions of these on-duty straight cops.

I recorded scattered observations by hand as I moved along the crowd lining the parade route in 1988. Referring to GOAL members as they passed by, one male on-duty cop said to another, "What a shame." A male cop asked his male partner, "What do you think of them?" His partner replied, "Not much, what is there to think about fag cops?" In a group of five plainclothes officers standing together one female said to the others, "I gotta see these guys." She laughed and smiled. Another female officer walked over to her colleagues and said contemptuously, "I'm afraid to go over any closer." At Fifth Avenue and Fifty-seventh Street three cops lining the parade route somberly crossed their arms precisely at the moment GOAL passed by. Farther along, one white officer said to his black partner, "They don't represent us." The black cop nodded his head in agreement and laughed. A male cop said to his male partner, "Glad I didn't see anyone here I work with."

In contrast, a female cop upon seeing a former GOAL president said to her male partner, "That's Charlie Cochrane. He's a nice man. He's done a lot for them." Two uniformed cops approached a GOAL member and shook his hand. Three other cops along the parade route also shook this particular officer's hand. Two of them worked in his precinct.

I took down the following comments and observations at the 1989 Gay Pride Parade. One on-duty cop said to another, "What a fucking disgrace. Thank God there's not many of them." Another cop said to his uniformed partner, "Hey Jimmy, come here, you see your partner there. You'll be shocked." One cop remarked loudly in front of four others as the GOAL contingent passed by, "The fucking pits." One female cop said to another female officer, "That's interesting, there's not a lot of women." "So what," the other female replied, as she walked away. Another cop asked his partner, "How do you feel about them?" The other cop said nothing. The first cop said, "Oh, look there's _____" (referring to a co-worker). Standing together along the parade route three Highway Unit cops turned their backs as GOAL members marched by.

This last recorded incident was strikingly similar to one that occurred during the 1987 Gay Pride Parade, when members of the NYPD's Mounted Unit contemptuously turned their horses around so their rears greeted the GOAL contingent as it passed by. This particularly blatant display of aversion was observed and recorded not only by GOAL members but by other homophile groups and the news media. The incident, later reported in local newspapers and in the *GOAL Gazette*, eventually resulted, I was told, in the guilty officers' being punished.

Notwithstanding the above-cited negative comments and reactions, among the hundreds of police officers stationed along the parade route only a relatively small percentage of those I observed made overtly unfavorable comments about or gestures toward members of GOAL. Most simply expressed a curiosity as to the identity of those marching. These observations lead me to believe that it is an oversimplification to state that all police hold rigid, automatic, and invariable views of their homosexual co-workers. I would argue that attitudes and reactions toward gay cops are socially and contextually situated.

This chapter has identified and brought together a number of information sources that convey to gay police officers their deviant status in the police community. While the homophobic messages flowing from these sources may indeed by scattered, isolated, and truly individualistic, their cumulative impact can lead the majority of gay cops to believe they are surrounded by an outside world in which antigay sentiments abound and by a police subculture that reflects these beliefs more strongly.[17] For other gay officers, there is the perhaps more realistic impression that only a limited segment of the larger police population in New York City is blatantly and decidedly antigay. Yet even these men and women soon come to realize that this antigay segment, small though it may be, is capable of influencing others whose views of homosexuality may only be marginally negative or even passive to follow in their biased footsteps or to remain silent and tolerate antigay behavior, thereby creating the distorted image of widespread police homophobia. It is also important to bear in mind that in the police world there are probably many homophobic straight cops who privately hold rigid, stereotypical views of homosexuality but who, out of fear of official departmental repercussions, are committed to silence. It is perhaps because of their awareness that both the overt and the hidden homophobic police groups exist that the majority of gay cops in New York City choose to hide their sexual orientation from most of their colleagues and superiors.

Five
Staying
in
the
Closet

Harry didn't discuss his private life with his colleagues. He appeared the typical officer. He drank beer with his partners after work, dated women as a cover, and sought refuge in his work, thinking that if he became an exceptional police officer, no one would question his masculinity. He was ostensibly living a very straight life as far as society was concerned.[1]

lfred Kinsey once wrote, "The world is not to be divided into sheep and goats. . . . The living world is a continuum in each and every one of its aspects." Restated from the perspective of this study, there are variations in the sexual identities gay cops choose to assume on the job and in the ways they fashion and then present those identities to the nongay world. As suggested in the preceding pages, the decision to conceal or expose a potentially discrediting secret stems in large part from gay cops' assessment of how both they and the police in general view homosexuality. The issue is one of perception; that is, how gay cops perceive themselves as well as how they believe others perceive them. What others *actually* think becomes less important. Concerning those, such as gay police, possessing hidden social failings, Erving Goffman summarizes the problem of identity management: "The issue is . . . that of managing information about [one's] failing. To display or not to display; to tell or not to tell; to let on or not to let on; to lie or not to lie; and in each case, to whom, how, when, and where."[2]

The stages or sequences through which a homosexual cop moves from complete closetedness to public openness do not emerge abruptly or spontaneously. Rather, they are tailored to each individual's needs, priorities, and sometimes changing expectations of others' reactions, and they evolve gradually over time. Each step along the way receives careful consideration. This movement, or passing, through the various stages of openness (including the beginning process of learning how to keep one's homosexual identity hidden) can best be viewed as problem-solving behavior.[3]

Gay officers do not act passively with regard to their homosexuality but take an active role in shaping the identity they present to others in the workplace. They do this by controlling information about self that they send to co-workers. Should this strategy fail to fully safeguard their secret identity or should their cover become an intolerable burden, closeted gay cops may attempt to alter the meanings others attach to their discreditable status, hoping that this will serve to reduce the moral significance of their homosexuality. One way this task may be accomplished is by first earning and then playing up the designation of "good cop" while at the same time playing down or disavowing the stigma attached to sexual differentness. Whatever form this information control or meaning alteration takes for individuals, if they are to successfully shape their destiny they must be able to influence the construction of reality among their work associates.

THE TEMPTATION TO MAINTAIN A DOUBLE LIFE

To understand the process of coming out fully, it is important to define the boundaries of each stage as it emerges. In this initial phase, gay officers guard their secret identity from others in the workplace so thoroughly that often it is even hidden from other homosexual cops. Knowledge of the social relationships of secret homosexuals and details of their off-the-job life-style and sexual activities becomes privatized. To use the metaphor of the closet, the totally secretive cop strives to keep the closet door shut to all at work. At this stage, straight co-workers, especially, are given no reason even to suspect the closeted individual of being homosexual. Consequently, these unsuspecting colleagues pass by the closet door and make no attempt to pry it open to see who is inside.

Generally speaking, those who possess a hidden stigma may have to deal with the realization that others (normals) who accept them do so unwittingly; that is, they do not know of the stigma and should they come to find out, their acceptance may turn to rejection. In order to avoid the possibility of rejection, some opt to keep their stigma hidden.[4] While justifications and reasons for staying in the closet vary from individual to individual, under them all lies either uncertainty of the reactions of fellow officers and supervisors or a belief that their reactions will be decidedly unfavorable. These closeted men and women feel that they live in a society that condemns their sexual desires and life-styles, and they fear that most of their co-workers will reflect this broader societal view in their reactions. As one fully closeted cop put it, "American society keeps pounding into our heads that gays are perverts, mentally disturbed. They see it as a sickness. Cops see it as a sickness, too."

Another officer draws a sarcastic comparison. "You see the way they react to gays. It even comes from the bosses. It's the only minority group that they are allowed to talk about, make fun of. It's okay to discriminate against. You couldn't make a remark about a black person but you can about a gay person. It's laughed at." There is a parallel between the situation when blacks first entered policing in the late 1960s and that of gays today.[5] Members of this newest minority, many of the officers in this study believe, cannot escape discrimination as long as they remain stigmatized. As with other minority newcomers to the police world, there is among many gays an acute and persistent fear of rejection in its broadest sense, should one's purported moral failing be revealed at work. Ridicule is one of the most anticipated forms of rejection.

I thought at the time it would create just so many problems. I believed I would have been ridiculed all the time. I don't like being ridiculed. Officers get picked on for being female. Others get picked on for being fat. I don't want to fight battles every day. What's going to be next, you know? It's a shame.

Unlike the black cop whose stigma was visible in the workplace and may have curbed openly disparaging remarks, the closeted gay officer is not known to possess a stigma. Consequently, unfavorable remarks about gays in general will not be toned down in their presence, and they may come to feel that they are surrounded by a work force that is truly homophobic. A young male cop reflects on some of the more offensive comments he has heard that convey to him a powerful message about how he might be treated if he unveils his secret at work.

You hear the derogatory comments and things like that. It's just that they don't know there's someone gay in the room so they speak real freely about it. You know cops say real disgusting things like they [gays] should all die or they should be put away somewhere or something. That closes the door a little more. That sort of solidifies why I shouldn't come out.

A female cop explains that she remains in the closet "because of the way they talk about gay people. There's not a day that doesn't go by when someone doesn't say, 'Look at that faggot, look at that butch, who's doing who, that muff muncher.' 'That faggot' is a common everyday thing."

Some of these closeted cops believe that what is being said openly would later be said behind their backs if they decide to come out. Imagining the comments of other cops, and then exaggerating the negative reactions to disclosure, may be even more frightening than the reactions themselves. As a closeted officer put it, "One can only imagine the things others will say. I don't like people talking behind my back. I've seen the cruelty that cops do to other cops. I know what they can say behind your back and I don't want to be subject to that."

While it is one thing to live in constant fear of gossip and back stabbing, believing that it is constantly going on around you, it is quite another to be publicly confronted and ridiculed. This experience can be especially painful and frustrating when the offending officer is one's supervisor. One respondent recalls an incredible story of just such an incident:

There's this one guy I know. I was present at roll call and the sergeant calls out his name. The guy says, "Here," and the sergeant says, "Tell me truthfully, are you really a faggot?" This was at roll call. There were about thirty-five people that he said this in front of. The guy didn't say anything. You know people are cruel.

For some closeted male cops the belief that stereotypical images associated with male homosexuals would automatically be attached to them once they revealed their true sexual orientation was equally painful. It is in this context that a transit officer explained why he believes most gay cops remain closeted at work.

I think most [gay] cops stay in because they do like the job and the fact that they don't want the label. . . . Because a lot of people in this world picture gay people as having a very high voice, very loose hands and for some reason we're supposed to

swish like a woman. But in reality the majority of gay male cops are masculine.
. . . That's why a lot of people don't come out because people will start to see you as
a different type of person and you're not.

A woman presents a lesbian officer's side of the picture. "I didn't want to be labeled as a bulldagger or macho. No matter what, I was always inside a woman. People wouldn't perceive it that way. Guys can be so freakin' cruel and make fun of females." Despite her feminine appearance, this female officer felt that she would suffer the indignity of being labeled a pseudo-male. She based this assumption on the personal experience of a fellow lesbian cop. "There was this one female, a bull-daggish type, you know. They labeled her, made fun of her. They were OK in front of her—but behind her back they would like dog her, both men and women. I denied it because I didn't want to be labeled like _____ was.

A number of officers, in justifying their closeted sexual identity, referred to the police world as an extended family and spoke of the intense need among cops, *both gay and straight*, to be included and accepted as part of that family. They kept themselves locked in the closet out of fear that disclosure would bring rejection and social isolation at work; in short, banishment from the family. This feeling is typified by an officer who said, "I think it's a personality trait that cops need to be accepted. . . . It's a tough job and you need to have that acceptance from each other because sometimes you have to do things that you know other people don't experience that are very hard on your heart and soul. And cops need support from each other no matter what. And I needed that too."

Another officer similarly implied that, should his secret become known, he would automatically have to forgo that sense of acceptance and belonging to the police family he so greatly cherished and personally needed. "I was scared. I wanted to be one of the group, one of the crowd. I didn't want to be labeled or tabooed. Being a token, I didn't want to be made fun of. I wanted everybody to like me."

Still another officer, unsure of whether he would be accepted or rejected by his colleagues despite an experience when acceptance was already demonstrated, chose to remain in the closet.

I'm so uncertain of what their reaction is going to be. It's too risky to ever chance
it. . . . I would think the old-timers, the bosses, would freak out. But I don't

really know. When I was in the _____ Precinct, we took a sergeant out for dinner
right around the corner from [a gay bar]. One of the cops with us leaned over
and said, "Is this where you bring all your gay friends?" He was young, twenty-five,
twenty-six. He probably saw me come out of [the bar]. But nothing changed
after that. He's still very friendly. There was nothing put on my locker. Maybe I
might be very, very wrong about being accepted as one of the guys. But it's still a
big risk.

Others spoke of the loss of friendship among their police colleagues that they felt would surely follow disclosure. "I do not volun-
teer that information to my straight co-workers because I don't want
to lose my friends because of my sexuality. So I haven't told anyone."

A few also expressed the related, and perhaps more serious, concern that they would experience difficulty finding anyone willing to
be their steady work partner. As one woman put it, "It's a feeling of
discomfort working among people who might not talk to you as if you
were a fellow officer because of the fact that you are gay. Or, maybe
they may choose not to work with you, not because of your ability as
a police officer, but because of your sexual preference."

One man believed that his status as a professional police officer
would be called into question should he come out because other cops
would no longer take him seriously. As with others in this study,
there was the feeling that the gay officer's professional worth would
have to be earned all over again.

My professionalism is very important to me. I don't look at this job as being just a
job. I look at it as a profession and I feel that my professionalism would be un-
dermined seriously if it came out that I was gay. I don't think a lot of people would
take me seriously for at least a while.   I would have to gain their respect
and confidence back. And that would be devastating for me.

Yet some of the cops who were still totally secretive about their
homosexuality at the time of the interviews did express an intense
desire and need to come out at least to their immediate partners.
What stopped most of them was the underlying fear that their secret
would somehow be betrayed to others in their precinct. One noted
that "inexperienced cops can very rarely be trusted. Sometimes they
are the biggest washwomen. That's why I haven't confided in [my
partner]."

But even with this concern looming large in their minds, a number of officers still seriously considered coming out to their close partners. Some had even gone so far as to plan for the moment and choose the words they would use. In each of these cases, however, a disturbing personal experience or series of events kept them locked in the tenuous security of their closet. One officer (who eventually did share his secret with his partner) explained why he had a last-minute change of heart. "One guy I know came out to his partner. The very next day his partner requested a squad change. And then the shit hit the fan. He started getting obscene phone calls at home and shit put all over his locker. . . . So naturally I decided that it's safer to stay in."

Rejection can come in a variety of painful and humiliating forms. It may mean, for example, having to endure a spate of cruel pranks and comments, which can, over time, chip away at one's self-esteem. "I'm not ready to bare myself and face whatever demons will come upon me. The collective mentality is kind of Neanderthal, juvenile. . . . The snide remarks, pranks, the worst would come out."

Pranks in the form of demeaning, anonymous phone calls can be especially disturbing to individuals who are targeted solely because of their perceived moral failing. A number of respondents assured me that, should they ever reveal their homosexuality, they would be subject to harassing and degrading gestures. One officer explained, "I know they find a way of getting your home number. They call people up and harass them and then you have to change your number again and again because of it."

One reason why this particular form of harassment is so prevalent in the police world and so appealing to the homophobic cop is linked to an important aspect of police work itself. All police officers are required to provide their home phone numbers to precinct personnel in the event an emergency arises and the officer, or his or her family, needs to be notified. Thus, potential victims of prank calls from other police officers are, in effect, denied the option of having an unlisted number. Even if accessibility to an individual's home number is limited to select precinct personnel, mischievous officers could simply request the number from the telephone company. One need only provide the company with a fictitious name and police ID number.

Another fear that keeps some cops closeted is that their personal property will be vandalized should they disclose their homosexuality. A few have expressed the concern, for example, that they will find their lockers turned upside down or stuffed with toothpaste; others, that feces might be smeared on their lockers or that personally de-grading messages will be stuck to them. The former president of GOAL, Charlie Cochrane, expressed the fear that if he came out, someone might destroy his car, burn his house down, or urinate in his locker.[6]

One officer was effectively deterred from exposing his homosexuality because of just such a locker room incident experienced by a male colleague who was only *suspected* of being gay. This officer reasoned that the same could easily happen to him. "Someone wrote 'faggot' on his locker on five different occasions. He was mortified. He asked me, how could they know. I then thought of them doing that to me."

These direct and anonymous forms of harassment are, to some homosexual cops, the most insidious of all because these officers become, for the most part, helpless victims. Although they may have suspicions, they generally cannot positively identify the culprits and engage them. To do so could be embarrassing and risky. They may wind up accusing the wrong person or spreading further suspicions as to their true sexual orientation should word of their protestations filter back to others in the precinct.

There is the related concern of making waves in the precinct. To report an incident of anonymous harassment could provoke an internal investigation, thus subjecting the reporting officer to further alienation from colleagues. This fear has prevented a number of gay cops from reporting these incidents to higher-ups in the department. One male officer explained that

after the locker room incident [in which someone wrote "homo" on his locker] I had to start psyching myself out as to how to deal with the situation. My heart sank right into my stomach. I thought of my father. I thought of all the fears I had about coming out. . . . That's when I started to think what would happen if I went to [his lieutenant's] office and told him about my locker . . . putting it on paper and really following through with it. . . . The mentality of this job is not to make waves, not to get involved. The cop that does is going to find himself alienated. That's what it comes down to. And it's because of this reason I decided not to make a big deal about it. I thought it would create more problems than it would solve and I would find myself completely alienated.

A female cop, having suffered harassment at the hands of some of her male colleagues soon after she was outed by another female officer, explains that she was reluctant to register a formal complaint because "I was a rookie and I knew that if I made a complaint, I would be called a rat. Nobody wants a cloud like that over their head for twenty years. So I put up with it." The story of another female officer who did report instances of discrimination against her supports the above woman's fear of being labeled a rat. Her office was ransacked by her colleagues, and "they wrote 'dyke' on my bulletin board. . . . They threw files all over the floor. It looked like the place had been burglarized. Then I filed the complaint. After that, I was considered a rat and no one would talk to me."[7]

Moreover, it is common practice among some cops to continue or even to increase the incidence of anonymous harassment once they have someone on the run. Subjecting their victims to further humiliating and degrading forms of harassment becomes, for these officers, not only a game but a challenge to see how long they can evade discovery. It is, after all, the macho nature of policing to accept dangerous challenges.

The unwillingness to file a formal complaint against a fellow officer is, however, motivated by more than the fear of being labeled a rat. In the police department accusations of antihomosexual bias are tantamount to coming out, and these officers simply do not want anyone to know what their sexual orientation is. It is perhaps a telling indication of the marginal status lesbian officers occupy vis-à-vis the informal structure of policing today when, of the fifty or so complaints of discrimination brought to the attention of the department's gay and lesbian liaison officer over the past five years, in none has the complainant sought disciplinary action against her harassers. Many simply transferred out of the troublesome command.[8]

For some closeted gays there is the additional fear that harassment could spill over into the actual job of policing—a cop may be dispatched to handle a dummy call or unnecessary job or have his radio transmission blocked during an emergency. One sergeant felt certain that even though he was a ranking officer, knowledge or suspicion of his gayness would expose him to such on-the-job persecution. "Cops probably would start harassing me, calling me to jobs that I really shouldn't have to go to. I got enough hassles just working without having to put up with shit like this."

A few officers expressed the feeling that exposure could jeopardize their present assignments or restrict their opportunities for advancement to coveted units, such as the detective bureau.

One of the reasons I'm in the closet is because I'm afraid that I would lose my
detail if they found out about me.

I don't want it to affect any movement on the job, my career. It would give them
ammunition. It would affect details, and I would not be free to move around.

One man believes to this day that he was passed over for promotion
after being discovered in a gay cruising area some years ago by two
uniformed officers.

Two cops stopped me in [a gay cruising park in] Queens and ran my license plate.
I never told them I was a cop, but it was a cruising area. This was during the
Son of Sam investigation. After that I had passed the sergeant's exam and was
passed over. There was some mention in the papers that the cops caught a priest
and another cop in the park.

Even patrol officers, who occupy the least desirable position in the
police department, expressed concern that should their secret be discovered, they would start receiving the lion's share of unpleasant
assignments and duties that are inevitably part of every precinct's
daily routine, such as guarding dead and sometimes badly decom-
posing bodies until they can be removed to the morgue. One officer
explained, "I'm just afraid that I'll start getting all the shit details in
the precinct. I was on the verge of coming out because I was feeling
good about myself. Then I realized I have sixteen years left to go in
the department. Sixteen years of shit details."

Of paramount concern to most closeted officers is that, if they
come out to their co-workers, their personal safety at work could be
endangered.[9] It is crucial that cops on patrol feel secure that, should
they need to put in a call for assistance (backup) in an emergency or
life-threatening situation, other cops will respond immediately. A
timely response is especially critical for cops who frequently work
solo, as is the case with transit and highway patrol officers. The fear
that homophobic co-workers may drag their heels when summoned
to respond to a known gay cop's call for assistance is a very real one
for these men and women.

I can handle myself very well only because I came from a very bad neighborhood,
a lot of street fighting to survive. But in this job, especially in transit, you need
a backup. In transit, you work without a radio sometimes. You work by yourself. I
would want them to respond to my calls.

GAY COPS

Cops known to be or even suspected of being gay can find themselves victimized on the job in other, more potentially harmful ways as well. Although admittedly rare as a form of victimization, cops have, nevertheless, been known to attempt to ruin a fellow officer's reputation or even his career by planting contraband in his locker or private vehicle, then anonymously notifying the department's Internal Affairs Division. No matter how infrequently these sorts of incidents occur, this fear alone kept some officers from telling anyone at work that they were gay.

Because of the homophobic that might want to open my locker. They might plant drugs in my locker. The possibilities are endless so I am proceeding with caution. A lot of people think we are not worthy of the job, that we are evil, we're this, we're that, we're deviants.

Others worried that disclosure might result in some false accusation of having violated departmental rules and regulations or, worse, of having committed a criminal offense. A female officer referred to an incident she personally knew of as evidence of what can happen when cops want to get back at a fellow officer whose behavior has been judged by them to violate conventional moral standards.

This white female cop was dating this Hispanic man and they [some cops in her command] were calling up and making allegations about her. There were twenty-six accusations made against her over the course of six months to the point of drug taking. . . . I know how cruel cops can be, and they can get away with it.

Many of these same officers also worried that the well-being of people related to them could be jeopardized should their homosexuality become public knowledge at work. Most often mentioned was the fear that an unknowing family member would be anonymously informed of the officer's homosexuality. That fear of now being a liability, in some instances, was sufficient to keep them locked in the closet.

It would be like finding out you have AIDS. Now, you have to go back and explain to your parents you're gay. I don't know how I would handle it.

The only reason I don't come out is because of my mother and father. I have no other reason anymore. If I came out, my parents would be told, they would find out.

A lesbian officer whose mother, she claims, abhors homosexuals is especially concerned about protecting her from the truth. Like the officer quoted earlier, this woman now lives with the constant fear that if she came out, one of her co-workers would intentionally and maliciously expose her homosexuality to her mother.

My mother is the main priority in my life. So I keep it hush-hush. My mother is
very happy and proud of me, how I've made it in the department. I wouldn't want to
tarnish that. She's very old-fashioned, set in her ways. She believes that gay
people should be shot. . . . If I went public [at work] I feel somehow she would get
a whiff of it. There are some people [cops] out there who are deceitful and
would not hesitate to call up your house and say, "You know, your daughter's gay,
she's hanging out."

One officer felt certain that disclosure at work would somehow be leaked to his home, thereby exposing his mother to sanctions from other family members. "My family would do a number on my mother if they found out. That's why I stay inside. If I had no family, there's the possibility I wouldn't keep it a secret." Another cop who kept up the front for the benefit of his mother explained, "The job I can deal with. I live at home with mom and she's old and sick. She doesn't need another shocker. . . . I have to live with this lady, OK? If something happens to her I don't want to feel the guilt that, hey, this was the straw that broke the camel's back. This is why she got sicker. That, I can't deal with."

And still another respondent was concerned that his father, a veteran member of the department, would find out and suffer embarrassment. "I have to respect my father's position in this job. He's extremely well respected and very well known. He's the only one in the family that doesn't know about me." Interestingly, it is almost always the mother, rather than the father, whom the officer was most anxious to protect from finding out about his or her homosexuality. Yet when a decision is made to tell a parent about one's homosexuality, it is generally the mother, not the father, who is told.

A number of the men and women I spoke with also said they considered their sexual preferences nobody's business but their own. This belief provided, in many instances, an added rationale for staying in the closet. Some went even further, stating that it was important that they keep their professional world separate from their personal life. These sentiments, well captured in the following quotations, suggest that there is among gay police an awareness of the possible interaction between a person's perceived moral and professional status.

Basically, you become a police officer and put on the uniform. That's one aspect of your life. My sexual preference is another. That's nobody's business.

I have this ethic about work. You don't shit in your living room. I work with these guys and that's it. Because of that I have decided to keep my professional life professional, and my personal life personal.

Another common response was that one's sexual orientation is simply irrelevant in the workplace, that it has nothing whatsoever to do with how one performs on the job. Moreover, as a few of these officers pointed out, almost as an afterthought, homosexuality should not be singled out as a point of contention since heterosexuals' preference for the opposite sex has never been brought up in relation to the performance of police work.

It's nothing I go about and say, "Hi, I'm Jim and I'm gay." I don't think it's anyone's business. Just like a heterosexual person doesn't go around and say, "Hi, I'm Steve, I'm heterosexual." My sexuality is personal to me. Why is it necessary to make a public statement? Do you [heterosexuals] come out and say you're heterosexual?

A concern expressed by a few officers touched, not surprisingly, on the sensitive and potentially threatening issue of AIDS. Mostly men, they said that they were aware that many of their straight colleagues were obsessed with the fear of becoming infected with the virus through job-related contacts with homosexuals. Such an obsession, which they attribute to unresolved homophobia, manifests itself in both derogatory comments about and the avoidance of both intravenous drug users and people who are openly homosexual. These officers are both angry and fearful that, should they disclose their homosexuality to their straight co-workers, they will be perceived as liabilities and socially isolated at work.

One officer's remarks, illuminating the sources of his fear of coming out, are particularly relevant.

It really bothers me when you hear over the radio, "Respond to such and such a location," and some cop chimes in, "It's probably an AIDS case." My partner, he's got the idea that even if a person looks at you, you can get AIDS from him. I've tried to talk to him time and time again, but there's no telling him. He knows what he knows.

This officer concluded that disclosure would in all probability lead to categorical imputation as an *AIDS carrier* and subsequent banishment from the police family.

You know that he's not the only one with these irrational fears. A lot of cops have stereotypical homophobic attitudes about AIDS, how to catch it. This is in spite of all the training the department gives. So my fear is that if I told him, he would ask to be transferred. He would tell everybody else and then nobody would want to work with me.

Another male officer expressed a similar rationale for staying in the closet.

My biggest fear, no one will want to work with me on a steady basis, that I'll have to work solo or on a foot post. Straight cops have all the *mis*information that all the straight people have. They have the information that you're going to get it [AIDS] by touching somebody. A [gay] friend of mine in the _____ Precinct, who is out to a few of the guys, told me that he went to kiss his female partner on the cheek and she said to him, "Don't kiss me, I don't want to kiss someone who has AIDS." So its simply easier for me not to confront the AIDS thing with all the shit that's passed around about homosexuals.

A municipal police officer in Middlesex County, New Jersey, who is out to his police colleagues, describes the extreme fears that many straight officers share concerning AIDS. "Yesterday I went to work with a stuffy nose, and my partner said, 'You're not going to infect me with AIDS, are you?' The department thinks that just because I'm gay, I have AIDS."[10]

The above officer's comments illustrate the socially destructive belief that homosexual men are AIDS carriers simply because they are gay and consequently should by segregated from their co-workers.

Fear of experiencing isolation and loss of friendship and support in the precinct because one is revealed to be a member of a stigmatized social category is for some gay officers sufficient cause to seriously reconsider exposing their true selves to their work associates. This fear is often combined with the more serious life-and-death concern that exposure as a homosexual could disqualify the gay officer from lifesaving treatment from their straight colleagues should he or she suffer a line-of-duty injury, especially one in which blood is flowing or in which the gay officer requires mouth-to-mouth resuscitation. The officer's desire to reveal his homosexuality may be permanently thwarted when considering such life-threatening situations.

One respondent expressed the extreme view that the fear of contracting AIDS through even casual exposure to homosexuals was so great among the straight cops with whom he had worked that a *known* gay officer's safety and even survival in the streets would be jeopardized should he or she suffer a serious injury.

There are a lot of cops out there that won't touch anybody, not even another cop who is suspected of being gay. This they have told me. So if I'm injured I don't want these cops to be the ones that respond to the scene and do nothing to help me. . . . That's another reason why I stay in [the closet].

Another male officer exhibits the same concerns.

No fuckin' way would I tell these guys today [that he is gay]. Suppose I get shot, stabbed, or get into a serious car accident chasing someone and I'm
bleeding? They know I'm gay and they'd immediately say, "I'm not going near him." Quite a few guys have told me that they wouldn't treat *anyone* who looks like a junkie or a fag, no matter who they were.

Another male officer further reasoned that, given the extreme homophobia concerning homosexuality and AIDS, because he was not HIV positive, there was no moral reason to reveal his sexual differentness to even his closest colleagues. But in an ironic twist, this same officer, when pressed, conceded that if he were to become infected with the AIDS virus his attitude toward disclosure might be very different. He attributed this reversal to the belief that being HIV positive would now make him a liability to his co-workers and as such it would be morally proper to inform others in his command.

It is, in a sense, a contradiction, albeit an understandable one, that some of the men and women who condemned the fatalistic attitudes of their straight colleagues toward homosexuals and AIDS were the very same officers who expressed serious reservations and even reluctance to treat accident and injury victims who were bleeding. A

ranking officer recalls a recent experience in which he resisted his
instinctive compassion to come to the aid of a person who was injured, bleeding, and clearly in need of treatment.

I flew [was temporarily assigned] to the Ninth Precinct this year. It's ten o'clock at
night and the door opens and in comes some local from the street covered
with blood and he's got his head opened up somehow. My first reaction is, oh,
shit, and I get up and go over to help this guy. And I stop dead in my tracks. I
physically, for the first time in my life, stopped. I thought that the guy may be
a junkie and I don't want to go over and touch him. I got an ambulance. I'm not
putting my mouth on anybody, and I'm not touching anybody's blood or saliva.

It is important to note, however, that the majority of the officers in
this study, both men and women, simply approached injury cases
cautiously, minimizing their exposure to wounds. The following comment is typical of their stated views on treating serious injuries of any
kind as well as known AIDS cases:

There's a safety factor that has to be considered. Although I'm not a big advocate
of cops wearing rubber gloves all the time and panicking to do a simple aided
case [accident or injury] or AIDS call, you do have to be careful. You just have to
use good judgment. That's what this job is all about.

For those homosexual officers who know they are HIV positive,
the world of policing can become doubly stressful. There is the constant concern of becoming a liability to one's partner and other work
associates, which has to be balanced against the risks and hazards of
disclosure. (Although I am not aware of instances in which gay cops
confided in their partners or co-workers that they were HIV positive,
no doubt such disclosures have been made.) In fact, it has been related to me that those gay officers who know they are infected with
the virus go to even greater extremes than most closeted officers to
protect and conceal both their homosexual identity and their medical
condition in the workplace. As an example of one such extreme
measure, gay cops suffering from AIDS have reportedly admitted to
paying for relatively costly medication out of their own pockets rather
than using their police union's prescription drug plan in an attempt to
avoid discovery.[11]

Driven by their fears of rejection and professional vulnerability,
gay cops who have chosen the relative safety of the closet begin to

adopt strategies based upon pretense, deception, and precaution that will help them evade discovery. They have, in short, organized much of their workday around the fact of their homosexuality.

MASKING HOMOSEXUAL IDENTITY: STRATEGIES OF INFORMATION CONTROL

The officers in this study and, no doubt, *all* closeted gays in policing use various protective mechanisms and strategies to avoid exposure and its uncertain or anticipated negative consequences. In their constant struggle to escape detection, they employ protectiveness or information control to varying degrees. Some go to great extremes, constructing elaborate fictional biographies and chronicles of their sexual activities and social relationships, while others take only minimal precautions to conceal their homosexual identities.

Research into the problem of information control has revealed a variety of tactics available to discreditable individuals to conceal their stigma from others. Avoidance strategies are perhaps the most frequently used. These may involve avoiding *contact* with "stigma symbols" or signs that suggest or reveal a deviant condition. For example, homosexuals may try to pass as straight, avoiding contact on the job with *known* gays. Similar strategies can involve avoiding *situations* in which one's stigma is likely to become visible or an issue. The closeted homosexual could avoid the subject of homosexuality when it comes up in a conversation or refuse to mix socially with co-workers, fearing that intimacy in a social setting could lead to accidental disclosure. In each instance, the primary concern of the secret homosexual is never to relinquish control over information about self.[12]

Constructing a cover is another strategy selectively used by secret gays to hide their stigma. This occasionally involves enlisting the aid of others who are wise to the person's secret to play along in concealing the stigma—as when a homosexual brings a member of the opposite sex (perhaps another gay friend or relative) to a public event or social get-together.

Role distancing is yet another tactic employed by gays looking to conceal their discreditable identity. For the male homosexual who seeks anonymity at work this might involve intentionally, albeit jokingly, behaving in a manner associated with homosexuality stereotyping, such as making passes and putting his arm around other men. The expectation is, in part, that others will interpret these actions simply as joking behavior. As Plummer suggests, "Such distancing allows the homosexual the opportunity to behave homosexually while others assume he is basically heterosexual."[13]

The way most gay cops cope with their socially discredited status, however, is to construct and maintain a *convincing* heterosexual front. In the macho world of the police officer, it is not uncommon for conversations among men (and, to some degree, women) to center around such topics as dating and sexual conquests and prowess, all, of course, with the opposite sex.[14] With male cops these ubiquitous conversations are sometimes punctuated by flirtatious behavior and sexually suggestive remarks made to or about women, both co-workers and civilians. To avoid being suspected of having a different sexual agenda, closeted gay cops frequently mask their true sexual feelings and desires by playing along in this macho sexual bravado. This staged presentation of self as one of the guys (or girls) serves to reinforce a heterosexual image in the eyes of co-workers. As a female officer confided, "I flirted with the guys and they flirted with me. I never went any further. I never had to. They just assumed from that I was straight."

Another female officer reports that some lesbians have been known to sleep with their male colleagues in order to protect their hidden sexual identity from discovery or to dispel rumors that they are lesbians. Those who reject a male colleague's sexual advances, especially if he is a ranking officer, may experience discrimination. "This lieutenant used to come into work and tell me about a dream he had had. I told him I really didn't want to hear about it. He used to make me sign out whenever I wanted to leave the office. It was like being under house arrest." This woman eventually requested and got a transfer to a different precinct. The lieutenant responsible for the harassment called her new command, however, and informed her fellow cops that she was a lesbian. "I wasn't even out at the time; I had been seeing a guy in the unit. But he made up this totally absurd story that he saw me grinding in the kitchen area of a precinct behind some woman."[15]

A lieutenant, now out to members of his command, reminisced about his earlier days of masquerading as straight. "Yeah, oh God, did I go through the pretension stage. I did, yes. I would sit there when guys talked about women's tits and asses and play along."

In order to successfully sustain a false heterosexual front, it may also be important for the closeted male officer to occasionally accompany straight cops as they make their rounds of such male entertainment spots as topless bars. "When I went out with the guys to those bars and places where the girls have their tits out and stuff like that, you have to play it out. I was feeling guilty about that. I really was."

Some of these same officers also choose to wear wedding bands to work, believing that this symbol of conventionality—or to use Goffman's term, *disidentifier*, would validate their identity as heterosexuals.[16] "I would always wear a wedding ring. There were no questions asked. They saw me as a married woman." Another lesbian officer masquerading as straight spoke of the extreme importance she placed on convincing her superiors that she was heterosexual. To this end she provided them with fictional accounts of male relationships and consistently feigned interest in men in general.

You would have to put up a front. Oh yeah, I'm seeing this guy and, oh yeah, he's cute. . . . Around a boss I would say, oh yeah, he's cute, whatever the case may be. I wouldn't want bosses leery about my life-style. You know how bosses are on the job. They would be blackballing you.

She continued:

Or, we would be watching TV programs and a boss would be around and they would be admiring the girls and guys that work out and I would say, "Look at the body on this guy and that guy." You have to sometimes.

For a gay person to pretend that he or she is dating or having sexual relations with someone of the opposite sex means the individual must first have a mental image of how the staged heterosexual self should be presented.[17] This image can be conjured up in the case of the man or woman who has never experienced a cross-sex relationship, or it can be summoned up from earlier heterosexual affairs. One officer, however, expressed his discomfort in promoting this sort of pretense. "I generally try to avoid these conversations [about dating women], but the cops are always talking about it and always asking me about my dates. I just look back on past experiences that I had."

As my interviews along with my own experiences in the police department suggest, conversations among male heterosexual officers concerning the opposite sex are usually explicit and carnal. Given the appropriate verbal or visual cues, the straight male cop will quickly shift to personal accounts of his sexual exploits, which often involve a description of the women's erogenous body parts and of the couple's sexual activities. Other men present during these accounts are expected to either participate in the storytelling bravado, or at least to appear interested in others' sexual conquests. All this is part of the machismo ritual of male bonding, separating real cops from the others. Understandably, for the gay officer trying to pass as straight, these expectations can require enormous expenditures of energy. To get some understanding of the difficult and uncomfortable predicament a closeted gay cop constantly has to contend with, consider this hypothetical situation: Instead of a heterosexually dominated society, we are living in one occupied mostly by homosexuals. In this inverted society the straight cop becomes the deviant and, in order to fit in, must pretend that he is normal, that is, *homosexual.* This pretense is crucial when in the company of his male co-workers who, he must assume, are all accepted gays in this inverted world. Consequently, this closeted straight must feign (or even vocalize) an interest in fellating other men and must appear sexually aroused at pictures or graphic descriptions of men's genitals. When in mixed company this heterosexual must pretend to flirt with other men, while publicly rejecting and privately suppressing any sexual interest in the women around him. He must watch his every word and gesture lest he signal to the majority that he is not the person he purports to be. It would only take one slip for his secret to be exposed.

Another widely adopted strategy used to help create this fictional heterosexual identity for the closeted cop is to occasionally attend police social functions or get-togethers in the company of a member of the opposite sex. One officer who continues to carefully shelter his true sexual identity from others at work recalls a recent affair to which he brought, as his date, a female relative. "Not long ago I was invited to this [cop's] wedding and I ended up taking my sister-in-law. I passed her off as my girlfriend. There was no problem with her because she already knew I was gay."

Others in this group of secret homosexuals have similarly experienced the stress that accompanies living a lie, of constructing fictional relationships to convince heterosexual fellow officers that they are straight. One lesbian, who is now out to a handful of her co-workers, speaks of her lover, also an officer in the NYPD. Her lover is not out, so, "when we went to precinct rackets she would introduce me as . . . her cousin. She's not homophobic or anything. She doesn't care if the whole world knows except those two hundred people who work in that building [her precinct]."

Social situations such as precinct rackets (for example, promotional or retirement dinners) often magnify anxieties and tensions because the closeted officer who comes unescorted must guard constantly against any slip that could reveal his or her true sexual identity. Thus what should be an otherwise quite ordinary and relaxed social atmosphere, as it is for the heterosexual officer, often turns into one that requires constant vigilance. "Yeah, you've got to be real careful that you don't slip. It's always in the back of your mind when you're talking about your private life. You can be talking to someone from work and even before I mention to them something I did the night before, I've got to think it out and make sure I don't slip and tell them about my lover."

Given the strain of having to be continually on guard, it is not surprising to find that some closeted cops, as a protective strategy, tend to forgo most group get-togethers, especially such liquor-consuming activities as barhopping with the guys or gals after work. For these officers there is a gradual withdrawal from contact with their heterosexual workmates, a drifting away from their colleagues and their social activities when off duty. "I don't go out with the guys that much anymore after work because I have to pretend for eight hours, and I don't want to pretend for another three. You go out and you have a little liquor, and you might say something accidentally that you will regret later."

A further self-demeaning and certainly stress-producing strategy involves listening to and possibly even participating in a seemingly endless stream of homosexual jokes and antigay slurs. For the closeted gay cop to appear even mildly disturbed, offended, or disinterested in this degrading humor could cause others to suspect him or her of being gay. One female officer candidly admitted that on occasions such as this she "has to at least put up with it so you're not labeled a homosexual." This officer even feels compelled, in some instances, to partake in the vilification of gays, though this behavior leaves her troubled. "I even joke around with everybody when they talk about gays and make fun of them. It bothers me."

To help maintain or even strengthen a false heterosexual image in the workplace, some gay males strive to appear overly masculine. One veteran officer, reflecting on his earlier days, said that at the time his method of covering up his homosexuality was to excel in sports. He admits now that even he then subscribed to the commonly held notion that if one were an athlete participating in manly sports, one could not possibly be viewed as homosexual. "I was really concerned in the [police] academy. In the gym I compensated for my gayness by being overly masculine. I guess by as far as the different sports activities I made damn sure I was up in the front of my class." Overly masculinizing his speech pattern was another way this officer chose to convey a heterosexual identity to his police colleagues. He said he "tried to be more aggressive" in his speech.

Another widely adopted strategy to help avoid discovery at work is to simply refrain from discussing or getting into arguments involving the subject of homosexuality. But intentionally avoiding such conversations can leave one feeling extremely frustrated and ego-damaged. The behavior can also have the counteracting effect of actually heightening suspicion as to the individual's true sexual orientation should the avoidance become patterned and visible. Thus the effectiveness of this strategy is debatable, as one officer notes. "I tried to avoid these discussions whenever I could. But one day one of the cops I work with accused me of being a homosexual since I never said anything against them."

This comment, along with others I collected during the course of this research, strengthens my hypothesis that for a cop, either gay or straight, to avoid even the suspicion of being homosexual, it is not enough to remain neutral on the subject of homosexuality. A cop must actively participate in the denunciation of gays and their reputedly deviant life-styles.

Precautionary measures designed to evade discovery can and do extend beyond the confines of the officer's immediate work world. One extreme measure is to steer clear of areas in the city where gays are known to hang out. Most of the men and women in this study say, however, that this is not a viable alternative for one intent on pursuing a more stable homosexual life-style. Consequently, when they frequent these known gay locales, as most do, their chief concern is how to avoid drawing attention to themselves from police on patrol. Virtually everyone I spoke with has, at one time or another, taken precautions not to be recognized by other police officers while socializing in homosexual areas of the city. One man, now out, reflected on feelings he experienced during the closeted stage of his police career.

Three years ago when I was looking for an apartment I was down on West Eleventh Street by the river [a well-known gay area]. So I'm with a friend of mine, a guy. He's gay. I park the car and we're going to walk a block or so to the building. As we're walking down the street there's a van from Manhattan South Task Force. I froze. I absolutely froze. I didn't even want to get close enough to find out if I knew anybody. The chances were fifty-fifty that I was going to know somebody in the van. . . . So we stopped and went around the corner.

Likewise, when entering or leaving a reputed homosexual establishment, the closeted gay cop is always mindful of being seen by other cops, regardless of whether or not he knows them. The same officer elaborates, "I used to avoid them [the cops]. I would definitely look over my shoulder going into a bar to see if there were any radio cars coming down the street. Silly stuff, when I look at it now."

Another male officer's deep-seated fear of being seen entering his favorite gay bar by the police seems to border on paranoia. "I remember going to [a gay bar]. I was looking around thinking there was a camera watching me and other gays to see if any gay cops came in the place." The most common way of dealing with the ever-present possibility of being recognized when nearing a known gay bar or club is to quickly turn away when a police car approaches or to simply keep walking past the establishment as though it were not one's destination.

I'd be discreet if I saw a couple of cops in uniform or a car go by. I'd walk by the place till they left.

At one time I was really nervous. I would turn the other way when cops were around and I was, say, down in the Village. I would look at window displays.

Some took the extreme action of intentionally covering their faces when approached by officers in uniform. "When I was really closeted I was in the Village with my friends and anytime a radio car would pass by or when we passed a cop on the street I would find myself sort of looking off to the side, covering my face so I wouldn't be recognized. Really, I used to hide my face like a common criminal."

Still others would quickly duck into hallways, storefronts, or the gay bar itself through a side or back entrance to avoid detection by patrol officers whom they may or may not know. A lesbian reports the anxiety she experienced from the simple act of attempting to enter a gay bar:

There's this place [a lesbian bar], and right across the street is a bar owned by a former transit cop, and a lot of cops go there. So one time I'm walking down [this] street and ready to go into the bar and all of a sudden I hear, "Hey _____, how are you?" Oh, my God, I thought. Let's just make the first turn around the corner and go in the back way. . . . And so now if I'm going to go into that bar, I make sure the whole street is clear and then I duck into the place. Leaving is tough, too. I've gone back into the place a couple of times when I saw some cops.

Even after having inconspicuously and safely entered a gay bar, there is no guarantee the closeted cop will not be recognized by other cops on patrol. The same officer explains, "I was inside this place one time when an RMP [radio motor patrol car] stopped in front of the place and the cops came to the door. I had to duck down."

Moreover, the police may, at any time, be called to a gay establishment in response to a complaint or call for service and then, coincidentally, encounter a co-worker as one of the patrons. "Yeah, I've seen the RMPs stop by [a gay bar]. I've heard of cops going into the place, so it's not a safe haven even once you're inside."

A gay officer may also be seen and recognized by a cop he or she knows when leaving a gay establishment. One officer reported getting

caught once. I walked out of a place on Second Avenue. I walked out the door, a gay bar, and there's the bouncer standing there talking to a . . . patrol sergeant sitting in his car—the guy I grew up with in the neighborhood in Queens. And I walk out and I say, "Hi, how are you doing." And he goes, "Hi, _____," and I walk down the street and I get into my car. . . . I've seen him since and neither one of us have said a fucking word. . . . I know him well enough so he could have said, "What the fuck were you doing in that place?" Maybe he was out to lunch and didn't know it was a gay bar.

Even when they are merely spectators at gay events, closeted cops find they must keep looking over their shoulders and stay alert as to who is around them at all times. As most of these public events are heavily policed, there is a persistent danger that the secretly gay officer will bump into a cop with whom he or she worked in the past. These occasions often call for even more evasive actions.

I went to the Gay Parade with sunglasses on. I had to duck every time I saw some cop I knew. At one parade I was walking on Christopher Street and a guy from the _____ Precinct who I know saw me for just a quick second. I had to hide from him, so I ducked down behind a display case. . . . It was just a split second he saw me.

When gay officers are off duty and out socializing, the type and degree of precautionary actions they take to avoid being recognized by on-duty police often depend on the appearance and mannerisms of the person accompanying them. As one transit cop explains:

What I did, I was careful who I went out with. When I went to discos, I don't have a car so I had to use the subway. I remember I would always take the longer route [to avoid my police district] when I was with an effeminate friend. If I was with a straight-looking friend, that was not a problem.

The fear of being seen and recognized while frequenting a gay area is not limited to the moment a patrol officer passes by or responds to a job, as there is a strong possibility that he or she will not know the gay officer. On these occasions the fear is projected into the future, should the two wind up assigned to the same command or meet accidentally at a police social function. Although even then the possibility of recognition of the other by either officer is slim, it becomes a reality that keeps the gay officer ever vigilant and self-protective.

Understandably, the most risky areas for being discovered are the more unconventional gay cruising grounds, such as parks, tearooms, and waterfronts. Unlike being spotted in other settings, such as gay bars and social clubs, the simple act of being present in these areas exposes one to the risk of being stopped by the police.[18] In these unconventional settings the possibility of being victimized (for example, robbed or assaulted) is high; consequently, the police are more prone to stop individuals who frequent these areas and check their identification. This is one of the closeted gay cop's worst fears. To avoid such unintentional discovery many closeted as well as some openly gay cops in this study who cruised these unconventional set-

tings claimed that they rarely, if ever, carried their police identification or weapon on their person. The following rationale offered for
this practice is typical: "Yes, I took precautions. I never carried my
shield and ID with me. Wouldn't even carry the gun. It would be in
the car. In case I got stopped in a cruising area I knew they would
toss [search] me."

Gay cops, especially those who are secretive about their sexual
identities, and who routinely cruise public areas of the city, are
acutely aware of police tactics in these places. To successfully handle
the problem of being stopped, questioned, and subsequently identified as police officers, some of the cops in this study actually devised
false biographies and phony reasons for their presence in these
areas. A few even went so far as to rehearse the answers they would
provide should the police stop and question them. "You have to create scenarios as to how you would deal with a situation, what you
would say to the cops that stopped you."

All of these comments suggest that closeted gay cops may experience far more stress navigating their homosexual social world than
their work world, for greater risks of exposure exist because of the
visible nature of homosexual life-styles and relationships. Thus, their
social world, even though it may be separated geographically from
their workplace, may not be the comfortable refuge for the closeted
officer some gays seem to think it is.[19] For the closeted gay cop intent
on pursuing a life of secrecy, conditions of ordinary social interaction, taken for granted by straights, take on a special meaning. These
situations are, above all, a cause for heightened awareness and sensitivity to the possibility that they could accidentally give away their
sexual identities. This type of information control takes its toll on the
closeted officer in the form of fear, strife, and alienation from both
self and others.

Given the amount of energy expended and quiet suffering experienced creating and sustaining fictional biographies and accounts of
self both at work and at play, it is no wonder that some closeted cops
eventually seek relief and comfort by sharing their secret with others
at work. While these men and women are not yet ready to make a
public declaration of their homosexuality, they take a decisive step in
this direction by coming out to a select few of their co-workers.

Six

Coming

Out

Tentatively

at

Work

I'm not out publicly, but some cops are suspicious. . . . One guy said recently, "I know you're messing around [with other gays]." . . . But they don't care because they see me as a good cop, not a bad cop. There are good cops and bad cops.

Between the extremes of being totally secretive and publicly, fully out of the closet lies an in-between stage I have labeled "tentatively out." Passing from the first, most secretive phase to this one can be accomplished in a number of ways. Once again, the metaphor of the closet is a fitting way to chronicle the steps of this passage. Barring any outside intervention, the closeted gay cop largely controls the opening of that door, from first crack to fully flung open. These officers have a number of options. They can open the door all the way, fully revealing their homosexuality to as many or as few work associates as they choose. In this variation the closeted officer alone controls access to the door.

In a second variation, the still secretive cop can choose to open the door only partially by leaving a series of clues or thinly veiled suggestions of his homosexuality around the precinct. These pointed clues are usually not left with the specific intent of exposing oneself but are allowed to surface solely as a result of the officer's frustration with and unwillingness to continue living a lie. By taking this veiled action, the gay officer can now take some control over the opening of the closet door. Once these clues are allowed to filter into the officer's command, even without unequivocal proof of homosexuality, suspicions among co-workers can become so strong as to provoke not only rumors but an irresistible urge for some to try to pry the closet door open even further. If the curious prying of co-workers leads to evidence of a cop's homosexuality, that officer could lose control of his or her secret. At this point, however, the gay cop inside that closet may have the option to reshut the door before co-workers have a chance to confirm their suspicions. This can be accomplished either by denying the allegations of homosexuality or by concocting believable explanations for the purported (or even observed) homosexual behavior. If the closeted cop is unsuccessful in squelching the suspicions and rumors through logic, he or she may have to drop the staunchly straight front and admit homosexual tendencies. This is often the case when the clues left are so obvious and blatant that they belie any counterclaims.

In the third and final variation, the gay officer alone, with full awareness of the consequences, opens the door intentionally. The specific goal here is to reveal that he or she is gay. In this instance, clues deliberately planted in the precinct are designed to increase one's visibility as a homosexual without the officer's having to actually come out and say it in so many words.

CONFIDING IN ONE'S HETEROSEXUAL PARTNER: SELECTIVE DISCLOSURE

Divulging such highly personal biographical information as a non-conventional sexual orientation to a straight co-worker can be a relieving and reassuring experience for the closeted gay officer. Once the secret has been divulged, the officer no longer has to be on guard, nor does he or she have to continue to avoid stigma symbols or to use disidentifiers. Yet the decision to disclose such a discreditable secret is also fraught with uncertainties and fears. There is, first of all, the question of whom to tell; that is, which co-workers can be trusted with this potentially career-threatening information, and which cannot. Once that decision has been reached there are the questions of how, where, and when to reveal this information.

Not unexpectedly, the great majority of officers said that they chose to share their secret with only one or at most a select few close working partners. When asked to define the term *close partner*, they cited the following qualities most frequently: a partner who (1) was considered a friend as well as a work associate; (2) had already shown that he or she could be trusted with confidential information; (3) had demonstrated some compassion for other stigmatized groups, such as minorities or the visibly handicapped; and (4) was not overly judgmental, but who displayed understanding, maturity, and intelligence. In short, they described a person they felt safe with and had come to consider family. When, because of the nature of their assignments, closeted subjects did not have a close partner, they chose to reveal their homosexuality to a steady partner. This was someone who, though not necessarily close in terms of friendship, was nevertheless someone they had worked with often enough to feel that he or she would not betray the gay officer's secret. Only two officers said they disclosed their homosexuality to cops with whom they worked only sporadically.

Most of the closeted officers elected to tell their partners of their homosexuality while at work, either in the locker room when no one else was present or when they were alone together in the radio car during the quiet hours of their tour. A smaller group revealed their secret after they and their partners finished a tour, usually after having first stopped off at a local bar for a few drinks. In these instances, the liquor no doubt served to instill courage and ease the apprehension the gay officer was experiencing about the impending revelation.

Given the uncertainty as to what kind of reaction disclosure might bring, the most important question is *why* these men and women decided to expose such a potentially discrediting aspect of their personal life to a workmate in the first place. The officers offered a variety of reasons that they claimed collectively, over time, triggered their decision to open the closet door. Most said they were driven by resentment from living a lie and having to be on all the time, especially with close partners who were also considered friends. As one frustrated officer put it:

You develop friendships and you don't want them shrouded in lies. Eventually, if you are that close to someone you should reveal yourself, including your sexuality. It's not fair for you to lie about women and who you laid and how many girls you made love to when it's all a lie. He deserves the truth.

A lesbian described the circumstances surrounding her unmasking. She too was tired of leading two lives while in the company of her close partner.

We were in the precinct awhile and she took to me. I got very close to her. She was always saying, let's get together, bring your boyfriend, your husband. At first I played along with it, and I always declined invitations. Enough was enough. I was getting tired of the pretensions and I said, "If I can go there's somebody I'd like to bring if it's all right with you." I said it was another woman. So I told her and said, "If you tell anybody I will just have to deal with it."

Two men explained their decision to come out by pointing to the pressure and personally disruptive effects of having to maintain a constant pretense of heterosexuality:

It was finally on a four-to-twelve [tour] and I had to stop at eight o'clock and make a date for later on. I got back in the car after making a phone call and he [my partner] said, "What's up?" I said, "Nothing." What happened is that I was lying to my partner all the time. That really bothered me. That relationship doesn't work. And it was hurting me. And it was obvious to him that I was hiding something. So I just told him. . . . It was very difficult for me. I'm even a little emotional now telling you about it. I was worried that he was going to reject me, that he wouldn't want to work with me, that he'd tell everyone in the precinct. I was also the PBA delegate. This would be the end of my political career.

I felt like a goddamn schizo. It was crazy for a thirty-three-year-old man to have to lead a double life with [his partner]. It was driving me crazy. It's not even a matter of having to live a lie. You're in your mid-thirties and single, innuendo takes over.

The daily pretense, the need to be constantly on guard and to appear attracted to members of the opposite sex, took its toll on another officer, finally compelling him, as well, to come out to his partner. Once out, he said he felt considerably more relaxed and found that he could finally be himself on patrol. He said his only regret was that he did not confide his homosexuality to his partner sooner. He went on to describe what life was like at work once he was finally out to this officer.

So now while he was looking at a woman going this way, I was looking at a guy going that way. Now he'd be talking to me and I would say, "Shut up, I'm trying to pay attention to this guy." Or, we would be going on a job and I'd be flirting with guys and not worry. We'd go to radio runs and we'd go in and take a look around and he'd say, "You're handling this one," because it was obvious we were in a gay man's home.

Some of my subjects view their relationship with a close partner as a marriage of sorts involving such deep feelings as mutual trust, commitment, and honesty. Precisely because of the depth of these relationships, these men and women came to believe that it was not morally right to continue to hide their secret from their partners. One officer explained it this way:

> We were best friends, close partners. I thought he had a right to know that I was gay. We were so close. He was closer than a brother, and he had a right to know. I trusted him. He understood me and was never judgmental.

This same officer, however, held off telling his partner (as most others have done) until the most opportune time. In this case, that moment came when they returned from a vacation they had taken together.

> I remember we just got back from a trip to Mexico and we went up to his house, still celebrating, drinking the Scotch we bought. I was going to spend the night there and it was a perfect vacation, and we were just talking, and I said, "Tommy, there's something I want to tell you," and I just told him that I was gay.

Similarly, another detective noted how the sense of closeness he shared with one of his co-workers, and consequently his need for honesty and openness between partners, brought him to disclose his homosexuality to that partner. In this case, as well, disclosure occurred during a friendly, festive occasion and was precipitated by the consumption of alcohol.

> I went to his retirement party and we were drinking. . . . I thought it would be easier to tell him there. We were off to the side. I told him in relation to my marriage, why it was not working, why we [he and his wife] had problems. I had worked with him over the years, and we were very close. I had a need not to hide it anymore from him because we got so close. You have a marriage in police work. There is trust with your partners.

As noted earlier, an important element of trust between partners is the conviction that any shared personal information, particularly that of a potentially discrediting nature, will be held in utmost confidence and not be passed along to others. For the typically cynical police officer this depth of trust does not develop easily and never spontaneously; it should not automatically be assumed to exist in every working relationship. Trust in one's partner, when it occurs, is a quality that emerges only through positive experiences and over time.

It was on the midnight [tour]. It was as dead as a doornail. There was nothing
going on. So I told him. There was some concern about him telling others. It did
come up. But deep down inside I knew he wouldn't because our friendship
and our partnership was such that we had discussed things in reference to people
at work as well as people we knew, and nothing that I had ever told him had
passed him. So I knew that if I told him something this important, I knew he wasn't
going to go back and put it up on the board.

In a few instances disclosure was made to a close partner because the gay officer was experiencing a serious personal problem in his or her social life and had a powerful need to confide in a close friend. In a partnership where closeness and mutual trust have developed over a period of months or years and where the straight partner has freely confided personal problems or intimate facts of his life to the gay officer, that officer comes to feel comfortable enough to reveal his or her own secrets. In one instance the gay officer's money problems were an entry into exposing her true sexual identity to her partner. This was coupled with her male heterosexual partner's previous sharing of his own personal problems.

He didn't have a steady partner so one day I asked him if he would like to ride
steady with me. We got our own sector after six months and we were
riding together every day. . . . When you spend eight hours or more a day you begin to talk to each other and get to know each other personally. Well, one day
after I broke up with my lover, I was so upset I needed to talk to him, tell him
about the breakup. I now had an apartment I couldn't afford and had to face
the idea of having to find another one, on top of the emotional hurt. That's when I
confided my homosexuality to him. By then I knew about his family problems,
and it was easy to tell him about me.

Another cop's disclosure was motivated by sudden depression over a lost lover and his need to share this sorrow with someone close. "My partner and I had worked together for three and a half years. We were very, very close. I had just lost my first lover, and I was depressed because it was true love on my part, and it hurt me very much, and I just didn't know how to shake the feeling. I had to talk to somebody."

Closeness between partners generally emerges through the camaraderie derived from the intense challenges and dangers of policing. But misunderstanding of what that closeness means does occasionally surface between male and female officer teams. For example, closeness can be taken out of the narrow context of policing and misinterpreted by one or the other partner as an expression of sexual interest. A closeted female officer had just this experience when she began receiving signals that this closeness between her and some of her male partners was being perceived as heterosexual attraction. To set the record straight she chose to come out to one of them.

There were a few guys at the precinct who liked me. I had to constantly make excuses to them. Some guys really persisted, and I had to go into these really nasty lies. . . . I really liked these guys. I started to really care about their feelings and I saw that they were starting to really care about me. . . . There was this one particular guy at the precinct who liked me, really liked me. I got tired of being dishonest, leading him on. I finally told the guy. I was not going to keep lying.

Along the same lines, another female officer explained that she simply grew tired of a male partner's persistent sexual overtures.

When I was in the _____ Precinct I worked with a guy on a steady basis and he was constantly hitting on me, and I got fed up with it. So I said, "Look, honey, this is how my situation is. My preference is not men, it's females. You label that any way you want, OK. I'm not interested in you other than a partner and a friend. Other than that, it's not going any farther. And it has nothing to do with whether you are good looking. It's just that you're not my sex."

Judging from the comments thus far, it seems that a gay officer's perception of how he or she is viewed by a co-worker can become a powerful determinant of how that officer manages a homosexual identity at work. This perception-action linkage is most evident when gay officers believe they are viewed by a close partner as a "good cop" and because of this favorable image entrust the partner with information about their gay identity. These men and women expressed the feeling both directly and indirectly that their reputation or standing as good cops would override the stigma attached to homosexuality and insulate them from co-worker discrimination. Stated another way, the good cop would become the "master status"[1] that would validate to close work mates the gay officer's social worth in the precinct.

To be designated a good cop, police officers must possess personal traits and professional skills that are central to survival in their line of work. These qualities are not born of society's rules, nor are they necessarily endorsed, at least not publicly, by those in high administrative positions. (Indeed, as we shall see, they are often in conflict with the needs and interests of the public and especially of those in political leadership positions in the city.) They are, rather, cops' rules made by cops, sanctioned by cops, and *enforced* by cops.[2]

Because my standing as a ranking member of the police department was firmly established before the interviews, most of the officers felt no compelling need to elaborate on the term *good cop*. There was a built-in assumption that when they used the term, I knew what they meant. However, I asked them to clarify their understanding of what it meant to be a good cop to see if their definitions squared with my own. There was no significant difference. A good cop was characterized in the following general terms: an officer who (1) backs up partner and co-workers in emergency situations; (2) covers up partner's or co-workers' indiscretions or misconduct at work or, (3) at the very least, does not give up (betray) a fellow officer who is suspected or accused of having engaged in misconduct of a departmental (or, in some instances, even criminal) nature; (4) is a risk taker, not afraid to deviate from departmental rules to get the job done; (5) shares in the workload, especially in the handling of routine or tedious jobs; and (6) does not look for others to do his or her work. In short, the designation *good cop* reflects the needs and expectations of others who work in a world that is extremely hazardous. Summing up the expectations of street cops in general, the police chief of Portland, Oregon, said, "Most police officers could not care one way or the other whether someone is a homosexual, what matters as a street cop . . . is whether you'll be there to help when things get tough." Those cops who fail to live up to these informal rules, like prison inmates who become informers, face rejection and social isolation by their peers.[3]

While it may be true that some of these qualities can be demonstrated in most commands, certain assignments, such as patrol and investigations in which members of the department are most directly and continuously exposed to the routine hazards of the street, afford officers a greater opportunity to prove their worthiness of the designation good cop. On the other hand, those cops who work out of headquarters or who have other inside or desk jobs and consequently are not involved in the dangerous world of the street cop may forfeit the opportunity to earn the reputation of a good cop. Insofar as this designation remains questionable in the eyes of other cops, for the gay officer who is not assigned to patrol or other potentially hazardous duties to reveal his homosexuality to others in the workplace may mean that his professional or overall worth will now be determined largely, if not exclusively, by his status as a homosexual.

This study conditionally supports the argument that there is a relationship between self-perception and self-presentation in the homosexual cop's work world. This linkage is often mediated by the officer's role or assignment in the department. Among the segment of cops who were either tentatively or publicly out at the time of the interviews, the overwhelming majority were assigned to either patrol or investigative duties when they made their disclosure. These cops believed strongly that the partners to whom they chose to reveal their homosexuality saw them as good cops both before and after disclosure. Moreover, many of these same officers mentioned that one of the primary (if not the key) considerations in their decision to come out was the belief that their reputations as good cops would somehow ease their transition to greater openness by diminishing the relevance others might attach to their homosexual status. As one precinct officer put it:

It was something I was concerned about when I first got here. But I eventually had a chance to prove myself in some tough situations and I always came through. My partners always had the impression of me as someone who could be trusted, you know, someone who could be counted on if the shit hit the fan in the street. I would always back them even if they fucked up. . . . It's not anything the guys tell you, but you just know that you're considered a good cop. So I played on this when I told my partner [about being gay]. I was a little leery but I felt that my reputation with this guy was solid. So I took a chance and told him.

A transit officer, also believing that he had earned the reputation of good cop among his peers, reflected on how this perceived status impacted on his choice of a confidant.

The first person I told was my steady partner. We were partners for six months
and we went through a number of major capers together. He felt I was a
good cop, that I could be trusted [to keep his mouth shut], and I felt the same
about him.

A female officer offered a more sensitive insight into the image of a
good cop as it may apply to some women in policing; that is, the
ability to seem down to earth and possibly, to some male partners,
less threatening.

This guy chose to work with me rather than with anybody else. He saw me as a
good cop. Men tend to act very macho and they like to work with somebody who is
down to earth. Well, the macho guy believes that his shit doesn't stink. He
tends not to listen to the real problem but only what he thinks the problem is.
He tends to instigate things a little bit more and he deals with his muscles rather
than his brains.

As the interviews have shown, the process of coming out in the
workplace is accomplished in varying stages. As the gay officer
travels through the uncharted waters of these difficult life segments,
he or she finds that each one brings with it a new set of complications
and stresses. One stress-provoking and ironic consequence of choosing to come out to a close partner is that in doing so gay officers
inflict the same burden of secretiveness on their partners, themselves
now faced with the pressure of how to deal with this information
while attempting to function normally in the perceived homophobic
world of policing. The ambivalence and perhaps even guilt felt by the
gay officer for placing this unasked for burden on the straight partner is graphically and poignantly detailed in the following account of
an off-duty incident.

My partner [whom he told last year] and I were just leaving this bar with a couple
of guys from the precinct. Two guys were walking toward us, holding hands.
One of the guys [cops] made a loud remark, something like, "Look at those sick
motherfuckers!" I could see [my partner] was real embarrassed. He just kept walking as if nothing had been said. I felt real bad for him, but I guess he really
couldn't have said anything under the circumstances. He's not the type to start any
shit. . . . They would have thought that he must be a faggot too. So we just left.
. . . Nothing was ever said [about the incident].

In such situations, the straight partner becomes entwined in the same dilemma as the closeted gay cop; that is, how to deal with anti-gay slurs or homophobic behavior by straight cops. Whether these disparaging remarks or behaviors are directed toward homosexuals in general or toward a particular police officer suspected or known to be gay, the knowledge imposed upon the straight partner now sets that individual apart from the unknowing who make up the bulk of the command. The informed straight partner is thrust into the position of having to make one of several no-win decisions: either to stand by and listen silently to the degrading comments, knowing they refer indirectly to a close partner, thereby possibly experiencing a sense of betrayal for not having said anything in defense; to join in the ridicule so as to avoid appearing suspect in any way, but thereby knowingly insulting his partner; or to simply, sheepishly walk away, as described in the previous detailed incident. A fourth choice, that of taking a stand in defense of the partner, as is reported to have occurred in the following locker room incident, clearly carries with it its own potential for repercussions among the straight officer's colleagues.

I told my partner a few months ago and there was no problem at all. . . . I felt I had his loyalty. One evening we were all changing [in the locker room] to go home and there was this photo of Rock Hudson hanging on a locker [of a suspected gay cop] and someone had drawn a picture of a big dick sticking up his ass. It was a fairly big drawing. Some of the guys were crowding around the photo, laughing and saying how fucking sick people like this were and how he got what he deserved (I guess they meant he died of AIDS). . . . [His partner] looked at me and went over and ripped the picture off the locker. He said, "I'm not gay, but I don't think this kind of shit is funny." One guy made a few remarks. Then everyone got quiet. . . . I was really taken back by what he did, and I told him later that I appreciated it. It took a lot of courage. He said it was no big deal.

Like the ripples made by a stone cast in water, the secret, once revealed to a co-worker, can impact on the gay officer and his straight partner in unintentional and unforeseen ways. For the closeted cop, both betrayal or support, in varying degrees, must be considered and weighed as possible outcomes before deciding to divulge the secret to a trusted partner who is also considered a friend.

Along with those officers who have *chosen* to expose their homosexuality to one or more of their partners is a smaller group of subjects who fall into the second tentatively out category. Although most have not confided in anyone in particular, these officers are still, for various reasons, suspected of being homosexuals.

Most of the men and women in this group felt that they had done nothing intentional to arouse suspicions in their workplace. Indeed, a few even seemed genuinely surprised that rumors of their sexual differentness had begun to surface. What then did constitute grounds for suspicion and rumors? One key factor, uncovered in the interviews, was a positive change in the way they were beginning to perceive themselves in relation to others in the precinct. The result was that they simply dropped the facade of heterosexuality from their self-presentations and interactions with others at work.

As pointed out earlier in this chapter, important tip-offs to a person's true sexual orientation are the social relationships he or she either openly maintains or attempts to present when in the presence of straight cops. Gay male officers who make a point of attending social functions in the company of women, for example, are obviously seeking to convey the impression of heterosexuality. Likewise, a male officer who receives phone calls at work primarily from women is hardly likely to be suspected of having homosexual inclinations. On the other hand, the male officer who is known to receive calls predominantly from *men* may indeed become suspect. Rumors may begin to circulate that the recipient of these predominantly same-gender calls is not the heterosexual he professes to be.

When asked specifically how suspicions of their homosexuality first began to surface, a number of gay officers felt that it was because colleagues at work noticed that they were constantly receiving same-sex calls. As one female officer summed it up, "Cops working the T.S. [telephone switchboard] and who calls all the time? Other females. They get the message."

Male officers concurred:

How did they come to suspect me, even though I haven't told anyone? I don't have women calling me up at work all the time. I don't have a long list of [women's] phone numbers they [straight cops] do.

I don't have girls calling the district and stuff like that. People do pick up on things. Girls don't call me ever. Some guys suspect.

Attention was drawn to the possible homosexuality of one officer when a few of his co-workers began to notice that the great majority of people calling and asking for him at the station house were not only men, but a particular ethnic group of men. "Basically, rumors [circulated] to the fact that Asian men are always calling me. Other cops pick up the phone and want to know why only Asian guys were calling."

Another clue to a hidden homosexual identity can be an individual's same-sex roommate. By itself, this living arrangement is not unusual today and should not necessarily arouse suspicions. But living with a member of the same sex (or even living alone) can, when coupled with other suspect information, trigger suspicions as to an individual's real sexual preferences. Moreover, if an individual is already under suspicion—for instance, for failing to meet conventional gender-image requirements, such as appearing feminine—and the discovery is made that the individual's living arrangements are not *distinctly* heterosexual, then suspicions may even be magnified. As a female officer explained:

If they see a woman who is not too feminine and who doesn't have a wedding band on or who doesn't talk about her boyfriends or dates or who is not slutting around with everybody at work, they will assume she is gay. They are going to say, "Oh, she's gay."

In addition to biographical clues, behavioral characteristics can provoke suspicion. For instance, repeated failure on the part of a male cop to comment in the time-honored, manly way about women's bodies or to make sexually suggestive remarks about women is certain to alert his male partners that something is *different* about him. One lieutenant who, before confiding in his partner, had almost totally ceased participating in the pretense reflects on the suspicion his behavior aroused.

When you spend eight hours and thirty minutes with cops on patrol and they're looking at every woman walking down the street and I'm not, I think it's the nature of a cop to notice that his partner never makes comments about big tits, or nice ass, or nice legs. And they notice that while they're looking at some females, I'm looking at some red-headed guy.

A further clue that a male co-worker may not be what he purports to be is the absence (or removal) of pictures of scantily clad or nude women on the inside of his locker. "One of the telltale signs is if he does not talk about girls all the time and doesn't have five thousand nude pictures in his locker. I'm the only one out of 150 cops in my command who doesn't have these nude photographs." In addition, if a male officer appears bored, uninterested, or uncomfortable when talk among his male colleagues centers on women, it may be taken as a sign that the officer is not really one of the guys. "The [captain] in the precinct is also single and he loves to womanize. And he knows I'm single and he keeps telling me all these stories about these women and these parties and I'm bored to death. So I believe he finally figured it out [from that]."

Because, as indicated earlier, the majority of still-closeted cops go to great lengths to protect their anonymity when frequenting known gay areas of the city, it is not surprising that most of them have successfully managed, when in these areas, to elude police detection. A few, however, did report being recognized by on-duty officers either in a known homosexual area or at a gay-sponsored event. In a frantic attempt to cover up their hidden homosexuality, they later denied ever having been in that homosexual setting. One officer reported, for example, that "someone said to another guy that he saw me at the gay parade [as a spectator, not as a marcher]. . . . I went up to the cop and confronted him. I had him backed in the corner and he graciously put it off as a joke." As this incident suggests, if a suspect officer is aggressive enough and successful in refuting what someone claims and believes they saw or heard, then the officer's secret identity may remain temporarily intact. But if, on the other hand, the closeted gay is caught red-handed in a more intimate situation (for instance, observed kissing a same-sex companion), there may remain little choice but to stand up and admit one's homosexuality, at least to the witness, and hope that the discreditable information will not be passed on to others in the precinct. A female officer finding herself in precisely this predicament recalled her first reaction: "He had just seen me with her. He asked who she was. . . . I said she was just a friend. He said that she looks like she's a little bit more than that. . . . (He saw her kissing me.) My immediate reaction was to ask him who else did you tell about this."

Of those officers in this study who had already come out to a select few colleagues and who were contemplating eventually going public, most stated that they preferred to make that final transition on their own terms and in their own time. It is clearly crucial for these men and women to feel in full control of the circumstances that could so dramatically alter their lives.

I don't want it to be like we were onstage and I'm on the sidelines watching and someone shoves me in the middle of the stage and now I gotta act. You do and I freeze and go the other way. It's like learning to walk. You gotta crawl first.

SELF-INITIATED RUMORS AND SUSPICIONS

Sometimes, to facilitate the coming-out process, gay cops themselves instigate rumors of their homosexuality. This signaling process, however, may be first confined to other suspected homosexuals in the precinct as a means of gathering support. One demonstration of this is the female cop who deliberately wore to work a souvenir T-shirt inscribed with the name of a resort known in the homosexual community to be a gathering spot for gays. She explained that this choice of action was her way of feeling out the climate before making a more public statement.

Sometimes you wear a T-shirt that says something. That's what I did. I walked into work one day and I wanted the lesbians to know I was gay. The shirt said, "P-Town," a large gay population, a vacation place. It would be something the men and women would recognize. So they did recognize it, the lesbians did. They didn't acknowledge it right away, but at the end of the tour, two females were waiting for me. They said, "We noticed your T-shirt." They had smiles on their faces. They had no idea I was gay. I didn't look butch, I flirted with the men, and they flirted with me.

Similarly, a now fully open transit cop reflects on the messages he sent to prepare his straight partner for disclosure of his homosexuality.

We were talking about girlfriends. He was telling me about his girls, you know. He knew I had a roommate. I stopped talking about girls, lying. When he would talk about women, I wouldn't say anymore, "Oh, she has nice tits, look at that woman there." I wouldn't say anything. First, you stop saying things like that. Then they notice that you're not saying things like that and then they start getting

ideas, you have a roommate and you never talk about girls and you don't have a
girlfriend. They know you're not dating anyone. They know everything about you.
. . . Anyway, I think that what happened was in the end he hinted that me and my
roommate were something else than roommates. And I told him that's the case.

One ranking officer noted that holding a position of higher authority in the police department can actually ease the process of disclosure, as it allows that officer to respond officially, rather than
personally, to any displays of homophobia in his command, such as
derogatory comments spoken or written on walls. He said that on a
number of occasions he used this authority to put a stop to the use of
homophobic terminology in his presence.

The next day I'm talking to a cop in the precinct and he starts carrying on and uses
the term *faggots*. And I stopped him immediately and told him that I objected to
that term. . . . I said, "It's not appropriate in the workplace," so I could rely on the
rules, not on my own personal sense of justice.

As with the female officer's choice of T-shirts, this lieutenant's defense of homosexuals aroused suspicions among the officers in his
command as to *his* true sexual identity. Soon after the above incident,
this same lieutenant corrected another subordinate who used the
term *faggot* in describing a known gay bar in the precinct. However,
in this case he went even further toward revealing his own sexual
identity by bluntly acknowledging that he had heard about this establishment through gay channels.

We were talking about bars in the precinct and he tells me about this club and it's
all faggots. I said, "Don't use that term. I just had to correct somebody
yesterday." He was kind of flabbergasted. I said you can say gay bar or gay crowd,
that's acceptable. I told him I knew about that location because they advertise
in the gay press. So in terms of telling anybody in the precinct, no I haven't run up
the flag. I didn't put anything up on the bulletin board *yet*. But I think I have
certainly dropped enough clues.

Besides helping him make the transition from being closeted to being out, his correcting others served as an educational tool in the
workplace.

Once a cop was driving me and he knew I lived in the Village and he asked me if
there really were a lot of faggots in my building. I would say, "What?" I would

make him say it again and again until he stopped using the word *faggot* and used the word *gay* or *homosexual*.

A female transit officer went even further toward revealing her true sexual identity when she challenged two male officers who had arrested and then physically abused an obviously gay male she let into the subway station.

I let this guy through [the turnstile] and two cops on a plainclothes detail grabbed him and started beating him. These jerks, these fucking morons grabbed him, threw him against the wall, threw handcuffs on and bashed his head against the wall. I went over and said, "What the fuck are you doing?" They said he was a fucking faggot and started beating him again. Usually cops are supposed to back up other cops. Well this bitch didn't back up shit. I pushed the two cops. "OK," I said. "Now call a boss and let the handcuffs off of him." I told the guy this was police brutality and he should file a lawsuit against the city and use me as a witness. That got me so pissed. He was a fucking human being. What are you abusing him for?

As another way of intentionally arousing or heightening suspicion in their commands, a few subjects decided simply to refrain from disputing the rumors about or accusations of their homosexuality. The following comments reflect a variety of styles of nondenial used by emerging gay officers when confronted by co-workers who suspected them of being homosexual.

I was in the locker room and one guy says to my face, "Hey, _____, someone in this place is a faggot." I turned around to him and said, "Other than me I don't know of anybody else here."

When people at work asked me, I'd look at my calendar watch and say, "Only Thursdays." This one guy always asks me. The next time I think I'm going to say, "Is this a proposal?" And I'll just take his hand.

When the topic came up I didn't deny it. . . . One guy told some others that I was a faggot. . . . And I was approached by them and asked why is he saying this. I responded, "If that's what he's doing it's the last time I'll let him suck my cock." You see, I never confirmed it or denied it.

The deliberate and provocative actions of these officers are only a small step away from full disclosure. In quite a few cases evidence of homosexuality had been accumulating, and it was only a matter of time before some of their co-workers would directly confront them.

One significant difference between this group of subjects and those who are publicly out is that the latter group has openly acknowledged their homosexuality while the former group is simply *not denying it*. This tentatively out group also retains the option of denying co-workers' suspicions and even direct accusations. They may still choose to attempt to reestablish a heterosexual front. The absence of any absolute evidence (such as a witness to a homosexual act or a public admission of one's homosexuality) provides these marginally closeted individuals with room to maneuver, or so some have come to believe. In actuality, only a few are successful in their attempts to quash these disreputable suspicions should they have a change of heart. Their fate as reputed homosexuals is virtually sealed by their act of opening the closet door and allowing others to look in. Now, no matter how loudly they protest or how vehemently they try to reestablish a false heterosexual identity, they will never be permitted to return to the ranks of the so-called normal and conventional. As two close observers of the homosexual community put it, "There is no court of law [here], only the court of public opinion."[4]

Some gay officers may, nevertheless, delude themselves into believing that their protestations or counterclaims of heterosexuality have been successful. But this delusion only exists in their own minds as a result of others in the precinct having carefully avoided letting on that they now know. An observation by one of the officers in this study draws upon the linkage between being known as a good cop and being able to insulate oneself from the negative sanctions attached to homosexuality to support this supposition.

There are a couple of guys and this one female cop in the past few commands where I worked who started to come out and then had a sudden change of heart. . . . This one guy left so many clues around you would have to be blind not to know that he was gay. Then one day he starts to put on this "straight" act as if people are real stupid. Nobody said anything because he was a good worker, but they all knew. They just let on that they didn't.

INDIVIDUAL REACTIONS TO ACKNOWLEDGED OR REPUTED HOMOSEXUALITY

Although it is certainly important to describe straight cops' reactions to the discovery of a partner's true sexual identity, it is equally important to attempt to explain these reactions. Most closeted cops, as we have seen, experienced a great deal of anxiety when telling even their closest partners of their homosexuality. However, when asked how they were received after disclosure, despite their many fears and concerns, most of these men and women felt accepted rather than rejected and despised. In fact, in only three instances reported in this study did a straight partner react with rejection.

In those few cases, however, rejection was both total and unequivocal; the straight partners requested an immediate team or assignment change and then betrayed the gay officer by divulging his secret to other members of the command. One possible explanation for this hostile reaction is the fear of being unwittingly contaminated by another's moral failings, or experiencing what Goffman calls "courtesy stigma," in which a failing spreads from the stigmatized to the normal.[5] The normal male (straight cop) fears moral contamination should he continue to work or even associate with a person he knows possesses a disreputable status. He fears being labeled a "fag lover" at the very least, and, at worst, he fears that his own sexuality may be called into question by others in the precinct should his partner's secret somehow become public knowledge and co-workers discover that he knew about it all the time. These fears, real or imagined, become the basis for action that is aimed at preventing their actualization. In this case, the knowledgeable partner not only disassociates himself from the gay officer, he also tells others of the officer's discreditable status, hoping these actions will sustain or even strengthen his reputation, image, and ties to others in the command. The contamination process was illustrated by a transit officer:

When my steady partner found out, when I told him, he immediately asked for a transfer. He went to another detail. . . . They don't want to associate with you after that because they know they are going to be ostracized if they do. Other cops might think they're gay. They will ostracize your partner.

This officer went on to tell how his worst fear came true. "I was mainly concerned that he was going to tell others. I didn't want other people to know. And he did tell them. Some other guy told me." Soon after he told his partner, he began receiving sexually explicit mail at work. "I got a postcard of a guy, one of those African carvings. A picture of an African guy with a big huge dick."

Another respondent, experiencing a bad reaction, spoke of being cut off from his partner soon after he informed him of his homosexuality. This gay officer had little doubt that the informed straight partner (someone he had worked with for a period of months) promptly told others in the precinct of his acknowledged homosexuality, because soon after his disclosure, he began to experience harassment at work. Anonymous co-workers "did things like putting things on my locker. They would put any type of gay [media] article that would come up. . . . They would change names, insert my name or photograph or Xerox of my picture. Some of it was extremely sick."

One officer who was strongly suspected of being gay was reported to have experienced substantial harassment and ridicule because, in spite of growing evidence to the contrary, he persisted in maintaining a heterosexual front. In this rare instance, the young male officer in question projected a definite femininity in his mannerisms, appearance, and even speech. His lack of manliness in the eyes of his straight co-workers was further magnified when he requested and was subsequently granted a safer precinct detail, one normally assigned to limited-duty or near-retirement officers. His story was told by a female officer.

I believe they continue to ridicule him because he keeps denying it. He's not out and keeps denying it to the guys. He's also a "house mouse." He's been in the precinct for a year pushing paper. He's also a busybody. You want to know something that's going on, you go ask [him]. The guys look at him like a washwoman. It's usually the women that do the gossiping. Now you have this guy who's very feminine and he does the gossiping.

As she suggested, it may not have been the gay officer's reputed homosexuality that aroused the antipathy of others in his precinct as much as his inept and possibly even irritating attempts to maintain a pretense of heterosexuality. When he combined this hypocrisy with the less than manly role he chose to assume in the precinct, this officer surrendered any claim he may have had to being a good cop and was judged exclusively by his perceived moral failing.

Despite the many fears and apprehensions expressed by these gay officers before they came out to even the most trusted in their command, the overwhelming majority of those who did open up to a partner reported that they experienced decisively positive reactions reflecting not just tolerance but genuine acceptance. In a few instances, however, these positive reactions were initially punctuated by displays of surprise and disbelief. This suggests that, at least with some of these straight partners, there were no suspicions of the closeted officer's homosexuality. A lesbian, for example, described her partner's initial reaction when, while driving home from work one night, she finally confided in him. "He said, '_____, I'm happy for you. I'm really shocked but I'm happy for you.' We got closer after that. He invited me and my lover to meet his wife for dinner."

Two other women experienced similar reactions from their male partners—surprise followed by recovery and then eventual acceptance.

He was surprised. He said, "What?" Then he didn't want to talk about it to me. After a while we worked together and we got along great. One day we had this conversation, and we became very good friends.

I had a straight [male] partner. He was attracted to me and we worked close together and that attraction grew. We used to have fun—long dinners, long lunches, together. One night we went out and I got really plastered and I told him. I think he was shocked. I started crying. We worked together for six months and I hadn't told him. He said, "Don't worry about it." He took care of me as a partner would. I don't think he told anyone else.

A highway patrol officer recalled his partner's response at this difficult moment. "He said, 'No, get out of here.' We sat in the car. He just couldn't understand. But he accepted me. To this very day we are still close friends."

The straight partners of this group of gay officers appear to have accepted the news that the person they had been working beside was a homosexual with a minimum of discomfort. Indeed, beyond these initial reactions no evidence of hostility or rejection was reported. And for another group of gay officers, only acceptance, support, and, in some instances, even words of encouragement followed disclosure. The following reported reactions are not unusual for this group:

I said, "Let's say if there's rumors, what they're saying is true. Does it matter?" He said, "It doesn't matter. We're friends. We came on the job together."

We had just finished dinner with his wife and he walked me to the car. I knew he desperately wanted to ask me. Before he could form the question I blurted out "yes" I am. I'm a homosexual. I'm gay. After my acknowledgment we remained seated in the car, both crying and sobbing. The next several hours were spent talking and listening, smiling and laughing; crying and feeling free.[6]

One of the primary explanations offered by these gay officers to account for this immediate acceptance and support was their reputation as good cops, which all of these officers believed they had earned. This reputation, they are convinced, was paramount in the eyes of their partners and superseded or obscured any stigma attached to their sexual orientation. In many instances this rationale was directly conveyed to the gay cop.

I waited until the very last minute before I got out of the car. Then I somewhat tearfully told him. And I just said, "Listen, there's something I gotta tell you. You know I've been seeing someone." And he said, "Yeah, I know, what's the big deal? Who is she?" I said, "It's a guy, I'm gay." I don't know what happened next. It wound up that he said, "It doesn't matter, you're still a good cop. You're still the same person I wanted to work with two years ago." His response was accepting. It was, hey, it's no big deal. He was like, "When do I meet him? I wanna meet this guy."

A lesbian, confiding in her male partner, reported essentially the same, almost matter-of-fact explanation of acceptance. Her credentials as a good cop were sufficient to override any negative attributes thought to be associated with her sexual orientation.

Initially, he turned a little red, I guess from embarrassment about the subject. But then his statement was something to the effect that I was going through a difficult time and that anything I can do for you, just let me know. He said, "What you do outside with relationships doesn't matter. You do your job well and we work together. That's all that matters." We are still in touch with each other.

A male officer elaborated further. Speaking of the favorable reaction he experienced upon informing his close partner he said he felt that this acceptance was linked, in large measure, to the fact that he was known to be a "worker"; that is, someone who did not try to shirk his share of the precinct workload. This officer told yet another

partner. Although the reasons offered for this other partner's acceptance differed, the reactions were basically the same.

> I teamed up with my partner, who was the PBA delegate. One day we were talking
> and I told him about a friend of mine who was gay. . . . I remember he said to
> me, "Well, you're gay too." I said, "Yeah," and that was the end of it. It didn't
> bother him at all. We've been partners ever since. . . . He trusted me on the job. He
> knew he could count on me, confide in me.

Of perhaps equal importance to their known reputation as good
cops is, as noted elsewhere, the fact that these officers were *not* seen
as limp-wristed, lisping "faggots" or, in the case of most of the
women, overtly masculine "dyke" types. Thus, at least some of
the popular homosexual stereotypes were shown to be incorrect. As
one precinct cop put it:

> You know what these guys think of us, that we all carry ourselves like girls, the
> way we walk and how we speak. . . . The [gay cops] that I know are not like that.
> That's proof that it's all a misconception. . . . I remember [his partner's]
> reaction when I told him. He shook his head in disbelief and said, "I would never
> have guessed it. You don't fit the mold." I think that started him thinking
> about all the other things homosexuals are supposed to be. . . . We talked about
> this a lot.

One high-ranking police officer in New York raised the same point
in an interview with a reporter.

> Most people fear the unknown. . . . Homosexuals conjure up all kinds of visions
> of gross perversions and erratic behavior. But out of nowhere steps Charlie
> [Cochrane], a well-liked, normal street cop with a consistently steady track record,
> to proclaim he's gay. Suddenly, many of us are forced to reevaluate our opinions.
> I can't think of a single cop who hasn't changed his mind about this particular
> homosexual on the job. Charlie is as perfect an example of a normal homosexual
> as you can find. If all gays were like him, it wouldn't be an issue.[7]

There is indeed something to be said about the ability of male
homosexual cops to dispel some of the commonly accepted, negative
images that a significant sector of the straight population finds unattractive about gays. Yet there is one popular image that cannot be
readily dispelled; that of homosexuals engaging in what many

straights consider unnatural sex. Such overt public behavior as intimate hugging, kissing, and hand holding among gays serves to
conjure up visions of this unnatural behavior and arouse deep-seated
revulsion toward gays. The officers in this study are aware of such
linkages, and consequently many of them shy away from such behavior when meeting a friend or lover while in the presence of a partner
who knows of their homosexuality. Their restraint is based on the
reasoning that full acceptance may be jeopardized by visible demonstrations of love and affection, even though they are common practice among heterosexuals.

Even those gays who are fully out to their close partners and who
are now comfortable enough with their sexuality while riding on patrol to make sexual comments about same-sex individuals on the
street are careful not to go overboard in demonstrating their sexual
desire for members of the same sex. They too reason that, although
merely admiring another person from afar while in the company of a
straight partner may be acceptable, graphically displaying an intense
sexual attraction may indeed make the straight partner very uncomfortable. Like other minority newcomers to policing, they are cautious about invoking strong negative stereotypes that have in the past
played such a dominant role in isolating them from mainstream society in general and from white-dominated police departments in particular. For most of these men and women this is a small price to pay
to gain acceptance in the world of policing. For others it is a major
concession and one they are unwilling to make. These officers do not
see their sexual life-style as unnatural or immoral, nor do they care
what others think. These men and women are at the forefront of a
newly emerging radical movement among gay cops throughout the
country.

A major theme emerging in this research is that the decision to
present oneself authentically to a partner and the subsequent reactions of that partner are linked to the basic values and corresponding
needs that form the core of social relationships in traditional police
settings. The unique demands of the job, for example, require un-
wavering trust, loyalty, honesty, and commitment between partners.
When these work characteristics are present, each partner can define the other as a good cop. In this positive relationship the repertoire of interactions between the two can, and usually does, expand to
include nonwork-related matters. The two partners in such a team
will often exchange personal thoughts and intimate facts about them-

selves, further strengthening the bonds of mutual trust, support, and commitment. Gay officers in such a relationship may feel comfortable and secure enough to confide their sexual secret to their partner, knowing that they have already established a bond that is linked first and foremost to their reputation as a good cop. Likewise, straight cops may be so heavily influenced by their partners' demonstration of loyalty and so on that they are willing to play down their moral failing or even to ignore its relevance to their relationship altogether.

Seven
Coming
Out
Publicly
at
Work

Bigotry can be eliminated. A low-ball estimate: There are about 20,000,000 lesbian and gay people in the USA. If each of us were to come out to the twenty people who love us the most and only half of them could handle it, we would then live in a country where Two Hundred and Twenty Million people do not hate every lesbian and gay they know. That's the road to freedom.[1]

In the process of coming out, gay cops at or moving through the second stage have either revealed their homosexuality to one or more of their colleagues or are suspected by co-workers, in varying degrees, of being gay. In stage three they have fully disclosed their sexual orientation. This state is achieved when an individual proclaims (for instance, by announcing it on the "Arsenio Hall Show") that he or she is gay, demonstrates it publicly by unmistakably clear actions, or merely allows the trait to be guessed.[2] Not all homosexual cops proceed from stage one (fully closeted) through the second stage and then the third. In rare instances, some move from the first stage directly into the third. Only two officers I know of made such an abrupt leap. Equally uncommon is the decision of a gay cop to publicly announce or demonstrate his or her homosexuality when first entering the police world. Only one officer stated that he let his homosexuality be known to his fellow officers while attending the police academy as a recruit.

THE DECISION TO COME OUT FULLY

Many of the same motives that played a crucial role in the individual's decision to come out tentatively—for example, the need to reduce the stress and tension associated with having to maintain a constant pretense of heterosexuality—eventually contribute to the gay cop's decision to take the final step and publicly declare his or her homosexuality. As one female cop stated, being constantly on guard was more than she could handle. "It was just too much work. It was hard saying different things to people and then trying to remember what you said to who."

Another cop, experiencing the anguish of dishonesty to both self and others that accompanies sustaining a false heterosexual image, chose to reveal his homosexuality.

The problem I had was hiding my personality, which was being gay. What I mean is by attending these social and after-work parties, I would have to put a lot of makeup on [that is, pretend he was straight] and I couldn't be honest with myself. I'm not a pretender. I don't feel comfortable going along with the jokes and myths that gays and lesbians have to put up with.

After shedding his heterosexual mask, another man expressed the relief of finally being able to present himself authentically to others at work.

Like every time the conversation came up about girlfriends, I had to take it, you know. Now, there's much less anxiety about who I am. I can now play with the rest of them. I can look at guys and make comments like guys do about women.

As this officer implies, coming out may mean that the gay cop no longer has to experience the hypocrisy of having to constantly feign interest in members of the opposite sex. For some women, coming out also serves to insulate them from sexual overtures and unwanted passes from straight male cops in their precinct.

I think it's good in that I don't have to worry so much about who I'm saying what to. I think it has helped me in that I don't like being hit on constantly by a lot of men. They used to hit on me. They haven't since I've come out.

Well, for me, the guys just stopped hitting on me. . . . Some guys just don't take no for an answer. They persist on and on and on. You can tell them enough is enough and they wait a couple of days and they come back to square one all over again. Now they leave me the hell alone, that's for sure.

Dispelling the uncertainty over what co-workers' reactions will be can also be a compelling reason for some gay cops to come fully out of the closet. One officer, for example, said that he came out because he wanted to get rid of his own confusion as to what to expect from other members of his precinct. Of paramount concern to him was his personal safety should he find himself in a life-threatening situation at work. He needed to know that should he call for back-up assistance in the street, his colleagues would be there for him.

I was always wondering how they would react to me. You find out who your friends are. Mentally, it takes the burden off your shoulders. Are they going to back you up? If you're out you have all the answers to that question. You don't have to deal with wondering anymore.

A few officers who maintained an open homosexual life-style with their lovers and gay friends when off duty began to feel that it was immoral to continue to "live a lie" at work. They developed a strong need to be open about their homosexuality in *all* aspects of their lives. By taking this posture they hoped to preserve both the integrity of their personal relationships and, should they at some point actually be seen with a lover, the trust and support of their co-workers. As one lesbian officer who eventually chose full disclosure at work explained:

I didn't want to live with a lie any longer and worry about being exposed. It was better to tell people about myself than to be seen walking down the street or be in a public place with [her lover] and be found to be living a lie.

For another female officer, the daily irritation of verbal gay bashing from her unsuspecting colleagues finally proved intolerable.

I decided to because one thing that bothered me about police officers is that the typical gay joke is calling each other faggot and stuff like that. I hoped that it would happen less if I did [come out]. I was prepared to tackle the whole job—go the whole nine yards.

Two officers chose to make their homosexuality public soon after being promoted to ranking positions in the department. Their reasoning for coming out at this juncture in their careers was that they had acquired reputations as model employees and were now in positions of authority. Consequently, they felt they had nothing to fear from the department as a result of their disclosure. As one of them, now a lieutenant, put it:

The worst thing they could do was put me back on the desk. But they wouldn't. They couldn't because you know I've never been rated anything but above average. I've never been chronic sick. I've never had any disciplinary problems. By all objective standards I'm a model employee. So in that sense I'm no longer worried about my career.

He added that it is considerably less risky for a ranking officer to come out publicly because as one moves up the promotional ladder, the number of potential troublemakers in the department shrinks dramatically.[3] "The other thing that makes it easy is that I'm a lieutenant. There are only a thousand lieutenants. In that sense there's less risk."

A powerful motivation for one veteran officer to come out to his colleagues was his sense of moral righteousness; that is, as a homosexual, he did not feel that he was deviant or different in any significant way from his straight co-workers. He was thus less concerned with the consequences of disclosure.[4] "It was not a decision," he explained. "To me there was nothing strange about it. . . . To tell you the truth, I really didn't care about what some twenty-year-old ethnic kids from Levittown thought about me. I would do my job and then go home. I didn't make an issue about it. To me I was not strange or different."

A thirty-year-old female officer expressed similar sentiments. "I figured that if these people at work can't deal with it, well they don't feed me. They don't pay the rent. That's the way I am. If you don't like it, well I put [in] my eight hours at work with you and at the end of the day I'm going home." However, in her case coming out was eased somewhat by circumstances. "When I got to the precinct there had been this other woman—a lesbian. She had made a statement. She broke the ground for me coming out. It made it easier."

In some instances this ultimate and irreversible decision was motivated less by the individual's concern with having to live a double life than by the altruistic belief that coming out would, in the long run, better serve the needs and interests of the larger gay police community in New York City. By confronting head-on individual shame and guilt, they reasoned that other still-closeted gay cops might also mus-

ter the courage to unveil themselves. These politically spirited officers were united in the belief that heterosexual cops and supervisors
(especially those in high command positions) must be made aware
that there *was* such an entity as gay police. Furthermore, these unknowing groups needed to be informed that the number of gays in
the department was growing and that in time they would become a
political force to be reckoned with, as has been the case with other
minority police groups. Two officers in the study commented specifically on the importance of achieving visibility in the department.

I felt we have to be very visible. We have to show that it's not just one or two
people who are out. . . . Even the department feels there's only a few gay cops.

I want to be counted rather than have people [the department] count for us.

A related motive for coming out is the belief that publicly acknowledged gay cops can help dispel disparaging stereotypes about homosexuals in general and gay police in particular by showing that they
do not differ from straights in ways that make them less capable of
performing their duties effectively.

To let other cops see that I am gay and a good cop at the same time. They judge
you by what you know and do. . . . It can help other cops understand. For example,
I knew a gay cop and he was a good cop. A guy once said to me, "If you are gay
then there ought to be more gays on the job." I understood what he meant.

Like in situations when people are talking about fags. You know the faggots this
and the faggots that. And when I came out and said, "Well, there are a lot of us out
there," that changed their perception of gays. They had a stereotypical view of
us. Coming out educates them.

Increased visibility, or what some call a show of force by gay cops,
is thought to be important not only because of the implications it has
for helping dissolve negative stereotypes of gays but because these
openly gay officers can serve as role models.

I think it's terribly important for cops who are in the closet struggling to know that
there are gay people in the department; that we function normally in the PD;
that we contribute to the goals of the PD; and that we advance in rank and that just
like the rest of society we are everywhere in the department.

Implied in that comment and stated directly in the next is the feeling that coming out in numbers will have a snowball effect. In this context one veteran officer insists that there is much truth to the adage of strength in numbers.

If you show an "invisibility" say, of 2 percent and you are gay, you might say, "I'm not coming out." If you show a "visibility" of 20 percent, say, it gives the guy that sense of pride that he's not part of a small group, but of a larger group. You feel better about yourself.

Many of the officers in this study now also believe that management will back them should they experience harassment and discrimination on the job. They believe that times have changed to the extent that management now finds itself in the position of having to publicly support the rights of homosexuals and other minorities, even though many of the top-ranking officials in the department may privately feel quite differently. For example, one male officer believes

the precinct C.O. [commanding officer] knows today, that if something comes to them, if a sergeant comes to a precinct C.O. today and says, "You know, they're busting so-and-so's balls and they're putting notes on his locker, and I think it's some guys in his squad, the C.O. knows today he better do something about that. Because, if he doesn't he's going to have an OEEO [Office of Equal Employment Opportunity] complaint and it's going to affect his career. Years ago, the precinct commander could have laughed. He may still laugh today inside, but he's got to do something.

TELLING THE POLICE WORLD

Revealing one's homosexuality involves a variety of strategies ranging from public pronouncements to less direct but equally effective and revealing symbolic gestures. The most extreme approach to public disclosure is perhaps best illustrated by the action taken by Charlie Cochrane when, on prime-time television, he announced his homosexuality. This is the only instance I am aware of, however, in which a gay police officer revealed himself so totally and dramatically. Most of the now openly gay men and women in the NYPD approached the dilemma of how to reveal their homosexuality in a more circumspect or indirect manner. A transit cop explains, for example, how, after having confided his homosexuality to a few select partners, he gradually eased into the final stage of full disclosure:

> After that I kept doing the same thing. Whenever I would work with someone, like when we would see a girl and he would say, "Oh, look at that ass," I wouldn't say anything. It was like a process. . . . So I started first by not lying, and then people would ask me who do you live with? "I live with my roommate." "Do you have a girlfriend?" "No! I don't have a girlfriend." I would tell them that way, not lying. And then I started telling people just like that. They would ask me, "You married?" "No, I have a lover." "What's her name?" "Her name is *Hector*." That's what I did.

One detective came out gradually to the officers in his precinct through a series of informal discussions of gay rights. His pro and admittedly aggressive posture with regard to this controversial issue not surprisingly triggered suspicions and rumors among his co-workers.

> I remember a bunch of us, maybe fifteen guys, were sitting around a table in the locker room watching TV when Charlie [Cochrane] came out [in 1981]. The reaction of some of the guys [who didn't know he was gay] was, "What a pair of balls." I then explained what the gay rights bill meant. They had no inkling. . . . The younger guys were vehemently against the bill. The older guys were more liberal. They basically said, "What's the difference if he's gay, long as he backs me." Some of the younger guys got nasty, indignant, started banging the table. But I took a position then for gay rights, so you can say I started coming out that day. We had subsequent discussions, and I continued to support gay rights.

Suspicions as to this detective's homosexuality were soon confirmed when he marched in the Gay Pride Parade and was recognized by co-workers who had been assigned to work that detail.

Other than issuing a public statement attesting to one's homosexuality there is perhaps no more direct approach to coming out than marching beside other members of GOAL in the Gay Pride Parade.[5] As mentioned earlier, this is an annual event in which literally hundreds of cops from commands throughout the city are assigned to the parade detail. Indeed, many of the subjects who were not fully out chose this event as their way of both revealing their homosexuality and demonstrating their pride in being gay without making what they felt to be a difficult public statement. All of these officers were aware that the news of their participation in a gay parade would quickly get back to their commands. A veteran officer relates such an experience as he recalls the day his secret became public.

The first real statement I made was when I marched. A few sergeants [working the parade detail] recognized me even though I was wearing dark sunglasses. The day after, I called the precinct and asked for the day off. The one sergeant who had seen me said, "Why? Because your feet hurt?"

A female officer had a similar recollection of her coming out.

It was June and I decided to march in the parade. Anyway the Forty-third [Precinct] cops were down in the Seventies. I looked up and there was one of my female sergeants. I waved to her. It dawned on her. She waved back.

Another lesbian told of how a different aspect of the Gay Pride Parade precipitated her coming out fully.

Everybody in the [precinct] knows. What happened is that I just got into the command and I wanted the Gay Rights Day off. . . . I had to actually put that down on the 'twenty-eight [official excusal form]. That's how I came out. My 'twenty-eight was denied. I had to go to the PBA, the borough, my administrative lieutenant, my C.O. I finally got it approved.

By choosing to attend a meeting of the Mayor's Police Council as an official representative of GOAL, another closeted gay boldly made his sexual preference public. Present at this meeting was a high-ranking officer whose son was assigned to this officer's command. Another cop's homosexuality was revealed through his GOAL membership. "Two months ago I put in for a day off to attend a GOAL meeting. That's the first time I put it on paper. I made a public statement then. Just about everybody knows now."

As indicated earlier, one approach to disclosure is to wear buttons, pins, T-shirts, or other insignia ("stigma symbols") attesting to membership in or support of a gay organization or cause. A GOAL member reports his progress using this method. "I'm coming out more and more each day. I now wear my GOAL pin. I wear the gay flag on my uniform. I'm advertising slowly."

There are other ways in which gay officers can bring their secret homosexual identity to the attention of members of their command, and certainly other reasons for doing so. For example, in instances where off-duty closeted gay cops find themselves forced to take police action in known gay establishments, there is the risk of exposure should the incident escalate to the point where the police are called to intervene. In these instances the closeted gay cop may not be able to prevent a report of the incident from circulating among his co-workers. Faced with hard evidence of homosexuality, the officer may have little choice but to come out publicly. In all my interviews, however, there was only one reported instance in which a closeted gay officer found himself, while patronizing a gay bar, unavoidably involved in a police-related matter. In this case the gay officer's presence in the bar was for some reason kept in confidence by the cops called to the scene.

Although no doubt there have been occasions in which this type of information has not been covered up by other cops, I am inclined to believe that the traditions of solidarity and unquestioned loyalty are so compelling for some police officers that a gay officer's partially exposed secret would be kept in confidence. Especially if the discovered officer is of higher rank, it might prove beneficial for a cop to keep this potentially discrediting news from filtering back to the officer's command, for having something on a ranking officer obligates him to reciprocate with a favor or service should they wind up working in the same command someday.

THE COLLECTIVE REACTION TO DISCLOSURE: REALITY VERSUS PERCEPTION

As illustrated in chapter 6, individual reactions to a partner's disclosure of homosexuality have seldom taken the form of long-term condemnation and exclusion, the response anticipated and feared most by closeted cops. Rather, these reactions, largely positive, seem based upon these officers' actions at work, which have shown them to be worthy of the designation "good cop." The collective reaction of co-workers to the disclosure of a homosexual in their midst is, however, a more complex issue. It is not at all apparent what the general precinctwide reaction might be. On the individual level, partners of known homosexual cops generally have sufficient firsthand knowledge of the officers' professional worth to make fair assessments of their overall worth as persons. This may not be the case with those who are new in the precinct or who know the openly gay officer only superficially. The one thing they do know for certain is that the officer is gay. Without firsthand knowledge of the officers' professional worth, their discreditable homosexual identity may unjustly overshadow all else, designating to the larger group their overall worth as a member of the department.[6] There is also the possibility that, to some straight cops, the stigma of homosexuality is so compelling and discrediting that it cannot be effectively neutralized by even the best established social or work-related credentials. Or the gay officers' reputation as good cops may assume the role of "master status," thus relegating their homosexual status to a subordinate level.

The openly gay officers in this study indicated that, on the whole, co-workers were far more accepting and supportive than they had anticipated or imagined. When asked why they thought these reactions appeared to lean toward acceptance rather than rejection, most of the men and women in this group repeated the reason they and others had given earlier when addressing the question of individual acceptance: they believed their earned reputations as "good cops" had effectively countered the stigma of homosexuality.[7] A detective observed marching in the Gay Pride Parade, for example, recalls the reaction he received the following night at a dinner for a retired co-worker.

One guy came up to me and asked me what the fuck I was doing at the parade. He was really nasty. . . . After that the word spread. It was interesting because one of the younger straight cops had heard his comment and he came over to me and said that if anyone said anything to me again [about the parade] he would break their face. . . . After that, the guy comes over to me and apologizes, said he was sorry about what he said. A couple of the other guys came up to me and apologized for the guy. . . . I feel I had a lot of support from most of the guys in the precinct. I had been there about fifteen years, and the guys knew me. They knew how I did the job. If there was any trouble I was there. They said, "We know you."

That this designation, "good cop," can obscure the stigma of homosexuality is confirmed by a lesbian officer.

I'm a good cop. That's it. I do my job, help people. I get the respect of my peers. Other people I work with rely on me. If I weren't a good cop, people would pay attention to my sexual orientation. That's factual. That's true. I don't know why it's true and it shouldn't be, but I believe it is. If they like you and you're on the "in," you can be what you want. . . . I've experienced no discrimination over the years. I got close to them. I do my job. I'm a worker, someone who carries her own weight, someone who is not going to start trouble, rat a cop out. If I was a whiner, some slouch, they'd get on the fact that I was a lesbian.

A veteran officer who reported that he experienced few problems when he came out described how he believes others perceive him. "Wherever I went they all knew I was coming. If there's anything on this job, it's the phone call. I'm sure it went like this, 'He's a fag, but he's OK. You won't have any problems.'"

A young cop, one of those who bluntly announced his homosexuality by putting in for time off to march in the Gay Pride Parade, said some of his colleagues at work "told me I got a lot of balls, you know, things like that. They said, I don't think I would have done that if I were in your position." A lesbian considered a good cop by members of her command recalls her experience upon returning from having marched in the parade.

The next day my partner asked me and said everybody was talking about it. People didn't believe it, what you are doing. Then this other guy came right over to me and stuck out his hand and he said, "Congratulations for what you did." I was very touched. The people that truly cared about me came to me and said, "We heard." After that day everybody seemed comfortable. With time I was back into the group.

Sometimes cops who openly condemn gays for their life-styles may be inclined to put these prejudices aside in some instances.[8]

Even those people who hate me in the sense that they hate gay people and what they do, I hear comments from other people that they show some admiration for what I did. They recognize that you need a lot of balls to do something like that.

A female officer agrees, stating with confidence that, upon her coming out, the support and acceptance she received from most of her co-workers was due to the combination of her having had the courage to march publicly in the parade and her reputation as a good cop. Her negative experiences were minimal, as she explains:

GAY COPS

The only instance was in the locker room, you know those call lines, [telephone] sex lines. Somebody stuck it in my locker. That's the only thing that happened to me since I've been in the precinct and it's not even worth mentioning. . . . When I came back from the parade everybody was kinda like just looking at me. They all said hello. People came up to me, you know, [and said] you got a lot of guts. . . . Most people were supportive. I always held my own. I didn't take shit from people. Cops respect other cops who are aware of what's around them, cops who work, who have intelligence, integrity.

And still another male officer testifies to the importance of the good cop reputation when others judge an officer's overall worth in the precinct.

I would say the majority of cops don't give a damn if you come out. It doesn't bother them as long as you're a decent person to work with. That's all they care about. Do your job as you're supposed to do your job. You're there when they need you. Back them up. You're not fucking off someplace. They can rely on you. That's all any police officer wants.

The tradition of backing or supporting a colleague who has earned the reputation of a good cop regardless of his social failing as a homosexual is evident even when homosexuality was unknown in the department. The following story recalled by a veteran detective illustrates this beyond-the-call-of-duty support afforded an officer who was murdered during a homosexual encounter while off duty.

Back in 1972 or '73, in the _____ Precinct. It was a gay situation. The cop picked up this guy and went back to his [own] apartment. The guy tied his hands. The cop started screaming. Neighbors called the police. He shoved rags in the cop's mouth. He died of suffocation. The cop who responded recognized the dead cop. It was in the papers as a sexual escapade. The cop was single and lived alone. The department at first refused to lower the flag to half-mast or to give the dead cop a formal department funeral. The guy had over twenty years on the job. He was considered a good cop. He was also in the Marine reserves. Then pressure was placed on the department. Guys in the precinct were indignant. They called for a work slowdown because the department wouldn't allow the funeral. Guys weren't answering the radio. There was a work slowdown. The day before the funeral the department allowed the flag to be lowered at half-mast. The cop was allowed to be laid out in a police officer's uniform.

Yet most of these openly gay men and women went on to note that there are a handful in every command who will continue to respond to the gay cop solely in terms of his or her perceived deviant sexual identity. In these situations the gay officer's earned reputation as a good cop does not in any way alter these feelings.

But there's always that small percentage of cops that are vicious as hell. It seems to bother them that there are gay cops, either male or female. That's all that seems to matter to them.

I have more friends now even though there is a small, select group, and I mean small, who are very prejudiced against gays. I've been there a year and they have not once said hello or talked to me even though I was reaching out and being friendly. They still don't talk to me. They ignore me as if I weren't there.

Unlike other so-called deviant types, such as prostitutes, drug addicts, and alcoholics, who can change their ways and gain social redemption from others for their past sins, officers who publicly acknowledge their homosexuality may never be able to retrieve the status of normality. What they can do is demonstrate through words and deeds that their discreditable status should be considered unimportant and replaced by the good cop status. In order to successfully accomplish this transformation, openly gay officers must not only prove to others that they are worthy of the designation "good cop," but they may find that, unlike their straight fellow officers, they have to extend themselves beyond the call of duty. Their situation is in many ways not unlike that of blacks (and other minority newcomers to policing) in the past who felt they had to do more than was required of them to prove that they were equal to whites and deserving of the reputation of a good cop.[9]

Of course, not all black cops felt that way. In the early 1970s, a movement toward militancy, fueled by black nationalism and a growing sense of racial pride, provided some black cops with a reason to flaunt their heritage (for instance, by wearing Afro haircuts and by giving "power" signs to other blacks, both cops and civilians). By appearing to align themselves with other militant blacks, these officers became enemies of many whites who came to view them as political traitors.[10] So it is with some openly gay cops who have gotten caught up in the wave of homosexual militancy and pride sweeping the nation today. Indeed, my interviews indicate that some men and

GAY COPS

women in policing are now defiantly parading their homosexuality in much the same way as the more militant blacks flaunted their blackness in the early 1970s. And like these blacks, they are experiencing a backlash from many of their straight co-workers.

Most of the gay cops in this study do not appear to support these more militant tactics. They feel that these actions, designed to achieve respect and equality in the workplace, have in fact had the counterproductive effect of encouraging disrespect, rejection, and isolation from straight cops. As one patrol officer explained:

Straight cops feel more comfortable with people who don't throw their gayness in their faces. There are cops out there that are gay that, in a sense, try to ram it down people's throats. And they resent this because they basically feel that what you do is your business but don't shove it in my face or I'm going to retaliate.

One officer, speaking from his personal observations at work, suggests that even the good cop status can be nullified by playing up or flaunting one's homosexual identity.

The majority of cops don't give a shit [about someone's sexuality]. Just as long as you are there when they need you. A 10-13 [assist police officer], they want you there. Keep the crowds back. They just want you to do your job. What you do after you clock out, they don't give a shit. You could fuck a horse. . . . The other thing is that they don't want you to flaunt it in their face. . . . As I said, most cops don't care if you fucked the man in the moon, just don't shove it in their faces.

The good gay cop then is someone who not only behaves according to traditional subcultural standards but who plays down his or her perceived moral failing, or at least does not parade it around the workplace. Another officer, in speaking out against those who belligerently flaunt their gayness, evidences some of his own apparent guilt and shame regarding homosexual life-styles. "You can say they have to accept this. They don't have to accept shit. . . . Anyone that's doing strange, kooky shit, keep it to yourself."

Becoming too political or outspoken can also provoke rejection from other gay cops.

_____ sets himself up for a lot of things that happen to him. For example, all the drawings and captions on his locker and that kind of stuff. The way he is doing it is the wrong way, like he's doing it and fighting a battle and everyone's

against him. And he's doing it in a very antagonistic manner. I think he's being un-
fair to himself and to the job too. This world doesn't change overnight. _____
wants things to change overnight. It takes time. People have to meet each other
halfway. Anything you're doing that breeds a lot of hatred and antagonism
defeats the purpose.

In discussing the same purportedly radical gay cop, a lesbian co-
worker added another dimension.

Something was told to me that _____ was using the idea that he's gay to work to
his advantage, getting days off, getting things where other people couldn't. He
would say they were discriminating against him because he was gay [if he didn't
get what he wanted]. Meanwhile, now everybody's claiming that he's getting
more than others because he's using the fact to his advantage. Now no one wants
to work with him.

In an interview, this reputedly radical officer confirmed the negative
reactions of his colleagues. However, he offered a slightly different
interpretation of their source.

I don't have a steady partner now. You know what's happening lately, they're put-
ting me with the females or by myself. I think they are fucking with me now.
Now, I'm not just _____, the nice guy they used to go out drinking with. Now,
I'm the fag, and fags are supposed to be like this and like that.

A lesbian recalled how a colleague's similar blatant flaunting of her
homosexuality at work produced a wave of rejection.

She would throw it up at them. She would bring her girlfriend to all the affairs
right off the bat. Here's someone they just met in the precinct and she was going
around referring to her [girlfriend] as "my wife." That's why I think they like
me. I didn't flaunt it.

Such comments point to the potential danger to one's reputation
that can flow from flaunting or exploiting one's homosexuality. Yet a
distinction must be made between flaunting in a perceptibly bellig-
erent and irritating way and simply displaying courage and pride.
The two are entirely different ways of presenting oneself to others in
the workplace. In the former instance, gay officers are accentuating
their so-called deviance in the eyes of others in order to neutralize it;

in the latter, they are simply denying that their sexual orientation is deviant. Moreover, in the police world any changes that upset or attempt to alter traditional routines or belief systems, or that challenge the authority and dominance of the rank and file, generally meet with fierce opposition. When changes are attempted or made, acceptance comes slowly, if at all, and only then if members of newcomer groups pushing for change do so in ways that do not seriously threaten the status quo. Those who attempt to alter traditional belief systems or routines radically through pressure tactics, or who seek outside political intervention for their cause, for example, will almost certainly run into resistance and rejection from the rank and file.

In addition to being considered good cops and maintaining relatively low profiles regarding their homosexuality, there are other ways in which openly gay cops can insulate themselves from rejection and gain respect from their straight co-workers. For example, how one deals with antigay office humor can become a critical factor in shaping collective reactions to individual homosexual cops. In these situations, the gay officer may ingratiatingly act out before co-workers "the full dance of bad qualities imputed to his kind, thereby consolidating a life-situation into a clownish role." Gays may also use humor to disarm those who might feel uncomfortable in their presence. It can make light of tragedy and bring "the unmentionable into the forefront of conversation, and, in short, permit the heavy air of embarrassment to be lifted."[11] One veteran officer recalled, along these lines, an experience in which he turned the tables on a colleague who had just made him the butt of a homosexual joke. The important point here is that he confronted that colleague in *good humor*.

When I was in the academy I was in the yard practicing using the nightstick, which was awkward for me. One of the class jocks, very popular, young, and handsome, mooned me out the window. I came up to the classroom and very nonchalantly said, "Why _____, was that an invitation? Bend over and I will be glad to oblige." He turned purple, denied it had been aimed at me, at which point everyone laughed at him. Wit is better than an official complaint. I have dealt with antigay comments with my wit. That's why I've gotten along with people and made friends. Handling it well does more to win respect.

The rationale for handling unsolicited antigay humor in a loose, nondefensive manner is explained by another veteran officer.

Someone put pictures on my locker of naked men. This was after I had come out. I realized who it was. I approached him and said, "The next time you leave pictures could you make it 8 x 10 glossies so I can hang it up over my bed?" I felt that was a way of joking around, a way of "reading out," [i.e., understanding]. . . . No one really shied away from me. Actually, I've had quite a few partners who were very supportive.

Reactions of heterosexual cops to a co-worker's disclosure, although largely positive for most of the now openly gay men and women in this study, were initially mixed for some. One man, for example, spoke of the reactions a close friend experienced soon after he was seen marching in the Gay Pride Parade.

Some of the cops from the [precinct] were on the detail, and they applauded when he marched by. Some turned their backs on him. Some of the cops said to him that it took a lot of courage. Some wrote comments on his locker. Some hung condoms on his locker. A lot were very supportive.

However, in almost every instance in which the disclosure of a gay officer produced either negative or mixed reactions, those reactions faded once the initial shock wore off, and the atmosphere in the workplace became largely positive. Sometimes, reputations of trustworthiness and good standing in the precinct were temporarily damaged by disclosure and had to be reestablished.

The next day, after marching with GOAL in the parade and being seen by my partner, he said to me that everybody was talking about it. People didn't believe what I did. People were shocked. They didn't know how to handle it. It was uncomfortable for them. There were even a few negative comments. They would say lesbians just like to have oral sex. Jokes about the Timex watch, it takes a licking, something like that. That's about it, as much as I've ever heard. On my locker someone put, "Have a gay day" in tiny, tiny letters. . . . The bosses were very uncomfortable with the jokes, the dirty jokes which are part of our job. All of a sudden there's the stereotype of the lesbian as a political person that if you made a dirty joke they are going to report you. I was like a new person there. They had to find out how much they could tell me and what they could get away with. So I frankly just went over and told them that I was the same person as I was before. They were concerned, afraid to tell me anything because of repercussions about whether I would make a complaint or retaliate in some way if anyone made any slurs or derogatory comments. I had to prove myself as a cop all over again.

This comment also suggests the tenuous nature of the status of good cop as it applies to the gay officer who has just gone public with his or her sexual orientation. For straight cops who have earned a reputation as a good cop, that designation stands throughout their career, unless they *behave* in ways that prove otherwise, such as "ratting out" a fellow officer. For the gay officer, the mere discovery or disclosure of a discreditable status unrelated to the actual job of policing can call into question the officer's proven reputation as a good cop because of the negative qualities believed to be associated with some openly homosexual persons, such as militancy and untrustworthiness.

In a strange twist of events, one officer recalled that although he himself encountered few overt problems upon coming out, his straight partner began to experience guilt by association. Thus a close association with a known homosexual cop, though only work related, can force a heterosexual cop to *share* the stigma of homosexuality assigned to the gay partner.

His partner got calls at home asking if he too sucks dick because he worked closely with a gay cop.

Some guys had us [he and his partner] as lovers. They had us living together. The fucking stories they came up with. It's funny, but it's not funny. We were just friends.

Cops who are not partners of the gay officer can also experience a backlash should they demonstrate support for a gay in their command. A lesbian told of a female officer who "ripped down a sign that was meant for me and confronted the cop [who put it up]. She stood up and she herself became the victim of discrimination."

A comment that appeared in the May 1988 issue of the *GOAL GAZETTE* suggests that a straight female cop who works with an openly gay female and simply *appears* somewhat less feminine than the norm is prone to courtesy stigma, that is, stigma by association. "When a woman comes out, the heterosexual women, especially if they look a little masculine, are afraid the men will start joking and saying, 'maybe you're gay too, because you hang around her.'"

Appearing overly feminine is also no guarantee that a heterosexual female will not be subjected to courtesy stigma, particularly if other attractive lesbian officers have recently come out at work. Public disclosure of lesbianism in a precinct can, in fact, result in sweeping suspicions and generalizations among heterosexual male cops who may feel that most of their female colleagues are impostors pretending to be straight. This categorical label can impact negatively on the straight female officer who, through no fault of her own, suddenly finds herself under suspicion. And it can indirectly impact on the newly out lesbian officer, who may now find herself shunned by her female co-workers because of the trouble they see her as having instigated by coming out. As one lesbian explained the dilemma:

The women were very different toward me [when she first came out]. They got very catty. They were very threatened that the cops would think they were gay too. That _____'s good looking and she's gay; how many other impostors do we have among the females?

A negative reaction in the workplace, unique to gay *women* who have chosen to come out, is a sudden unwillingness on the part of some of their heterosexual female colleagues to change clothes in front of them. A number of female officers say they have observed this form of rejection directed toward other lesbians:

I have been in the locker room when there was another lesbian getting changed and there were two straight women in there and they just walked out. They said they refused to get undressed with her around. I said, "Why, why not?" They said, "She will be looking at you."

In the locker room, girls would watch her, make sure she wasn't staring at them.

This preoccupation among some heterosexual females with undressing in front of a known or suspected lesbian cop moved one gay female officer to alter the scheduling of her workday.

Other girls were very leery about changing in front of her. She was very cool about it. She would come in extremely early when no one was in the locker room and change. In the interim, if someone would come in while she was changing, they would wait for her to finish before they changed. There were others who didn't care. They would easily change in front of her.

A female officer assigned to a Manhattan precinct stated that nasty rumors followed her to her new command. She complained "that there were tough moments in the locker room when other women

were too embarrassed to change in front of her. Some thought because she was a lesbian she would automatically proposition all other
women."[12]

Yet another openly gay female said that she had never experienced such locker room problems.

> I thought that would be the first reaction I would get. I haven't seen it yet. I think
> there are only one or two women who are afraid to take off their clothes but
> I'm not sure whether it's me or anyone in general. . . . Maybe they don't expect me
> to be hitting on them. I don't stand there and watch them change.

Despite such claims from some lesbians that they never experienced serious locker room problems since they came out, it appears
that tensions in some New York City precincts have turned to harassment, reportedly forcing the department to create separate locker
rooms for lesbian officers.[13]

Another form of reprisal some gay officers expect upon coming
out tentatively or publicly involves the question of assignment. The
feeling expressed by a number of men and women in this study, and
one that no doubt keeps many gay officers closeted at work, was that
disclosure or even suspicion of being homosexual could result in the
officer's being transferred to a less prestigious unit or command or
receiving the most undesirable precinct assignments. These officers
not only anticipate unfavorable reactions upon exposure but are
tempted to impute meanings to those reactions that are related exclusively to the officer's sexual orientation and to avoid or dismiss meanings that may be work related (for instance, an officer with a poor
attendance record may believe that his new, unfavorable assignment
is due to his being gay, not absent).

As one officer explained his predicament, which is typical:

> I was bounced out of a plainclothes unit I was in. There were rumors around that I
> was gay. But you couldn't prove it. I heard the lieutenant was embarrassed I
> might be gay. People talk about certain things. If I ever brought them into court,
> they would deny what they heard. They got to cover themselves, and they
> couldn't open their mouths to me because it was against the rules. The reason I
> heard why they bounced me was that I was having problems at home and it was af-
> fecting my work and my activity wasn't up to par. So they had to make cuts, and
> I was the one they cut.

The question of where to lay the blame for an undesirable assignment, below standards evaluation, or unwanted transfer becomes even more problematic for those in law enforcement who possess multiple stigmas, such as black lesbians. For these suspected or openly gay officers, the question becomes one of identifying which of these traits, if any, was responsible for the unfavorable assignment or punishment.

SOURCES OF POLICE HOMOPHOBIA

Individual or collective reactions toward gay cops that can be classified as essentially hostile and intolerant spring from a variety of sources. Among the most common are parental convictions passed along to children; supporting media accounts of the unnatural nature of homosexual life-styles;[14] religious beliefs; and, more recently, studies and media reports that lay the blame for the spread of AIDS into the heterosexual population on promiscuous bisexual males.

The gay cops in this study believed that the most prevalent source of homosexual hostility among police officers, aside from the fear of catching AIDS from homosexuals, was the belief that gay sexual relationships were either "sick," "sinful," or "immoral." The typical imagery conjured up by straight cops, they explained, was one in which gays are not only preoccupied with sex but in which the sexual relationship itself was devoid of any expression of love and emotional involvement. Straight cops, they felt, do not or cannot visualize the wider picture that exists for many gays in which there is a need for a relationship that combines sex with love, tenderness, security, and a sense of commitment. In their eyes, the gay male, especially, is morally bankrupt because of this unnatural emphasis on deviant sex instead of love. This perceived moral failing and the revulsion it breeds is well captured in the following quotation:

Cops start to envision what it's like for [a gay officer] to be in bed with another guy
having sex. . . . The initial reaction is one of abhorrence because you can see
their faces when they talk about it. Oh, my God. And that's what it comes down to
when I tell you I'm gay. I tell you what I like to do in bed.

Another officer was considerably more explicit.

GAY COPS

When they think of gays, it's a blow job, a dick in someone's ass. This is the image they see—they don't see warmth, love, affection. And if this image is conjured up, it's always with one of the guys in a dress.

Yet some of the female officers would object to this stereotyped image of homosexuals. They claim that lesbian cops actually experience less rejection, whether public or private, from their straight male co-workers than do openly gay male cops. As a cause of this difference they point to the more subdued sexual imagery that women project publicly. In fact, as some have pointed out, men may even find an erotic element in the idea of two women having sex that is absent or even repulsive when they think of men engaging in sex. The difference, generally, between the perceived sexual acts involving two women and those involving men is explained in some detail by an openly gay female officer.

Society looks upon homosexuality and it's more accepted in women. Women are supposed to be nurturing, frivolous, soft, and weak and that kind of eroticism. And sex between two women is accepted in [male] society. The thought of you being next to a woman who does things to other women turns men on. But if you put a man on the inside, there are certain expectations from society, and the sexual act itself between men is not accepted. It's looked upon in a different way. When women have sex you don't think of any violent acts. Women are supposed to be soft. This is what you think of women, you think of soft sex, and men you think of hard sex that's violent, the act of penetration.

Another potential source of hostility, not only in the police world but perhaps in other occupations in which trust and loyalty are crucial bonding factors among co-workers, is the discovery that a work mate has been intentionally deceptive and dishonest. There is also the complementary element of being caught unawares, of feeling tricked by a co-worker who has been masquerading as straight. Largely as a result of their training and on-the-job experiences, cops pride themselves on their ability not to be caught by surprise. When this turns out to be the case, and when the deceiver turns out to be one of them, wounded egos may produce temporary hostilities. This is perhaps more likely to occur, as a number of gay officers pointed out, when disclosure comes without warning than when it emerges gradually.

You see when I came out I did it slowly, gradually, you know, leaving clues around. But there are some guys, and women too, that do it quickly. They don't give anyone a chance to digest it. I asked one guy why [another gay cop] was getting fucked over so much after being seen at the [Gay Pride] Parade and he told me that some of the cops in his precinct were shocked to find out he was gay, and they felt he had really pulled a fast one on them. He really had them convinced that he was straight. . . . It's as if he betrayed them. That's the way they saw it. . . . But all the shit stopped, the pictures on his locker, the phone calls, all that stuff. He said things are fine now. No problems.

As a few of the officers in this study have indicated, in instances of sudden, unexpected disclosure, most bruised egos do heal and the now openly gay cops are judged once more by their job-related behavior and professional reputation. But for other straight cops, being caught by surprise seems only to confirm what they knew all along—that gays are unreliable, emotionally unstable, and not to be trusted.

There is an important link between the foregoing sources of homophobia and instances of hostility actually displayed in the private spaces of the cop's work world—peer pressure. In the traditional world of policing, when cops get together in private areas such as locker rooms or elsewhere socially, a collective mentality is born. This mentality springs in large part from a multifaceted belief system and a set of subcultural rules and expectations that have traditionally bound cops together. One aspect of this belief system incorporates the view that those who possess certain moral failings, such as homosexuals, should be isolated and rejected by conventional members of society such as themselves. Once a part of this collective mentality, no individual wants to be singled out as a dissenter—in this case, the lone supporter of a deviant or immoral cause. Thus, although individuals in the workplace may privately tolerate or support the rights of others to be different or even refuse to see this differentness as a moral failing, they may *publicly* demonstrate an abhorrence for those who possess what others in the workplace perceive to be discredited traits. Their voices, like those of the true homophobic in policing, are sometimes heard loudly protesting the life-styles and sexual behavior of homosexuals. They may even join in the physical attacks committed against those known or suspected to be homosexuals in the streets, when in fact deep inside they feel no such compelling moral need or inclination. These men and women are the followers in the police world who have not yet mustered the courage to stand up for what they truly believe and break with this collective wisdom. To do so today would be, in their eyes, tantamount to expulsion from the police family.

I have only scattered observations to support my conviction that there are many of these followers in the department, men and women who care little about one's private sexual preferences but who, because of the powerful need to belong, join in the vilification of gays. The observations of the gay officer in the following quote capture my own views as well as those of other gay cops who are aware of the compelling nature of peer pressure among rank-and-file police officers.

It's amazing the stuff that goes on. I find that a lot of the guys who express these very strong antigay feelings, they express themselves in the locker room around a lot of guys. By themselves they are different. I find that the guy who talks all that stuff in the locker room, one night he just might be talking to a very obvious gay person very nicely. You know as a group there's this one consensus given off. As individuals you observe something else definitely. So, I think it's that mass type of pressure that you see a lot of this nonsense and then on a one-to-one basis sometimes it almost knocks you off your feet what you see.

In summary, in the social world of the precinct, alternating forms of criticism and support are directed toward the officer who is either suspected of being gay or openly so. In this socially constructed world, identity for the gay officer is often mediated by how great he or she perceives the risk of disclosure of sexual preference to be. Exposure as a "faggot" or a "dyke" for the officer in the lowest ranks could mean humiliation, ridicule, isolation, and decreased effectiveness. The interviews offer a graphic portrait of how fellow officers punish and marginalize those perceived to possess a moral weakness. Ranks close in conversations about sexual fantasy, in projections of heterosexual—and openly macho—conquests, and in vindictive scapegoating. For gay officers higher in rank, there is less risk, as the system increasingly insulates these officers from straightforward locker room criticism and discrimination. It is critical to note, however, that not all gay officers who have come out tentatively or publicly are mistreated by their partners and co-workers. Most of these men and women have carefully charted their process of coming out in ways that have provided maximum buffering against retribution.

When stepping back from the role of participant/interviewer to that of analyst, I find that the interviews themselves offer a striking portrait of the sociability of the police precinct or command with its different ranks. There is a camaraderie in these workplaces that supports the officer in a profoundly violent and dangerous occupation by transforming small talk into an index of sexual preference and prowess. The social world of the lowest ranking officer is one in which the locker room and other private spaces are critical for bonding. Much as in popular TV portraits such as "Hill Street Blues," the buddy system is critical and gossip has a profound impact on character assessment.

I also want to bring to the reader's attention the language that the interviewees use. Much of their disclosure to me—and I assume that I am both trusted and feared, as anyone would be who touches on such sensitive and emotionally volatile subjects—is in the vivid language of risk taking and problem resolution.[15]

Eight

The
Off-Duty
World
of Gay
Cops

My lover always thought of [his being a cop] as something sexy, being in uniform. He never asked me to wear the uniform to bed, although I have been asked that numerous times. It's usually said in jest, but not really.

The pronounced emphasis on camaraderie among police officers at work understandably extends beyond their work world. Officers who share intensely emotional and sometimes even life-threatening work experiences develop a special bond that usually spills over into their social lives and leisure activities—barhopping, attending sporting events, and such family get-togethers as weddings, outings, and holiday dinners. Indeed, for some cops who have worked closely together and who have developed over time an intimate social bond, there is an expectation that they will, at least occasionally, share in each other's off-duty social activities.[1] For the gay officer, and especially the officer who has kept his true sexual orientation hidden from his partners, these social expectations are often shrouded in conflict and stress. On the one hand, declining invitations to participate in exclusively heterosexual social activities can, over time, disrupt otherwise stable working relationships; the message received is that "I'm good enough to work with but not to socialize with." On the other hand, accepting such invitations carries with it the burden of having to continue to present and maintain a false self to others, of having to be on constant guard against the slip that might reveal one's true sexual identity. There is also the compelling need to spend one's leisure time in the company of other homosexuals where the gay officer can unwind, feel at ease about his or her sexuality, and, most importantly, seek out new sexual partners.

Although all of these cross-pressures operate to some extent in isolating the homosexual cop from his heterosexual counterparts, it is the last reason most gay officers offered to explain why they seldom if ever shared their leisure time with their straight colleagues. As one officer explained it:

Yeah, I did socialize with them [straight cops] once. They used to invite me out after work. But now I always decline. I don't want to hang out with them. I don't want pretensions. I think my time is better spent in a gay club. I think it's an imposition for me to have to go out and pretend. I want to go out with my gay friends where I can be myself.

Another male officer explained how one incident brought about a marked change in his socializing habits with his straight colleagues.

As a matter of fact I used to go out with the guys drinking, at least once a week. We'd all share stories [about women]. It was just bullshit. One night [after work] I said I couldn't go out to this one guy [in my command]. I said I already had plans with my girlfriend. He said, "Where you going?" I said, "To her house in Brooklyn." He asked, "Does she have a girlfriend? Can I come along?" I said no. He said "Come on, what kind of a friend are you?" This went on for fifteen minutes. I began to get sick. This guy kept on persisting, persisting. . . . I said, "There's just going to be the two of us. Do you want to be the third? Do you want to fuck my girlfriend? Why do you want to come along?"

Charlie Cochrane once said, "My cop friends aren't as shocked at my being gay as my gay friends are at my being a cop."[2] As his words suggest, a contradiction exists in the gay officer's social world that parallels the contradiction between the homosexual and police statuses that can produce conflict or strain on the job. At work the critical element is the officer's homosexual status, or perceived moral worth. Socially, however, the critical conflict-producing element is the officer's police status or perceived professional worth, his or her moral worth as a homosexual having already been established. Thus, in both worlds, there is an interaction between these supposedly incompatible statuses that often produces conflict and, for some gay policemen and policewomen, personal stress and torment.

In their work world gay officers are often able to resolve the dilemma of incompatible statuses by exploiting their professional worth as good cops, in hopes that it will neutralize their perceived moral failing as gays. In their social world they cannot exploit these same qualities to enhance their occupational worth for a number of reasons: (1) there exists in the gay community, as in most others, little understanding and appreciation of the qualities attached to being a good cop; (2) these same qualities (for example, not "ratting out" co-workers who verbally abuse or physically attack gays) often serve as catalysts for ongoing discriminatory police behavior directed toward members of the homosexual community; and, (3) very simply, gay men and women who have chosen to enter policing are viewed by some sectors of the gay community as traitors or conspirators, a situation paralleling that of the black officer who chose policing as a career in the late 1960s.[3]

Because they may not be known in the homosexual community as cops (as they most often are not known in the police world as gays), gay officers attempt to resolve their conflict through identity management, that is, by choosing, in their social world, not only whether but how and to whom to reveal their occupational status.

THE SEXUAL ADVENTURES OF GAY COPS

Though I will touch briefly on the broader socializing patterns of gay cops and identify the favored settings they frequent, the focus of this chapter is on the gay officer's adventurous cruising habits. This is because cruising patterns are more likely to be linked to and influenced by the officer's occupation than are his or her quests for friendship and emotional companionship.

I once did this scene with a guy I arrested—play arrested. I handcuffed him. I read him his rights. I took him home and fucked him. He loved it. But it bothered me. I never did that again. It doesn't work for me. If I want to fuck you, I want to fuck you. I don't want to spend the next three days and nights dancing. I just want to fuck you.[4]

From the interviews, two distinct cruising patterns emerge. The first involves fleeting encounters in such anonymous public areas as streets, parks, waterfronts, and back alleys. The second involves en-counters in more socially accepted locales, such as gay bars and clubs. While it can be assumed that most individuals frequenting the less conventional settings are also gays in search of sex that is expedient and noncommittal, it is a fact of life that these areas are more commonly frequented by muggers, thieves, street hustlers, and extortionists bent on victimizing unsuspecting gays. In the more socially accepted settings, an unsavory or potentially threatening element may still be present, but most of the clientele are legitimate homosexuals similarly seeking some form of social or safe sexual encounter.

While both settings do present a certain amount of risk for *any* homosexual, that risk is greatly magnified for the homosexual cop if he is closeted at work. To protect himself from victimization and subsequent exposure at work, the gay officer must not only devise strategies for presenting himself to strangers but plan how he will handle any problems that may arise in the course of pursuing a sexual encounter.

Cruising Nonconventional Locales

Certain parks, piers, streets, and back alleys are favored settings for gays in search of anonymous, impersonal, and quick sex. However, as already noted, these out-of-the-way places, which are often dark and sparsely populated, also make the gay individual a potential victim. A gay *civilian* who is victimized while cruising or actually engaging in a sex act in these public areas has a choice, depending upon the magnitude of the crime and on the individual's personal situation, of whether or not to report the incident to the police. Though, indeed, some homosexual victims do report crimes committed against them, according to David Wertheimer, executive director of New York City's Anti-Violence Project, 80 percent choose to remain silent, fearing either that the police will not act upon the complaint or that making a complaint could lead to humiliation, embarrassment, and public exposure of their sexual proclivities.[5] Moreover, there is no existing law in New York City that requires civilians to report a crime to the police. That is not the case, however, for those in law enforcement. By law, police are mandated to identify themselves and act upon or, at the very least, report any crimes committed in their presence. Realistically, of course, an off-duty gay cop in street clothes observing someone else being victimized can simply walk away from the scene, and in most instances no one would be the wiser. But if, while frequenting a known gay cruising area, that same gay cop becomes the victim, the situation changes. He or she now is presented with a number of options any one of which, if carried out, could prove to be career threatening or at least humiliating. Should the officer become, for instance, the victim of an armed robbery in which only personal property is taken, an instant decision must be made whether to resist the attacker and attempt to effect an arrest or, if the criminal flees, make an official report of the crime to police authorities. The decision to make an arrest or file a report obviously opens the door to the revealing question of what the off-duty officer was doing at that location in the first place.

The dilemma is that by taking legal action—that is, by arresting the offender or making an official police report—a still-closeted officer risks exposing the hidden homosexual side of his or her life. Even when the gay officer is out to co-workers, becoming involved in any sort of incident in a nonconventional cruising area could provoke damaging gossip in the workplace about the officer's social habits and moral character. Along these lines, one officer recalled an occasion in which a previously closeted police acquaintance was unwittingly outed to his straight co-workers when, after being victimized in a nonconventional setting, he made the choice to act based solely upon his occupational instincts and arrested the offenders.

One of the former members of the organization [GOAL] on three occasions left himself open. First occasion, he winds up collaring these two kids. What happened was he met them at a cruising spot. He thought they were trying to pick him up. When he felt that was the case he tried to pick them up. Something happened [to the car] and he got out of his car and he winds up collaring them. . . . He takes them to the station house. He was "in" then. Let me tell you something—he's out now. He brought the people in and one of the prisoners let it out that he was a fucking faggot who was trying to pick them up.

An alternate strategy to avoid unwanted outing is simply to not take any direct police action when in nonconventional, known cruising areas, or to avoid any actions that could jeopardize one's hidden sexual identity. By taking a course of nonaction, in most cases, the officer is only technically in violation of existing laws and

departmental regulations. For charges to be brought against the officer, the incident must first be observed and then officially reported
by another person. (The option of nonaction does not exist, however,
if during the incident shots are fired or the officer is in some way injured seriously enough to require hospitalization.) Another alternative to avoid unwanted exposure is to file a false or misleading report;
that is, one that states that the incident did occur but substituting a
more socially acceptable location and perhaps even altering the circumstances. However, by knowingly falsifying any aspect of a criminal incident, officers may be putting their careers in jeopardy. The
penalty for filing a fraudulent report can range, depending on one's
intent and position in the department, from temporary suspension to
outright dismissal. Yet in spite of these risks it appears from the interviews that most closeted gay cops would choose to put their careers on the line rather than to expose their secret homosexual
identity. The officer who related the incident with the two kids, for
example, went on to express not only his own feelings but those
of other gay cops as to how certain criminal incidents should be
handled by those intent on preserving their heterosexual front at
work.

I think he was foolish in deciding to collar those people. I don't care how much
damage they did to my car, I could always lie about it and say it was parked, and I
came out, and it was like that. Because the minute I take somebody in, the
person is going to say, "Yeah, he's a faggot." So I think it's foolish if you want to
stay in the closet. Unless there's a threat to your life, you get the fuck out of there.
Who needs the aggravation?

The one exception to this avoid-getting-involved approach is a life-
threatening situation. In this instance a gay officer who is in some
way personally involved rarely has any choice but to take official police action even though it may mean risking exposure. Yet even in
life-threatening situations, closeted gay cops may seek to protect
their secret sexual identity by attempting to scare off the attacker.

One day I almost got robbed. A knife was put to my throat. I was coming home and
there was this cute Hispanic kid, and I mean he was gorgeous. And I picked
him up, and we started to make out a little bit, and the next thing I know he has
a knife to my throat. And he goes to take my car. Luckily I was wearing sweat
pants. He told me to get out. I grabbed my keys and threw them to the ground,

and when I got out of the car I got my gun and scared the shit out of him. He ran away. I never reported it.

Employing this strategy of nonofficial intervention poses an additional risk, however small, that the attacker may retaliate by going to the police, claiming to have been the one who was victimized and naming the officer as the culprit. The attacker could also file an anonymous complaint providing the police with the license plate number of the officer's car and the known homosexual cruising location where he alleges the driver of the vehicle threatened him with a gun. Either of these possibilities could produce career-shattering results because, even in the case of an anonymous complaint, detectives are required to investigate the alleged incident. Although the officer in this case would not in all likelihood face criminal or even departmental charges if he were to deny the charges, the mere allegation that he was in a known cruising locale could prove both embarrassing and stigmatizing.

The question of whether or not to take action when victimized at a known public cruising area is more serious if the officer's gun, shield, or ID is stolen. Because a police officer cannot readily return to duty without this critical equipment, the theft of any of these serialized items *must* be reported to the department. If a true account of the incident is provided (one in which both the correct location and the circumstances surrounding the theft are fully revealed), then clearly the question of the victimized officer's sexual orientation will be raised. In light of this threat, the officer may, as before, opt to file a misleading report in which the scene of the robbery is changed to a different, less stigmatizing location. Or the officer could falsely state that the shield or gun was either lost or taken from the officer's apartment during a burglary. When reports of this nature are made, the officer faces relatively minor departmental sanctions for the loss of these items. But there remains the possibility of a worst-case scenario should the thief be apprehended as a result of an investigation or unrelated crime and subsequently confesses to having stolen the property while the officer was engaging the thief in a sexual proposition or encounter. The officer's problems are now compounded: departmental charges could be brought for knowingly and intentionally filing a false police report, and the conditions under which the theft took place could expose the officer's homosexual identity.

These dual risks of possible suspension and exposure at work loom large in the minds of those closeted officers who cruise noncon-ventional gay areas and become still another source of anxiety in their already complicated lives.

It's my nightmare that something happens when I'm in a gay setting and either I lose the gun and the shield or something happens like I'm assaulted or robbed and I have to go inside and report it. It's not a comfortable situation, but it's something we have to deal with all the time. If you're going to be in the life-style and be a cop in the city, it's something you have to prepare yourself for. If you don't you're a fool.

There's a serious dilemma in the person's mind whether to report it [as it hap-pened] because he was gay. And it's a hard decision to make.

Though a New York City police officer does have the option of resolving this dilemma by simply not carrying a gun or shield when out cruising, being unarmed in these often unsafe areas can present other problems. One officer said, "When I used to go out I didn't take my gun and shield at all. But lately, I've been taking my gun because of all the violence in the city."

Given the degree of escalation in urban violence, it could be ar-gued that it is safer and perhaps wiser in the long run for the closeted gay officer to be armed at all times. Should an incident occur, one could argue, the officer should simply be prepared to provide the authorities with a true account. Yet in such a case, interestingly enough, most *closeted* officers in this study said they would *not* tell the truth. The same answers were repeated over and over again:

Lie my ass off. Obviously, I'm not going to tell them the actual truth. I would say robbery and the guy fled. I wouldn't tell them the truth. I wouldn't say that I lost it. I would probably say that a female accompanied by a male robbed me. . . . But I would have to really plan that out. I hope I never get into that situation.

Oh, God, I'd lie. I wouldn't say where I lost it, or how I lost it. Definitely, I'd lie. No way would I tell the department the truth.

Though another man did state that he would report the theft of a gun or shield, he too was certain that he would not provide depart-ment investigators with the whole truth. He would "just report it missing. Say you had to relieve yourself in the general area. Cover yourself. You have a reason for being there. . . . If it comes down to it, it's his word against mine."

One officer (choosing to remain anonymous even to me) who had actually experienced the theft of his police shield while engaged in a homosexual act in a nonconventional cruising area said that the need to protect his secret sexual identity was so powerful that he did, indeed, falsify the circumstances of that theft. Though he was clearly aware that by lying to the authorities he compounded his risks, adding the potential for suspension or even termination, he rationalized the double risk this way:

Listen, I've leveled with you [so far] about everything. So let me tell you about this one incident. One night I was just fucking horny. I needed a blow job, so I picked up this trick on the West Side. . . . We were in my car and he was down on me. . . . My pants were down. When we finished, I checked for my money and shield. My money was there, my shield was gone. He must have sensed something was up because he was in the wind. Now, what do I do? Report it? I wasn't out then. . . . Fuck no, I told them [the investigators] that I must have dropped it in the street. . . . My only prayer, even today, is that the department never catches the guy who ripped me off because it will be double trouble for me.

Before filing a potentially revealing report of such a theft, the victimized officer has one further option: to personally go out looking for the thief and attempt to retrieve the property unofficially or off the record. A number of officers claim to have done just this. For example:

I had tied one on that night. I was drinking from the afternoon and started cruising the park at three o'clock in the morning. So I see this guy and I let my guard down and we had sex in the park and he fleeces me. . . . He got my shield. I was so drunk I came home. I went home and got my lover to help me find him. He said, "Let's go and do what we have to do." We went to different places, the cruising spots and we didn't locate him. I knew I had to report it. I didn't know what was going to happen. Was I going to get fired? Suspended? I didn't know. I never anticipated anything like this happening. . . . [Obviously the department doesn't know the truth.] The only thing that saved my butt was I had an excellent work record. I didn't call in sick, my clearance rate is excellent.

This course of action is precarious at best, as it carries with it the possibility of a violent confrontation with the thief, as well as the potential for further victimization through extortion. One female officer, who also chose to conduct her interview anonymously, related the following stress-provoking incident:

I know a couple of females who had problems. One ended up losing her gun and her shield because she fell asleep and she [her sexual partner] grabbed the tin [shield] and the piece [gun] in a motel. We looked for her. We finally got the gun back, but we ended up paying money for it. She didn't get the tin back so we gave her [the sexual partner] the beating of her life, and then we got all the shit back without escalating the matter. If we didn't get it back she would have had to report it, but it would have been embarrassing. I mean, how do you explain, "I was in a motel with a woman." It's different if you're in a motel with a man. This society is not ready to deal with gay people. What are you going to say, "I went to the motel room with this female to get my rocks and jollies off and while I was asleep the bitch took my shit?"

When asked why she did not simply claim that her sexual companion was a male, this woman quickly added:

So they catch the chick, then what? You have a major league problem. It's a perjury charge against you. It's totally different when you're a guy with another guy or a girl with another woman, because that's taboo. . . . Thank God we got our hands on that broad, and I use the term loosely.

It is important to emphasize that these risks of exposure and professional censure are attached only to the sexual life-styles of the fully closeted gay police officer. When an openly gay cop is victimized by a thief or mugger while out cruising, he has no need to be concerned about concealing his sexual orientation from the police if he has to make an arrest or file an official report of the incident. His situation now becomes similar to that of a heterosexual male cop who goes barhopping in search of a female bed partner and gets ripped off. For this cop, victimized by a female sexual companion, an accurate report of the incident in no way impugns his moral character. If the woman involved is later revealed to be a prostitute, the heterosexual cop may have some explaining to do, but he is not left as stigmatized as the homosexual cop caught in a corresponding sexual encounter.

In addition to the very real personal risk of being robbed, physically assaulted, exposed as a homosexual by that criminal element that preys on gays in public cruising areas, or all of these, closeted gay cops also risk exposure should uniformed officers patrolling these usually secluded areas come upon them while they are engaged in a homosexual act. Several officers expressed an intense fear of just this type of discovery, claiming that they had no way of knowing how any particular on-duty officer would react under the circumstances. Because sexual contact between consenting adults is not a crime in New York City (but public indecency is), the way in which the discovery of two same-sex adults caught in the act is handled is at the discretion of the patrol officers who encounter them. How the situation is eventually resolved depends, in large part, on the personal feelings and views that those patrol officers have regarding homosexuality. When one of the sexual partners turns out to be a cop, however, the strength of a patrol officer's loyalty and solidarity toward fellow officers can also enter the picture. It is perhaps because of this powerful sense of loyalty among police that in no instance in which one of my subjects was caught in the act by an on-duty patrol officer was the incident reported to his or her command. However, their experiences did range from on-the-spot humiliating put-downs to, in one instance reported by a male cop, kneeling and pleading with the patrol officer to forget what he saw. Despite no *reported* instances of betrayal by on-duty patrol officers, the possibility remains that a strongly homophobic officer, coming upon two adults in a homosexual encounter (one of whom is later revealed to be a cop), will perceive the gay officer as a disgrace to the profession and relish the opportunity to inform members of the officer's command of the cop's true sexual orientation.

Given the acknowledged dangers, one must ask why some closeted gay cops continue to use these admittedly high-risk settings for their sexual encounters. Several tentative answers can be offered: First, there is, compared to other U.S. cities, a relatively large population of gay males in New York and consequently a large and varied number of known cruising grounds. At least a portion of these gays routinely frequent these areas in search of sex that is quick, casual, and anonymous. Second, many homosexual males (some of whom are certainly cops) may be attracted to and find these settings tantalizing precisely because of the ever-present element of danger. As Laud Humphreys explains, "The chances they take add an element of adventure to the gaming encounters and, for many participants, serve as an aphrodisiac."[6]

Yet for most of the officers in this study, it is chiefly because of the increased risks attached to frequenting these areas that they claim to confine most of their cruising to the safer, more conventional settings such as gay bars, clubs, and discos.[7] As one of them explained:

If you come to the conclusion that you are not going to have impulsive sex [in these places] you have eliminated most of the problems of being a gay cop—of being afraid of losing your gun or shield, or being assaulted or robbed.

The Gay Bar and Social Club Scene

Compared to New York City's vast number of heterosexual gathering places, there are relatively few public spots where homosexuals can get together and comfortably socialize with other gays. The purpose of socializing in these places, for the gay individual is, as with the heterosexual, to meet friends, old and new, dance, listen to music, unwind with alcohol, enter into lively discussions, and pursue sexual relationships.[8] While the gay bar and social club fulfills all these functions, it is best known for its reputation as a hunting ground where sex can be found without obligation or commitment; that is, sex for the sake of sex alone. Indeed, as Bell and Weinberg note, "The gay bar far outshadows any other cruising locale as a free marketplace for sexual exchange."[9]

The function of the gay bar as a sexual marketplace figures prominently in the social agenda of gay officers. However, for an officer cruising these settings, the potential for danger exists with each new encounter. As Martin Hoffman put it, "If an individual picks up another man and takes him to his apartment, he really cannot predict what he is getting himself involved in. It may be a routine sexual encounter, and, in fact, most often is. But, it can also be a very disastrous encounter."[10] Though admittedly a potential for trouble exists for any individual regardless of gender or sexual orientation when meeting and engaging in a sex act with a total stranger, it could be argued that an off-duty police officer out cruising would be *less* at risk in these situations because he or she can choose to be armed. Even unarmed the officer is in a better position than a civilian to diffuse a potentially troublesome situation by simply making known his or her occupational status. Conveying the message "I'm a cop, so if you have any agenda other than sex or sociability, forget it" can forewarn any potential thief or mugger.

This immediate self-identification can serve still another purpose for the gay officer. It is well known in homosexual circles, for example, that many gay males desire and seek out sexual partners who exude a macho-masculine image. Thus it is not surprising that the police officer, shrouded in an aura of authority and militaristic masculinity enhanced by the uniform and occupational accoutrements, is highly sought after as a sexual partner. Michelangelo Signorile, a writer for a popular gay magazine, vividly describes the attraction. "The mere words [cop] increase testosterone and estrogen levels in the body as thoughts turn to nightsticks, badges, sunglasses, leather uniforms!"[11] Besides the sexual fantasy conjured up by the police uniform, many gays appear to be attracted to the image of police work itself. This image projected in stage, film, and TV cop stories is one of combined power (which can, incidentally, also be sexual) and the sense of safety that comes from being with a protector. Aware of this idolized image, it would seem that, for gay officers out cruising, revealing or even flaunting their police identity would be irresistible. Yet this is not necessarily the case. Because of the uncertainty as to how other gays may react to them as police officers, homosexual cops, when in the company of strangers, may choose to present themselves as something other than cops.

COMING OUT AS A COP: TO TELL OR NOT TO TELL

When meeting prospective sexual partners for the first time, a homosexual police officer will invariably have to deal with the question of *occupational* disclosure. Several options are available: (1) Because the gay officer is not in uniform when out socializing, he or she can sidestep questions about work by quickly changing the subject (this option, however, can create an uncomfortable atmosphere and inhibit further social interaction between the officer and the new potential sexual partner); (2) the officer can simply lie (as many have told me they do), claiming to be a teacher, social worker, or computer programmer; or (3) the officer can tell the truth, as some told me they have done. However, immediately revealing their police identity to strangers they meet in gay social settings also puts them at risk; the stranger could, for varied reasons, expose the officer's true sexual identity to the police department should that officer still be closeted at work, as most are.

The reasons some gay officers gave for knowingly putting themselves at risk need to be examined, as do the motives of others for choosing not to reveal their police identities at first meetings. The host of potential dangers facing both closeted and openly gay officers who bring a stranger home or elsewhere (a car or secluded public spot) for sex and the strategies adopted by these officers to avoid victimization also need to be explored.

In my interviews there was repeated reference to the powerful sexual imagery attached to policing. Being acutely aware of this favorable imagery and the sexual advantage it affords, some gay cops quickly reveal their police identity to prospective sexual partners in bars or clubs. The following statements from male officers provide some insight into this choice.

Simply, people are attracted to cops. It's a plus to tell them. There is a fantasy there. Oh, yeah. I think it's part imagination that they've seen good-looking cops, the uniform, the leather, the gun, the hat. So they use their imagination, and if they meet one, they want to do it just for kicks.

It's a big turn-on to people. They love it. They eat it up. The uniform, the authority, the image. You are on a very high pedestal as a rule. Guys like to say they went home and went to bed with a cop. That's hot. It's the fantasy thing to have a relationship, to have sex with a policeman. It's a big fantasy of most gays to say they went to bed with a cop. One guy told me he always wanted to pick up a cop, kiss a cop.

Most people get turned on by the fact that I'm a cop. It's the thing with the uniform. You would be surprised at how many people get turned on . . . they might say, "Oh, he's a cop, I always wanted to go to bed with a cop." The uniform, it drives them bananas. . . . It amazes me, the attraction it causes.

One man said that he and his nonpolice lover, mindful of the sexual imagery attached to policing, sometimes entertain themselves by calling homosexual talk lines and flaunting the officer's police identity. "Occasionally my lover and I will call up the gay line to talk. We just flirt, and I would tell them I'm a cop. And they would say, 'Oh, you're a cop.' And before you know it, everyone wants to meet you. It's a trip for them."

The sexual fantasy attached to the police officer's job and uniform is not confined to males, as the following lesbian officer confirms.

GAY COPS

"Some women enjoy it, too. It's a combination of gun and shield, uniform, the honor. I've had females say, 'You look so good in your uniform, sexually good. You look fine.' Some are turned on by that. Like some women love a man in uniform, some love a woman in uniform."

Virtually all of the officers in this study were aware when they cruised gay bars and clubs that their occupation (should they choose to disclose it) could provide them with a distinct sexual advantage over other homosexuals whose occupations might be viewed as less manly, such as teachers, accountants, or computer programmers. Should a gay male officer find himself in competition with another homosexual for the same sexual partner, it is commonly believed that if his police identity is revealed, he will usually win out.

That's a fantasy, turn-on. It's movies that made it a very masculine thing and obviously being gay you are attracted to the masculine. Nobody's going to fantasize about a relationship with a teacher.

The few I have met and told they were like, oh, yeah, wow. Those people were impressed. . . . I've been in a setting somewhere talking to a third person, and I'm a cop, and the other person is a schoolteacher. They're going to say, "Oh, you're a teacher. That's nice!"

The gay male officer has discovered that he can use his occupational status to entice potential sexual partners in much the same way that the heterosexual male doctor, lawyer, and Wall Street broker exploit their economically superior status on occasion to attract women. Thus, when pursuing a new sexual partner, some gay officers actually flaunt their line of work.

Of course, if you're out cruising it could get you over. To some people it's a fantasy. If it's going to get me what I want, I will capitalize on it. Straight cops do it all the time with women they meet.

A female officer agrees.

Definitely, I've seen some females at the club I go to have their gun where you can see the bottom of the holster. To me that's advertising, and if you advertise it's because you think it's going to help you in picking up women in the club. And for some women who have problems picking up girls, it's a foot in the door.

These comments suggest that it is not necessarily the police *person* who captures the interest of other gays but rather the trappings of the police occupation. Indeed, the profession itself can be such a powerful sexual magnet for nonpolice gays that it can make even an otherwise unattractive cop appear to be a good catch. "They like it. A lot of people have asked me to hook them up with a cop, *any* cop. . . . They want to complete a fantasy." A female officer elaborates:

I listen to other people talk about the so-called uniform fetish. You could be the ugliest person in the gay world and probably never had sex with anyone in your life. If you're a person in uniform you could get one or two people who would go to bed with you just because of the uniform. It depends on how much you want to advertise.

As an indicator of how powerful a component of the total sexual imagery the police uniform itself is to some gays, a number of the officers I interviewed reported having been asked to actually *wear* their uniform (all, or some select parts) while having sex. Some indicated that they did occasionally accommodate these requests.

Sometimes I have great fun with it. I go the whole gamut with them. Sometimes they just come right out and ask. The "blue magnet" works.

It's always been a positive experience for me. The reactions are very positive. People start expressing their fantasies, like, "I've always wanted to make it with a cop." They ask, "Is your uniform at home?" Some have asked me to put the uniform on. It's definitely a sexual turn-on, the uniform.

Yet others indicated that for them there is no personal fantasy or intrinsic sexual meaning attached to the wearing of their uniform while involved in sexual contact with another gay. For this smaller group, the uniform and its accoutrements symbolize only their work role and like the tools of any other trade should be left at the office. These men and women claimed that when they were asked to wear their uniform during intimate sexual acts to accommodate the fantasies of others they simply refused. One officer's standard response to this request is "I only put it on when I get time-and-a-half." He added, "I like sex without any clothes on. Besides, my mother washes my uniform—cum stains would be hard to explain."

For some in the homosexual community the image of a police

officer in uniform represents something more than mere sexual fantasy. To this segment, the more conventional aspects of the police role assume priority, though, as the following quote suggests, there still exists an undercurrent of sexual attraction:

I think a cop to them offers security and stereotypical masculine traits, like one who protects, guards over, one who knows what he's doing. . . . When you run into a cop, he's supposed to know what to do. You don't run up to a cop and hear, "Well, golly gee, I don't know." Kids are raised that if anything is wrong, go to a cop. He knows what to do. And you take that over as an adult and he's going to carry those things over to a sexual and emotional level.

Thus the image projected by the police officer of power and authority when coupled with a sense of protection can play a compelling role in attracting nonpolice homosexual partners. "Naturally they're impressed. The whole image, the uniform. The machismo. I think to some gay men it's an ultimate goal—to sleep with a cop. The image is the whole thing, what it represents. It represents power, authority, safety—nothing's going to happen to me if I'm with a cop."

Another belief shared by some gays is that because police officers have sworn to uphold the law, they are more stable, trustworthy, and perhaps even of higher moral character. "I think a lot of men feel they're meeting somebody who is reliable, someone they can trust. Because you uphold the law, you believe in the law."

Yet even when reflecting on qualities of higher moral character, there is still often an expressed undercurrent linking policing to the intoxicating mystique of sexual power. "A lot of guys look for someone who is assertive in a positive way, stands up for what he believes in, for his rights. They also lean more toward security. They perceive cops as being strong. The role cops play in the movies, hot lovers, gorgeous bodies."

For those lesbians who prefer to assume the submissive, "femme" role in a sexual encounter, the attraction to a female cop is obvious. Police roles such as those played by actresses Sharon Gless and Tyne Daley in TV's "Cagney and Lacy" and by Angie Dickinson in "Police Woman" have unquestionably contributed to the sensual/aggressive-assertive image of the female police officer. Simply being in the company of a woman who is known to carry a gun adds to that woman's sexual appeal, as noted by a lesbian officer:

There are a lot of lesbians who would be turned on if they knew that I'm a cop and I have a gun on my waist or leg somewhere. . . . It's safe being with a cop. It's a turn-on. The whole thing of not being afraid of dangerous situations. . . . They know you're not going to run away, that you can't run away. They're turned on by that feeling of safety. "Wow, this person has a gun." And a lot of it has to do with TV cop shows [about women]. It's the excitement. . . . The gun is a turn-on. The strength it gives. The power you have. And there's the stereotype of women being submissive and it exists. And if you're a cop and have a gun and behave with authority and confidence, some women are turned on by that.

This same officer stated that in her own experience, some lesbians were particularly vulnerable to the police image.

Latin women are especially turned on by that strength and power. A lot of Latin women are still into that butch and femme stuff. If you're a cop, you're probably butch and that whole power is going to attract the submissive woman who is going to get off on the fact that you're a cop and because you're strong and power-ful, you're going to take care of them, that kind of thing.

Yet many of these same men and women also concede that this first impression of the police officer as a virile sexual object and as one who possesses superior qualities and strengths may, in fact, be short-lived. They claim that this often idealized image begins to fade once a relationship has been established and the realities of the officer's job become apparent to the nonpolice lover. Confronted by the day-to-day uncertainties and very real stresses of living with a police officer, the partner quickly begins to see past the romantic mystique surrounding police work. Consequently, many officers in the study have come to believe that their occupational status, though possibly the instigator of a relationship, cannot alone sustain it.

Contrary to the popular notion that gays seek only transient, im-personal sexual encounters, there is a powerful and growing need among many homosexuals to establish relationships with lovers that are lasting and that go deeper than mere sexual fulfillment.[12] Gay officers seeking these more stable relationships feel this goal can only be attained when a lover develops an interest in and an attrac-tion to aspects of the officer's life and personality that extend *beyond* the trappings of the occupation. It is because of their sincere desire to establish a more permanent, bonded relationship that nearly half of the officers claim that at least at first meetings with a prospective lover they choose not to say they are police officers. When directly asked about the nature of their job, some said they felt it was to their advantage to lie or at least present a half-truth. As one highway patrol officer put it,

I don't tell people. . . . If they ask me, I tell them I work for the city highway depart-ment. Because, in general, the people you meet tend to be impressed by cops. I don't like that. I'm a person. I want people to know me as _____.

Another gay cop expressed the distressing feeling of being used after revealing his police affiliation. Now when asked about his line of work, he too lies.

I guess they think we change in a telephone booth and become Superman. . . . They see the uniform. They don't see the person. I'm a little wary of those types. . . . If he likes me because I'm a cop, that's a downer. That lets me down. It makes me feel that he's not with me but for the uniform. I need someone who is more sincere. So I don't usually tell them I'm a cop.

In short, there is a compelling need among this group of cops to be recognized and treated first and foremost as a person and not as someone's sexual fantasy, as this officer's comment makes clear:

I don't tell them, not at first. Because I don't want to fulfill someone's fantasy of going to bed with a cop. I want to be known as [his name], not [his name] the cop. I go to bed with someone because there's a feeling. Later on you can have your fantasy. . . . I would turn down someone who wanted me because I was a cop.

As is evident, many of the officers share a belief that premature occupational disclosure to a new sexual partner often limits that rela-tionship largely to sexual exchanges. Moreover, officers interested in establishing deeper, more enduring relationships encompassing companionship, friendship, and romance may, by immediately re-vealing a police identity, expose themselves to the possibility of being hurt or at least disappointed once the novelty of having sex with a cop begins to wear off. Along these lines one man confided that prema-ture disclosure of his occupation to some of the gay men he found attractive was the cause of a series of painful experiences.

I noticed that eventually I became kind of like a novelty. They would be interested
in me but only because of what I did for a living. And we would date, we would
go out, and I would get very emotionally attached. We would have sex and I would
get attached to them and then the novelty would wear off. And that was it. It
would leave me totally hurt. That's when I realized that was the problem here.
Now, if I meet a guy and he asks me what I do for a living, I tell him a white lie. I
tell him I work for the city. If I get to see the person a lot after that, then I start
to introduce the law enforcement aspect.

Like this officer, those men and women who resist early disclosure argued that their true line of work could always be revealed
once a more serious relationship had been established. By then, if
the lover is still attracted, the officer can feel at least somewhat confident that it is because of his or her own unique personal qualities, not
the more impersonal aura that surrounds the police as a whole. As
one of these more cautious individuals explained:

I would tell them I sell insurance, teach in a public school system. . . . I don't want
them to get off that I'm a cop, that they made it with a cop. I don't want them
to know me only as a cop. I want them to know me for who I am first. . . . My lover,
I would venture to say, we were dating close to two months, and I didn't tell him
what I did for a living. When I saw that it was getting serious, I thought that I gotta
let him know.

Another argument against early occupational disclosure is that it
can serve as a barrier to establishing wider social networks in the gay
community. This is because many homosexuals distrust and dislike
cops in general.[13] Thus, while for some the reality of meeting and
socializing with a cop may be an immediate sexual turn-on, for others
it may be a turn-off. A male officer said unequivocally,

No, I don't tell people. When I go out to a club I don't tell anyone I'm a cop because
first you get that eerie look, whether you're there to spy on them or socialize
with them, or you're there to try and get some information from them. So they become kinda leery. So I tell them I work for a large department, and I do
investigative work with missing persons. I let them think I work for a large insurance company.

A female officer experienced similar feelings:

My concern would be being rejected. Certain parts of our community, especially the political activists, those people I would hate to tell. I have been outwardly rejected by them. "It's nice to meet you" and then, good-bye. Another reason I would hold off on saying I'm a cop is because people already have a stereotype of what cops are, and they are prejudiced against me for being a cop. So I would hold off, tell them I'm in public relations, which isn't all that much of a lie.

A male port authority cop expressed his cynicism concerning some gays' attitudes toward the police by describing the rejection he had experienced upon revealing his police identity to other homosexuals.

I usually don't tell anybody anymore because they are going to have stereotypical responses. It puts a lot of blocks up. It interferes with communication. People have too many feelings about the police. Those I've told right away, I didn't like their reaction. Most of them, they don't accept the police. It's not popular to be a cop among gays.

A female cop was more explicit: "Some are turned on by that. Others are turned off. You're a cop. Ugh! They won't even look at you, talk to you, nothing. I had one female come up to me in [a bar]. She said, 'You're a cop, how could you do that?'"

The reported distrust some gays express toward those who identify themselves as police officers occasionally stems, in part, from the belief that the person claiming to be a cop is lying. These more suspicious members of the gay community view being both a cop and gay as so incompatible as to be almost inconceivable. Even when it is revealed that the gay officer is in fact telling the truth, there are those in the gay community who hold such strong antipolice attitudes that they perceive anyone in uniform, gay or straight, as the enemy, to be both feared and distrusted.[14] Like those who see the gay cop solely as a sexual object, these individuals often fail to see the person inside the uniform. These often inescapable dilemmas provide the rationale for presenting a false self in the gay bar and social club scene.

Especially, there are some people who cannot see a cop being gay. The first experience I ever had was in one bar and someone found out I was a cop. The first thing was, "What are you doing here?" I looked at him. The last thing people expect to find in a gay bar is a priest or a cop. . . . There are also people that are turned off [by cops]. We are the authority people. That's the way they see it.

They feel we shouldn't be doing what we are doing if we are cops. They see you
as a stereotype.

While a police career provides such benefits as job security, a daily
potential for excitement, and certainly a departure from the mundane
nine-to-five job routine, it also imposes on the officer the constant
threat of danger and a work schedule that frequently disrupts normal
socializing, eating, sleeping, and even love-making schedules. Some
of the officers in this study expressed uneasiness and doubt about
initially revealing their occupation to potential lovers and mates for
fear that they might automatically be rejected on the basis of these
commonly known occupational hazards and hardships. Two lesbian
officers explained how, when meeting other gay women for the first
time, the element of danger inherent in policing kept them from revealing their police identities.

A lot of females don't like dealing with a cop. They don't like the involvement, the
"one minute I could get a call, you could be dead." A lot of women don't want
to deal with that at all. They want to deal with a business person.

If they ask me what I do, I tell them I'm a zookeeper, because that's what I do. I'll
lie first. I don't think women are attracted to lesbian cops. As soon as they
hear cop, they think, not coming home at night, the threat of my lover getting
killed. The ones I've talked to are fearful of that unless they are in law enforcement.
They have told me this.

A male cop concurs. "Some gays are like straights in the sense that
they don't want to get involved with someone in law enforcement
because of the danger of the work."

A few officers pointed to the public's awareness of a police officer's
unpredictable work hours as a deterrent to premature disclosure.

They think, does that mean that at two o'clock in the morning when the phone
rings you gotta take off? It's like any marriage. They don't understand the
responsibilities, the duties that we do, like, hey, I got a collar, I won't be home till
after four o'clock. They say, "Fuck this."

Another male officer noted how having work hours that do not coincide with most people's schedules directly affects his social life. Because he often works nights and weekends, social events and dates

with nonpolice individuals are not always easy to arrange. "People are also initially concerned about cops having to work around-the-clock, having to work weekends, never being able to have a normal social life."

As police work involves such open-ended and time-consuming duties as investigating crimes, making arrests, and processing prisoners and transporting them to court, an officer's workday can, and frequently does, extend beyond the scheduled eight-hour shift. Criminal investigations and arrests may also require the officer to spend some days off preparing for trials and other official hearings. These routinely erratic elements of police work have long been exploited by the heterosexual male cop, intent on cheating on a wife or girlfriend. This same route of deception is available to the gay officer bent on philandering. But in the gay community it is not uncommon for nonpolice individuals who have had relationships with cops who cheated on them using job-related excuses to pass on their painfully won knowledge to their unattached gay friends. This networking forewarns others of the dangers and emotional risks attached to entering a relationship with a cop.

Through their personal experiences and conversations, gay cops realize that they share this reputation for dishonesty, which may incline them to conceal a police background during early encounters with a prospective lover or mate.

I usually don't tell anyone I'm interested in that I'm a cop right away. Because, this is a small world and the word spreads quickly about getting involved with a cop. Nobody in the beginning believes these stories about, "I'll be late. I've got a collar." They think you're out whoring around with someone else.

This general reputation for cheating on lovers, a character failing once confined exclusively to the male police officer, has now been extended through stories, rumor, and innuendo to the female police officer—suggesting, once again, that reputations or character assessments are frequently attached to statuses rather than to individuals. A female officer said lesbians she meets socially

have their concerns because of male cops. They have their wife at home and their mistress on the side. A lot of lesbians think that about lesbian cops. I've come across many people who know or question their lovers. Is she really in court and can't be reached? I found a lot of women that have that thought in their head.

They think that cops have a lot of interaction with a lot of people. . . . The cop has virtually the whole city.

A further reason for delaying the disclosure of a police identity to others in a social setting is the belief expressed by some nonpolice gays that becoming involved with a cop means they may be subjected to control and physical abuse. A male officer elaborated on this fear.

Some of the people I know run the other way when they find out you're a cop. Either they've had bad experiences with cops or physical abuse by a cop, or someone told them about their experiences. I've known guys who have had relationships with cops who physically abused them. See, when you tell them you're a cop they see the additional possibility for abuse with nightsticks, the gun in the house. I think they are in fear of that.

Similarly, although women are socially conditioned to be less aggressive, some lesbians perceive that because of the aggressive nature of the role of the police officer, there exists the potential not only for a misuse of power in a relationship but for manipulation and control. In this context, a lesbian officer confessed her own apprehension about getting involved with a woman in law enforcement.

Many people don't like dealing with female cops because they feel she can kick their ass. A lot of women think about that, you know. I thought about it myself twice and decided I'm not going to get hooked up with another female cop because you're dealing with all that dominance, that control.

Possibly the greatest single fear attached to early disclosure of one's police identity (and one that was expressed repeatedly throughout the interviews) is that imparting such information to a lover early in the relationship puts the officer still closeted at work at risk of exposure. For example, should the officer end the relationship or threaten to do so out of dissatisfaction with the lover, the lover may respond by calling the officer's command. One cop said he

never tells them right away because should you have to end it with the guy after one or two times because he's fucked up, not right somehow and he has fallen for you, you got problems. If he knows you're a cop and [that] you're in [the closet] at work, he could fuck you up good. All gays know how the department feels about them, so he's going to look to make life as miserable as possible for you. How does he do that? He drops a dime to your command.

Another officer pointed out that the possibility of being outed dramatically increases if the rejected, offended, or disenchanted lover turns out to also be anticop.

Most of the time I would not tell them I was a policeman. When they asked me, I would tell them I'm a schoolteacher. My reason for that is nobody has a bitch against a teacher. You never know who you are hooking up with. He could be a nut job and you know what problems it could make for you. They know this much about you, and they could go to your job. A lot of gays hate policemen. That goes back historically. And that's their way of getting back at you if things don't go well or if you don't come back a second time.

Because early disclosure of a police identity to a newfound lover can put the closeted officer at risk, some officers have found it wiser to get to know a lover for a while before trusting that individual with such potentially damaging information.

It's like at a certain point you want to tell someone yeah, I'm a cop. At the same time you have to realize that this person's gay and this person could drop a dime on you if you have a problem. And then you have a big problem and God knows.

It could come back to haunt me. It doesn't take much for you to say, well, I'm a cop and I work out of headquarters and out of the Missing Persons' Unit. It wouldn't take much for them to find out, and they then could call up and say something to someone in reference to your life that nobody knows about. Now you're out.

For cops who pursue impersonal one-night stands, the immediate advantage gained from exploiting the sexual fantasy attached to policing is, on occasion, overshadowed by the risk attached to early disclosure. One officer suggested that these cops are at the greatest peril of unwanted public exposure, and perhaps this is why they appear to be the most cautious about revealing their police identity to strangers.

I call it the "wolf syndrome." There are the guys who are out there trying to do as much as they can. Now those guys do not want people to know they are cops because they want to hit the scene, do their damage, and get out real quick. They don't want anyone to be able to tie them to police work.

Whether gay cops are out cruising the bars and social clubs for sexual partners or simply socializing for companionship's sake, there is the possibility that violations of law, such as drug use, will occur while they are present. Should others know of or become aware of their police identity, they may find themselves in, at the very least, an uncomfortable situation. Even though off duty, they may be viewed as cramping the scene. Thus, for some, anonymity is the best policy. "You go to these clubs and some people are smoking reefer and you tell someone you're a cop, they could go into a panic. So to avoid all that, I just don't tell anybody." Officers who do make their occupational identities known in public places where illegal substances are either openly displayed or used, but who take no official action, are also endangering their careers. Suspension or even termination are possible outcomes should any disgruntled or morally outraged patron or rejected suitor choose to inform the department that the officer was present when illegal activities were taking place and made no attempt to arrest the offenders.

Moreover, an officer need only be observed frequenting bars and clubs where illegal activities occur to constitute grounds for suspension or a departmental investigation. While the risk of being seen in these places and reported to the department extends to all police officers in New York City, once again the gay officer winds up in a no-win situation. Because official action (making an arrest or reporting the activities to the authorities) is not only impractical but risky in the sense that the officer must now explain what he or she was doing in a gay bar or club, the officer must often choose to sit by silently. On the other hand, the more conservative choice of frequenting gay bars and clubs where illicit activities rarely, if ever, occur severely limits the officer's cruising and socializing locales, thus restricting his or her circle of friends and sexual partners. These problems, it should be noted, generally do not extend to either straight cops or other nonpolice gays. My own experience suggests that straight cops prefer to hang out in cop bars that, for obvious reasons, discourage criminal activities from taking place on the premises. As for nonpolice gays, their risks are limited, for the police rules forbidding cops from frequenting places where criminal activities take place generally do not apply to them.

While the use of deception—that is, either implying or actually providing a false, less controversial, occupational biography—may allow the closeted cop to maneuver more easily through the gay social scene, it provides little or no protection against many of the other risks inherent in cruising. Consequently, some officers have found that along with keeping their occupational identity hidden when meeting other gays for the first time they occasionally needed to take more stringent precautions to protect themselves from victimization and exposure at work.

FURTHER CRUISING STRATEGIES AND PRECAUTIONS

The quest for sexual contact is, in varying degrees, always present in the gay bar and social club scene. Even officers who claim to frequent these locations in search of companionship or a long-term relationship admit that in the back of their minds always lies the hope that, along with meeting the right person, the evening will end in a sexual encounter. No matter how clothed, this ever-present sexual goal is always tempered by the concern among both male and female gays that voluntarily leaving a cruising spot with a stranger can leave them vulnerable to victimization.

[An acquaintance] had a one-night stand and she went back to this chick's apartment and she had another chick waiting for her. And they ended up trying to force her, like rape. She identified herself and they backed off. Out there, there's just too much shit going on. . . . Another friend of mine, she's a transit cop. Same shit happened. She went back with this chick and she started beating the shit out of her [the friend] for sexual reasons before she told her she was a cop. She was into S & M. She fought her off and just left. But before that she got fucked up.

You have to be careful. This is New York City. You just can't go around trusting anybody or everybody.

A gay sergeant recalls an experience in which a new sexual partner expressed this fear regarding him.

One night I met this guy at a bar. We went right to his place. We went to bed and started carrying on. I realized I had my belly band [holster] on. I said to him,

"Don't mind this, I'm a cop." He had a couple of drinks earlier. You should have seen this guy's expression. His jaw dropped a foot. He was terrified. He said, "Are you sure?" I had to show him my shield. He said he thought he was going to get ripped off, robbed, or killed. He said, "God, you never know who you are bringing home."

The stranger's comments reflect the ambivalence of gay men and women who find their need for immediate sexual gratification so intense that they repeatedly place themselves in situations in which they could end up becoming crime statistics. Their consciousness of this danger leads them to take extra precautions when out cruising or even just socializing in gay bars and clubs.

To begin with, a number of officers in this study claimed to rely largely upon what they variously labeled a cop's "sixth sense" or "gut feeling."

By virtue of my profession I think I have more of an insight into these people than the average gay person who's out there cruising.

Something you feel inside yourself. Something within you. I don't totally relax. . . . You develop that extra sense of safety. You're a little bit more aware than someone else.

I trust my police instinct in a bar when I meet someone. If I sit and have a couple of drinks with someone, I can pretty much trust my intuition and say whether or not this person is looking to hurt me. Especially guys who give you the "I'm just an innocent country boy" impression.

Many of these same officers indicated that when they found themselves in a situation with a stranger in which they sensed that something was not right, if they felt even slightly uncomfortable or threatened, they would immediately disengage themselves. One female cop cited fear itself as a deterrent to engaging in a sex act. "You have to trust your instincts. You see, if I'm not going to be comfortable with you, I'm not going to have sex with you."

The officers do not mean that the decision of whether or not to have a sexual encounter with a stranger is based entirely on intuition. Most of them claimed that they first attempted to elicit relevant biographical information from the prospective sexual partner. Not surprisingly, of primary importance to these officers was whether there was any indication that the stranger had been or was currently involved in illegal activities. One man briefly detailed his own personal checking-out process, which bears a distinct resemblance to the techniques used by police when confronting and questioning a criminal suspect in the street.

I am very cautious. The very first thing I do while I am in the bar with a new person is to stop, question, and frisk. Frisk with the eyes first. You notice his hands. Is he a smoker [grass]? Has he got yellow marks on his fingers from the joints? You question him. As you are speaking or dancing, you feel the body for weapons.

Elaborating on this checking-out process, another officer added, "What do I look for? I look at the guy, check his waist, ankles for a gun or knife. When I talk with a guy, I touch, I'm checking."

In addition to checking for something as specific as a weapon, some gay cops also look for indicators that collectively, if indirectly, suggest the stranger might be involved in some criminal enterprise. One man, although in an exaggerated way, identified some specific items that might link an individual to drug trafficking. "If I don't have a good feeling about them, for example, if someone is wearing gold chains, has a pit bull and a Porsche outside, he's probably involved with drugs."

The overall appearance of the stranger can also influence the officer's decision to pursue a sexual encounter. How is the person dressed? Is he or she clean looking? Does he or she appear generally healthy? Even physical size can figure into this decision and is of crucial importance to some. Should a dispute occur, the officer needs to feel confident he or she cannot be physically overpowered. This concern with differences in physical size was expressed over and over again by *men* in this study.

If I had any feeling that he could overpower me, I would not go home with him. If I felt I could handle him, I would do it, if everything else about him checked out.

I could never conceive of bringing someone home who I was concerned about whether they could overpower me or overtake me. If there was the slightest inkling about that in my head, they would never get anywhere near [his apartment].

A stranger's display of emotional and behavioral stability is a further indicator that sexual compatibility with the person may be possible. Officers who resorted to cruising to obtain sex said that they would usually pass over anyone exhibiting aggressive behavior. Another officer summed up his apprehensions about getting involved with someone who shows signs of being possessive.

We have a conversation. We talk, get to know each other. You get to know where the guy's coming from. You get to know who's possessive and who's not. . . . The worst thing a cop can do is get involved with someone who is possessive because he can cause trouble if you decide to see other guys.

Qualities in a prospective sexual partner that are perceived as negative or as indicators of possible trouble are, however, not always immediately apparent even to a trained police officer. In some instances such qualities may have to be carefully pried out. In trying to accurately size up the other person, officers said they often resorted to casual questioning designed to provide a general, albeit tentative, biography. The questions most frequently asked center around employment history, education, relationships with family and former lovers, and, occasionally, preferred sexual acts. One officer describes what he cynically referred to as his third-degree method.

I most definitely try to find out about him. In the course of our conversation I would ask him questions about his personality, job, and other things. . . . I would let him talk, give him enough rope to hang himself. I'm not exactly sure what I would be looking for, but when I found it, I would know. I would look to see if his head was screwed on really straight.

Another male officer explains similar precautions that he would take when first meeting a likely sexual partner, and why. "I would study everything. I would talk to him, draw him out, ask what he does for a living, his job, married or not, etc. I've met some pretty sleazy people in those bars."

A female officer who conceals her police identity when first meeting a potential sexual partner is more focused in describing the kinds of danger signs her veiled probing attempts to uncover.

Usually, I like to get into past relationships. It's worth knowing about. For example, if she hops into bed with every soul in the world, I'm not going to do it. Usually, if she doesn't know I'm a cop, I'll ask her if she does drugs. Usually, I'll make a snide remark about a cop and see what her reaction is. Maybe she will say I can't stand cops, I got busted last week. It will all come out. It will start flowing.

GAY COPS

To help elicit truthful information from a stranger, some gay cops in this study apply tactics similar to those used by seasoned detectives when questioning criminal suspects. They pose careful questions and verify an individual's honesty by casually and periodically reasking the same questions.

I do my own in-house sizing a person up. As the conversation goes on, sometimes things that were mentioned in the beginning of the conversation you check to see if it's the same as it is now. . . . I would try to find out as much truthful information about the person in this way.

This strategy is often combined with an assessment of both the stranger's body language and his or her reactions to carefully worded questions aimed at revealing more than just the answer, again, a tactic used by detectives to determine whether or not an individual is telling the truth.

If you're in a conversation you will be talking about things that he should be familiar with whether you are discussing the Gay Pride Parade, or other bars that you've been to. You may be asking him about his past. So I think also by virtue of our profession we're suspicious about most people. . . . You look at him, talk to him. Once again, that body language can really tell you a lot.

I go through absolutely a series of questions about where the person's from, how long they've been there, casual questions. It's a technique I would use in police work, but only if they're alone and in a very casual, nonchalant way. The person is not picking up that I'm getting so much from him. . . . I can tell they're lying by their movements. They get nervous. . . . I would just ask people to elaborate on different things they've done in their lives, different places they've been, to see if their stories make sense, if they're legitimate.

A more extreme tactic, and one that constitutes a serious violation of some departments' policies, is to check out a potential lover covertly through official criminal and motor vehicle records. These records are readily accessible to most law enforcement personnel and can be an important resource for the gay officer if other less official strategies prove unsuccessful. One detective now retired from the force candidly admitted to having used these official resources to check up on people he had recently met and to whom he found himself attracted.

I was just being honest and told him I'd like to get to know you better. We're going too fast and why don't we slow down. I'd like to meet again tomorrow for dinner and we can take it from there. . . . I took his [license] plate and did a criminal check on him; did a whole portfolio.

A female officer also said that she routinely inquires about and sometimes even personally checks out the living and working environments of likely sexual partners.

I like to find out where they live and where they work. What kind of place is it. Is it a hole in the wall? Do people do drugs in the back? Does it have connections with the Mafia, gangs, drugs? You inquire because you don't want to get wrapped up in none of that garbage. . . . That's what I normally do if I like the person. I don't take anything for granted because of my job. You have to be careful with whom you get involved.

To avoid many of the risks and dangers involved in picking up strangers, some gay officers claim to spend their cruising time in what they refer to as steady bars and clubs. Confining themselves to these places gives them the opportunity to become familiar with the regular patrons, who in turn become an added resource in identifying potential problem strangers. A related advantage in hanging out in steady clubs or bars is that, in time, they can establish relationships with management and employees as well. Should gay officers become interested in any of the regular clientele, they can tap these insiders for character and background information. For one lesbian officer, the management at her steady club proved useful in checking out a woman patron in whom she was interested.

In these places you get to know the managers, bartenders and they know everybody that comes in. Somebody knows somebody. . . . I met this girl at one of these clubs. I knew her first name, didn't know her last name. I wanted to know her last name. Why? Because I wanted to do a check on her. I asked the manager about her. The following week the manager gets back to me and tells me she's a secretary and she's an alright girl, but she's into drugs. That's all I wanted to know, end of story. I want to get more information . . . you know, the cop in me.

Despite the general acknowledgment on the part of all the officers in this study that strangers they met in any cruising locale must always be approached carefully, there are always moments when the

attraction is so intense that it overpowers the officer's better judgment. On these occasions a sexual liaison may begin before the officer has had a chance to check out the new partner's biography. Yet
even in these instances, all caution is not necessarily thrown to the
wind. A series of crucial and immediate decisions must still be made.
One of the first considerations, and often the most critical, is the
choice of where to go. Although a number of options usually exist,
the place most often agreed upon (for obvious reasons of privacy) is
one or the other's apartment. For the gay officer, there are advantages and risks attached to either choice. However, when asked
which of these two locations they preferred, when the encounter was
going to be with a person they knew little about, most indicated *their
own* apartment. This choice, they argued, offered a greater degree of
security. They could be assured at least of not walking into a setup.

Very rarely will I go back to someone's apartment. I feel more comfortable in my
own domain. I know what's here . . . I know what to anticipate here. You
never know what's waiting there. It could be something bad, like a setup. It's happened to plenty of guys before.

You also have to be especially careful of straight kids in gay clubs. . . . I prefer my
own apartment, because in someone else's apartment, someone could be
waiting for you in the hallway, in the closet. I know of instances, some cops felt
they were being set up. So I personally feel more secure here. I know what's here.
I don't know what's there.

When returning to a stranger's apartment there is also the possibility that one of his or her former or current lovers could show up
unexpectedly. It is easy to see how a confrontation might ensue and
quickly escalate into a situation in which someone calls the police.
Such an incident could clearly jeopardize the anonymity of an officer
who was trying to keep his or her homosexuality a secret from the
department. A female officer's reaction to this perceived element of
danger and risk of exposure is typical. In someone else's apartment,

I don't know who's going to call or stop by. She could be seeing someone else and
telling me she's not. She could be living with someone and they walk through
the door. I don't want to get caught in a situation like that because I'm a cop. I've
seen it happen with some of my friends. They'll pick up these girls from bars
and they'll go to their apartments, and the missus or mister will show up and the

shit hits the fan. You can lose your job or be found out, and it's not worth it over a sexual desire. It's not.

Despite these fully acknowledged risks, some cops still prefer the stranger's apartment, claiming the advantages outweigh the potential dangers. One is that, should the officer discover that for any reason the two are not compatible or begin to feel uncomfortable with or even threatened by the other person, the option of simply getting up and leaving is always available. A second is that returning to the stranger's apartment provides an opportunity to gain further insight into that person's character and life-style.

I'd rather go to her house because I could just get up and go when I want to rather than have to say, "Do you mind leaving," or "It's time for you to go." Once I was asked and I said, "Sure," and I went to her place. When I got there it was terrible. The place was just dirty and filthy, and I was like "Get me out of here," and I just left. I was there ten minutes, and I knew I did not want to be with this woman.

Personally, I prefer going to their place. Why? Because if you don't like them because they're duds, creeps, assholes, you can leave. They come to your house and it's kinda hard to get them out.

A few officers believed that there was considerably *less* chance of being victimized in a stranger's apartment than in their own. They reasoned that a person would have to be a fool to attack them in a place that could be easily located by the police. "I usually don't bring people back to my house. If I was going to sleep with them, I would go back to their place. I think part of this is out of fear. They really can't harm you or chop you up in their house."

Even for that group of officers that, for various reasons, claims to feel more comfortable engaging in a sexual encounter in a stranger's apartment, there remains the sticky problem of securing one's weapon. The police department regulation that officers must at all times see to it that their guns are safeguarded can become a problem when they find themselves in unknown territory.

If I had my gun on me and I'm at her place, where am I going to stash the thing so she's not going to know? With these one-night stands and what not you really don't know what you have. You might have an emotionally disturbed nut who's just waiting to grab your gun.

Consequently, in unfamiliar surroundings the officer cannot be casual about where the gun is placed. A stranger could get hold of the weapon and accidentally fire it. One obvious precaution is to simply leave the gun locked in the trunk of one's car, and some claim to do just that. But the car could be broken into and the weapon stolen, or the car itself could be stolen. In either case, the officer has failed to properly safeguard the weapon and would face departmental disciplinary charges. One male officer routinely uses an alternative strategy. "If I decide to go to someone's house, and of course I'd follow him in my car, on the way there I'd take the bullets out of my gun. I would not go to a stranger's house with a loaded weapon. I always make sure that my weapon is empty."

The problem of safeguarding one's weapon exists as well, though to a far lesser degree, for cops who choose their own apartments for a sexual liaison. When allowing a stranger to enter their home, officers have a precise plan to secure the weapon formulated in advance to avoid the possibility of theft, of accidental discharge, or worse yet, of finding themselves threatened by their own gun. Thus, some officers stated, when bringing a stranger back to their apartment, they immediately (though with utmost discretion) hide their gun, their shield, and any other valued property.

Also, being a cop I tend to be suspicious when I take someone home. I usually hide my wallet, and keys, and shield, and gun when they're not looking.

I put my gun in my favorite hiding place and that's it. You have to be responsible. In the door, off comes the gun and [when he's not around] on top of the china closet. It's just a response . . . second nature.

While hiding one's weapon can neutralize certain dangers for the officer, it can create other problems. For example, should the stranger have a hidden criminal agenda, or should a serious or even violent dispute flare up between the two, the officer may not be able to get to the weapon in time to prevent a theft, robbery, or physical attack. Precisely because of these possibilities, several officers stressed the importance of being able to retrieve their weapon. They always hide their gun with the thought of quick access.

How can you possibly get to know a person in two hours? What I usually do is put the gun in some location in the house where they can't find it, but in case of a problem I can get to it quickly. I put it under the sofa.

I keep my gun and shield under my clothes and keep an eye on them. Put your un-
derwear and socks on top of your gun and shield.

That the gun might be found (and, in a worst-case scenario, actually used) while the officer is, for instance, taking a shower, is of
paramount concern to both men and women in this study. As an
added precaution, some choose to unload the weapon and hide the
bullets elsewhere. Others lock the gun up or link handcuffs through
it to prevent it from being fired. Two officers said they were so fearful
that their weapons could be taken and used against them that, when
bringing a stranger home, under no circumstances did they ever
bring the weapon into the apartment. These officers chose instead,
even at the risk of auto theft, to leave their guns in the trunks of their
cars. A female cop explained why she chose this lesser of evils.

I don't trust anyone but my mother with my gun and shield. What I usually do is
take my gun and shield and lock them up in the trunk of my car. Of course, the car
could be stolen, but I prefer that over some bitch getting the gun.

Gay officers are also mindful that when they give a fictitious occupational identity to a stranger, they can never be certain that someone else in the gay social scene has not already tipped off the
stranger to their police identity. A seasoned detective spoke of both
the anxieties that surface and the extreme precautions he took in
such cases:

If I bring someone home I always put the gun underneath the bed so my hand can
drop down. On my side. And if they happen to wind up on that side, I always
watch where their hand is. No matter how wild the scene is or how intimate we
are, I always try to maneuver my body within range of the gun. . . . I also never let
them know there's a gun there. You never know whether someone knows
you're a policeman or not. Maybe someone already told them, and I don't know
that they know I'm not a teacher. You don't know who you're dealing with. You
have to cover your ass. It's the name of the game.

Extreme as it may appear, this detective's paranoia is not entirely
unfounded if one considers the growing number of violent crimes
committed against homosexuals throughout the country.[15] A gay who
is a police officer must be as alert to the possibility of victimization as
any other homosexual. This ever-present fear, which permeates the

gay scene as a whole, was expressed by virtually every officer in this study. As one of them chillingly summed it up:

All the time you have concerns the first time you meet somebody. Whether he's going to rob you or kill you. He can be on drugs, knock you out, clean out your apartment. It happened to friends of mine.

The possible theft of their personal property weighs on these officers' minds so heavily that before they bring a new potential sexual partner home they usually hide *all* their valuables. For some, the repeated inconvenience becomes so tedious that they eventually opt instead to test the stranger's honesty before engaging in sex. "When I take my shirt and pants off I will fold them in a certain way so that when I go to the bathroom I can tell if they have been moved." Concocting a story about a fictitious roommate who is supposedly not home at the moment is another strategy. "Now I'm more security conscious. I'm really cautious. I might leave the TV on if I'm going out and maybe meeting someone new. And if I bring someone home, I might say something like, 'My friend must have just left to go to the store.'"

One man said that when he allows a stranger entrée to his apartment, "I never let them out of my sight. Even when they ask to use the bathroom, I would always be alert to anything that could possibly happen." Another officer takes this precaution a step further. "I would never leave them alone. If they went to the bathroom to take a shower, I would stay near the door. I would never let them see me put my gun away. I have hiding places. Anything of value would not be out."

For the most cynical and apprehensive officer, every action the stranger takes bears watching. Suspicions are aroused by even the most ordinary movements and gestures.

I've always been very apprehensive when I'm home with a stranger. Why? Because I don't know what's in that person's mind. You can't know a person 100 percent by speaking to her one-half hour, hour, or two hours. . . . My guard is up, like when she goes into the bathroom or something and she takes her bag with her. My guard is automatically up.

As a further precaution against theft, several officers said that, when a stranger is present, besides hiding their weapon and valuables, they always made a point of locking the door. "Yep, I hide my stuff. I'll put money away, put keys away. I also double lock the door in case, let's say, I happen to use the bathroom and he's going to fleece me and get out of here." Locking the door serves a second protective function. "You bring the person home, you double lock the door from the inside. Put a chain on the door too. This stops others from coming in—his friends. Make sure also that all your money and jewelry are put away."

To circumvent some of the risks attached to either bringing a stranger home or returning to his or her apartment, officers sometimes choose a more neutral setting, such as a car or motel. But shifting the scene of the sexual encounter can produce another set of troublesome problems. Several officers complained, for example, that having sex in a car severely constrains body movement, limiting the enjoyment of the act. Engaging in sex in the semipublic atmosphere of a car also leaves one vulnerable to intrusion by voyeurs and criminals, as well as by police on patrol. Even the impersonal setting of a motel is not totally free of risk for the closeted gay cop. Unlike a heterosexual couple, an off-duty gay officer entering, checking into, or leaving a motel with a person of the same sex can attract attention and immediately brand the couple as homosexual. Once someone has observed the officer in this context there exists a witness who could, given the right set of circumstances, filter this information back to the officer's command.

In spite of these added potential problems, some officers still prefer vehicles and motels because of their anonymity and impersonal qualities. Especially for officers living with parents who are still unaware of their homosexuality or for those who have a live-in lover but still seek outside sex, preserving the secrecy of the affair is obviously paramount. In these instances a car or motel may, indeed, be the only option.

I live with my parents, so I can't go home with someone. And I generally won't go back to her place because I don't know what she might have in her apartment.

For me, I can't take them home obviously because I live with Mom. So that would be definitely out of the question. I prefer a motel because it would be a neutral ground for both of us. . . . I know no one's going to walk in, no surprises.

In addition to the very real concerns about being robbed, assaulted, exposed at work as a homosexual, or all three, the officers in this study also worried about contracting the AIDS virus through sex with strangers. For some this concern has turned into an ongoing and escalating fear, fueled by the media, by accounts of friends and lovers, and sometimes by relationships with lovers who had died from the virus.

You hear and read about it all the time. I personally feel almost apologetic about it to tell you the truth. I feel that it's almost inevitable that I will test HIV positive. . . . The fear is always there. It's something I live with every day.

I can't take a shower now every morning without looking at my body [for telltale spots]. It has just so invaded your consciousness.

For many of these men the fear of contracting AIDS is so great that they subject themselves to the stress of frequent AIDS testing and to the ordeal of spending anxious days or even weeks waiting for each new test result to come back.

I get tested all the time. About four times a year.

Physicals every six months or more even though that's no protection. I have a lot of friends that have been diagnosed having ARC. They also went for periodic tests.

Each time you have to wait to see what the results are. That's the hardest part, not knowing if the last guy you slept with had the disease.

It's the waiting that kills you. Like you have a lump and you go to a doctor for an exam. He takes a biopsy and then you sit on the fence waiting for the results. Those weeks I didn't do anything, maybe take some vacation days and just sit and wait.

The fear of contracting AIDS and the anxiety produced by that fear has convinced most of the men I interviewed to try to protect themselves from the disease. These officers claimed that they now practice safe-sex techniques when they are with strangers. For many, safe sex begins not with the use of prophylactics during sexual encounters but with discreet observations of the prospective partner's appearance. As one cautious male officer put it:

I was actually a little macho about it in the beginning. Then I began to look at these guys [potential lovers] carefully, look at their skin, their complexion, etc. You can tell a lot, but not everything.

Observation is often combined with questions aimed at revealing the person's sexual habits, preferences, and perhaps life-style.

I have to see if a person's really clean, if he looks healthy. . . . He could be the sex-iest guy in the world, if he doesn't look right, case closed. I would also ask a lot of questions. I want to know the truth. I ask them if they got their AIDS test, that kind of thing. Verbal precautions first, see the reaction when you bring up the AIDS question.

Even lesbian officers, whose fears of contracting AIDS are considerably less, are alert to a prospective sexual partner's appearance and usually ask discreet questions aimed at disclosing more about the individual's personal habits.

I would make sure the person was very clean, see how she dresses. Ask them about their habits. Or, you could be real sneaky and find out about their sexual practices, whether the person is flirtatious.

As when police check out a criminal suspect's statements, a gay officer often follows up on a prospective lover's accounts of past sexual experiences and habits, discreetly elicited, before having sex with him or her.

Then you try to find out what kind of guy he is. Is he sleeping around with every-body? You check this out with friends. Also, does he brag about the number of men he's fucked? These are the kinds of things I look for. A guy that's out there with everybody is not for me.

Even when they pass the initial checking-out process, strangers are still considered and treated by most of the male officers in this study as potential carriers of the virus. One male officer claims that it isn't always apparent who may be sick. Consequently, as do the others, he treats everyone he sleeps with, strangers as well as those he has dated before, as potential risks. For this officer, that means engaging only in protected sex. "Always, always, from day one, when I'm with someone I don't know that well, I'll have safe sex. I just don't exchange body fluids." Another man explains why he *never* has un-protected sex with any lover. "I would always do the safe-sex thing with a stranger and everybody else because everybody is a stranger. Who knows who else they are sleeping with or who they've been with."

Safe sex takes on a variety of forms for different men and women. For some men it may mean engaging exclusively in mutual masturbation or in other forms of sexual play that do not involve the exchange of bodily fluids. It is so crucial to these men to protect themselves while having sex with strangers and newfound lovers that if the extreme precautions they take are disruptive to the relationship, it is secondary to the safety factor.

The last guy I met, we went to bed fully clothed. I broke up with him because he gave me an ultimatum. He said, "Safe sex is one thing, but having sex through two pairs of jeans is ridiculous." I said, "I know you two days now. Well, this is the way I am. If you don't like it, you can take a hike." That's how it ended. If we can't go slow, then we can't go at all.

For most men I spoke with, however, safe sex simply meant using some form of protection, such as a condom. The following comment is typical: "I would never dream of having sex with someone without a condom. It's not within the realm of possibility. I take the maximum precaution even with oral sex."

The lesbian officers, who are significantly less likely than gay men to contract the AIDS virus through unprotected sex, also take precautions to avoid infection. Two women claim that they avoid any sexual encounters with females who confess to being bisexual. Others state that they use a protective rubber latex shield like the dental dams used by dentists.

I use rubber latex and put it over the genitals. You can have oral sex that way. Same as men using a rubber. But it's harder on women. It's a different dynamic, the sexual act.

In sexual encounters, there's not really much you can use for protection if you're a woman. I learned to cut off a piece of rubber and put it over the genitals. That's really all you can do.

As a final precaution against contacting the AIDS virus, some male officers said that they practice abstinence in the beginning of any relationship. These men weighed the threat of becoming infected through accidental exchange of body fluids against the potential loss of a new sexual partner or lover. All of them, it should be noted, had experienced the death of a close friend or lover from AIDS, a grim reality that has strengthened their resolve to abstain from sex with men they know little or nothing about. The pool of potential sexual partners that is available to these men because they are cops magnifies the dilemma.

AIDS is a hideous disease. I'm just as frightened about the disease as anyone else. That's why I choose abstinence in the beginning even though I lose a lot of the guys I could sleep with because of my job.

I'm just very afraid to go out and have sex with someone. Accidents do happen during sex. And I know I'm missing out because there are a lot of guys who want to sleep with a cop, like I told you before. So what has this done over the past few years? It has significantly decreased the number of men I've slept with right away.

So I deal with it [his desire for abstinence] during dinner. . . . And if I wind up talking to somebody who's looking at me like I got two heads, and they don't want to wait, that's the end of it. It's a very difficult situation for me being a cop, but I've had some people who were very close to me die. That sort of thing brings it home.

The comments in this chapter show that, for most of the men and women in this study, their dual identities *as gays and as police officers* link their work and social worlds in ways that produce constant and often inescapable interlocking conflicts and dilemmas. For those few who have chosen to reveal their homosexuality in the workplace, clearly at least some of these uncertainties and problems are eliminated in their social worlds.

RELATIONSHIPS WITH LOVERS

Twenty-six of the forty-one officers in this study either had stable, romantic relationships in the past or were seeking such arrangements. At the time of the interviews nine of the men and women were in long-term, stable relationships. This response pattern seems to belie the stereotypical belief shared by many heterosexuals that gay males, particularly, favor fleeting, impersonal sexual encounters over more enduring relationships. In the lesbian population the same preference seems to predominate. Hedblom, for example, reports that all but one of the lesbians in his study (sixty-four of sixty-five) preferred a stable relationship to any other.[16]

Some officers have an idealistic notion of what a relationship between same-sex couples should resemble.

I used to like one-night stands. But now, [he wants] a marriage made in heaven. Put the blame on society, the family. There is a belief that two people should stay together.

I prefer a long-term [relationship], no question about that. I've had one for three years and one for eight years. And I still have that kind of Hollywood dream. I know I sound like Donna Reed.

As the comments of many in the group imply, stable, coupled relationships among homosexuals are considered comparable to traditional heterosexual marriages in which there is a continuing sense of support for each partner's psychological well-being.[17] For a few of these men and women, the sharing and emotional bonding that a long-term commitment provides appeals most. "I want to be with someone I can laugh with, someone who will be home with you, cry with you, be with you. He becomes your family. You become a unit."

Two officers currently pursuing more permanent relationships compared this stable arrangement with earlier, more ephemeral sexual liaisons.

Well for me personally, there's stability, family, security, a sexual partner who's there for you all the time, a friend, companion, both growing together. Short-term relationships only feed the ego. They make you feel attractive, but you don't get any real substance from them, any real emotional fulfillment that comes with a long-term relationship.

Long-term, because the one-night stands, to me, are just for sexual pleasure, which I can also understand. I like a long-term because I like honesty, integrity, and I enjoy sharing my life with one person. It's love. It's not just sex.

While these men and women agree that short-term affairs or one-night stands satisfy one's immediate need for sexual variety, they point out that these brief liaisons are generally devoid of such essential elements as commitment, trust, and love. Moreover, in these loveless, fleeting relationships, there is little else than a seemingly unending search for new sexual partners. They are often fraught with stress and uncertainty. "The few that I had developed into a short-term. When it was over you realize that you gotta go out again and start cruising. And it's like a never-ending thing and you never know what you're going to find out there."

Perhaps it is this constant quest for new lovers and the attendant risks of being exposed at work or victimized in other ways that enhances the desire and need of some gay cops for permanency in a relationship. "I really don't like starting over and over again in my life. . . . The more you go out cruising, the greater the chances that something will happen, that you will eventually meet up with the wrong guy and then your problems with the PD begin."

Added to the many problems facing officers who choose the cruising scene and single life is the fear that they will end up alone at a relatively early age. To some cops in this study this fear is very real because of the inordinate emphasis the male homosexual community places on youth as a positive attribute. A correspondent to a popular gay magazine commenting on the perceived "aging crisis" among male homosexuals explained that "these youngsters seem to have the attitude that anyone over 25 is on the downgrade and anyone over 30 is dead sexually. . . . A straight is not considered 'over the hill' at 30, at least sexually, but for some reason a gay is."[18] This concern with aging and the accompanying loss of attractiveness steered some officers in the direction of seeking a more permanent relationship.[19]

You gotta realize that as you get older you're not going to be as attractive as you were twenty, thirty years ago. . . . I remember when I was in my teens and twenties, these older men who were trying to make me and how other people who were cruising would be very critical. I would say, "Hey, you're gonna be that age." They would call them *trolls*. They would use that term loosely, for someone that was in his forties, fifties. So I look for a long-term relationship so I don't have to go out constantly every night to look to make it with someone just to get my rocks off. It becomes a never-ending cycle. You're not happy with life. And as the years pass, you say to yourself, is this going to be the last good-looking one I made it with? What's the next one going to look like? Youth is a crucial factor.

Another officer expressed his views with a poignant observation on aging alone.

Youth is beauty. Old age is not. It may be dignified but no one wants to sleep with an historical personage. I would rather have sex with Mel Gibson than Winston Churchill. Just watch a fifty-year-old gay man in a bar. There's nothing more lonely.

A further problem prompting some respondents to seek permanency in a relationship was the fear of contracting diseases through repeated sexual encounters with strangers. Thus, for example, a disease such as AIDS has strongly reinforced their desire for a long-term commitment. As one man candidly admitted:

I've had them all [all kinds of relationships]. If you ask me right now, I would have to say a long-term relationship. For my health. Right now I wouldn't even consider having sex with someone unless it was going to be on a monogamous basis.

As mentioned earlier, a large proportion of the men in this study concur that AIDS in particular has impacted so strongly on the homosexual community that now most gays feel compelled to practice sexual restraint. Whether these male cops are, in fact, practicing what they preach by imposing more restrictive sexual standards upon themselves is problematic, given both the veil of secrecy surrounding their lives and the highly desirable sexual imagery attached to police in general that makes sexual partners more readily available. What can be safely assumed is that the increased publicity about and high incidence of AIDS in the gay community in recent years has produced a greater *inclination* among gay males on the whole to practice safer sex techniques.

Another factor motivating gay cops to pursue more enduring relationships is the very nature of the police officer's job; that is, the unpredictable work schedule and tours of duty that often require cops to work odd hours with relatively few weekends off during the year. This absence of normal socializing hours in the lives of most police officers eliminates many of the occasions for meeting potential partners, thus making a stable relationship more compelling.

I'm just starting to realize the importance of having a long-term relationship, being in this line of work. The first year I had weekends off and I could leave social possibilities open, to be with people. Now I'm working around the clock and it's ter-

ribly frustrating. So I can recognize the importance of having somebody you
love there all the time, be a cop's wife.

Accompanying the desire on the part of many to pursue a long-term, coupled relationship or marriage, as it is known in the gay community, is the realization that building such a desirable relationship is no easy task. The following statement is typical:

I prefer a monogamous relationship. I'm a romanticist. I want to fall in love and live
happily ever after. . . . I see these guys, thirty-five, forty, fifty [years old] and
they're still out tricking. I never want to end up like that. . . . But I never thought it
was possible for gay men to have a long-term relationship. What I saw in the
bars was guys looking for tricks. And then I started seeing it was possible. . . . Now
I'm going to work for a long-term relationship, one that does not mean only
sex. . . . That's my goal and I'm going to give it the best shot I can. I know it's not
easy. You have to really work at it. Now, I'm looking for Mr. Right.

For a few men who are currently coupled with other men, one of the major obstacles to sustaining permanency in a relationship is the compelling need, from time to time, to seek out new sexual partners. Several officers spoke of the ensuing dilemma of (and possible solution to) trying to simultaneously satisfy these two dissimilar and conflicting needs.

I'll say [his preference is] a combination of one-night stands and a long-term relationship. That's what I have right now. I've been with my lover for five years
and I've been going out with other people on the side. I don't think I want to stay
with one guy for the rest of my life and deprive myself of other people. And I
don't think I could go through one-night stands and not have anyone to come
home to.

I always felt that I needed someone there all the time, although I also found myself
getting turned on by diversity. Most gay people I know want monogamy. I like
the concept, but as I said I've always been turned on by other attractive men. I like
to find somebody cute and have sex with him. That's a conflict in my life right
now. . . . My lover insists on monogamy.

Interestingly, both of these men are in their mid-twenties and, by relative standards, exceptionally attractive. Perhaps because the combination of their visual sexual appeal and their occupation makes new sexual partners constantly available, they are, at this juncture in their lives, unwilling to commit themselves to an exclusively monogamous partnership with their present lovers. As one astute observer of the gay community sums up their predicament, "Since virtually the sole criterion of value in the homosexual world is physical attractiveness, being young and handsome in gay life is like being a millionaire in a community where wealth is the only criterion of value."[20] Thus, for these and no doubt other gay cops like them, there is a constant conflict between the personal and the ideal. Frequently this is resolved at this stage of their lives by actively engaging in multiple sexual relationships, while privately pretending to maintain a semipermanent, monogamous relationship with a lover or partner.

In contrast, a small proportion of male cops in this study reported that they have steadfastly resisted the temptation to be attached or coupled to one person. In a few instances it was because of a previous bad experience in which their lovers, in time, became overly possessive and dictatorial. These officers now see fealty as an undesirable restraint upon their independence.

The longest I've ever been in a relationship was six months. I like the ones that last a few weeks. It gets on my nerves when they want to know where you are every waking minute. I'm pretty independent. I don't like it when they're making plans for me. When I'm with somebody for a while, everybody else looks good to me.

Others in this group explained that they too tired of their lovers' increasing demonstrations of possessiveness and jealousy.

I found with long-term relationships they're very possessive. I found most people very possessive, very jealous. After a while they think they own you. I had one guy I was going out with and one night I was dancing with someone else. He said to me, "Sit down, what do you think you're doing?" I told him that nobody owns me. After a while they think they can run you. . . . Another lover I had, we had a fight one night. We were at a GOAL party. I was flirting around [with a civilian, not another cop]. As I was leaving, this guy shoves a phone number in my coat pocket. Richard [his lover] put his hand in my coat pocket and tried to pull out the number. He says, "Give me that." Says "I saw that shit." We had a big fight out in the street. I had to punch the shit out of him.

According to these officers, long-term relationships, while admittedly safer in many ways than one-night stands, are still fraught with risks. For example, an officer closeted at work may come to see couplehood as a liability in the sense that it could boomerang and become a source of exposure or extortion on the part of the sexual partner should the relationship sour and the officer threaten or attempt to terminate it. One man grimly recalled a number of unpleasant, unnerving, and potentially career-damaging incidents he experienced upon breaking up with his lover of a few years:

Story with my lover. It was coming to an end, our relationship. We were in front of his house arguing. He broke the windows of my car. I then broke his face. He didn't want me to leave him. Here I am, a NYC cop and here's this piece of shit. Why am I not locking him up. . . . Anyway, the cops responded. We were both bleeding. The sergeant shows up and says, "What's the problem?" I said there was no problem. Peter [lover] says, "Why don't you tell them what's going on?" The sergeant, an older boss, turned around to me, and he knew I had things under control. There were ten cops standing there. I said to myself, Oh, Christ. Peter is telling me to tell them what the problem is and I'm pleading with the cops to leave. . . . Anyway, they left, and I calmed down and then went home. Seven hundred fifty dollars damage to my car. Peter then started to call the station house and say, "_____'s a faggot." He would come to my house and ring the bell at five A.M. My fear was that if I had this guy locked up, my whole career would go down the drain. . . . Six months later this psycho was still calling me. I came closest to having a nervous breakdown over the fear that people [in his command] would find out I was gay. Finally I was transferred to [another command]. I was finally able to sleep. Then one night I had the desk. I got a call. "Hi _____, it's Peter." I put the phone down. What do I do now. . . . This is a year later. . . . Then he called me one evening and left a message on my machine saying he was going to call my new command and tell them I was a faggot. He called me back and told me he had called my precinct and told them that I took it up the ass. I came to work the next day and heard [one of the cops] tell another guy that some faggot called and said _____ is gay. I felt claustrophobic. So I stayed out in the field all day. I didn't even come back for meal. . . . I went on like that for three days and then took two days off. I went absolutely crazy.

Because of this ever-present threat of exposure, the closeted cop must always be cautious that conflicts or disputes with lovers do not escalate to the point that the police are summoned. Even minor disputes with lovers, when left unresolved, can lead to potentially career-damaging situations—for example, harassing phone calls or unexpected and revealing visits from the rejected lover to the officer's command.

One female officer, apparently unable or unwilling to settle a particularly violent dispute amicably, found herself in precisely this predicament. A man recalled the incident.

There was a situation in Brooklyn [some] years ago. Two girls I mentioned before had a very violent dispute and the girl that wasn't on the job went to her lover's resident precinct and by the time she [the cop] got to work the next day, her command knew all about it. Their suspicions about her being a dyke were confirmed.

Another female officer who broke off with her lover also experienced the pain of having information about her sexual preferences passed on to the department by her ex-lover.

One friend of mine, she was involved with a woman and at one point they were going through a terrible breakup and she [the lover] used it totally against her. Complaints, calls to IAD [Internal Affairs Division], everything. She said she was going to let everybody know she [the cop] was a lesbian, things like that. This woman was bent on letting the whole city know. My friend tried to soften the blow because of the fear of her calling IAD, etc. If she was not a cop, just any other person, she wouldn't have had these things hanging over her.

The fear of being exposed as a homosexual at work by a rejected lover may compel some closeted officers to continue in unhappy or conflict-filled relationships or in some instances to overlook or cover up personal victimization.

One case, a [cop] friend of mine was going with a junkie. When she found out the girl was a junkie, she tried to break up with her. So the girl goes and robs her of her watch and paycheck. She did not report it, just let her get away with it. She swallowed it.

Clearly, the threat of extortion does loom large over gay cops who wish to conceal their homosexual identities from their co-workers. While most of the closeted cops in this study who had entered into more permanent relationships with a lover have not experienced this form of *criminal* victimization, *all* stated that they were aware of how easily they could become victims of extortion in the event their relationship soured. Fearing exposure, most admitted that they would not press charges or even report a theft or assault committed by their lover. In this sense, some closeted officers actually suffer double victimization because they have chosen to keep their unconventional life-style hidden from the department.

In sum, because of society's continued prohibitions against the homosexual's life-style, closeted gay cops find themselves in a unique situation, one that separates them from openly gay as well as straight colleagues. Precisely because of their secretive status in the workplace, they are able to observe firsthand the reactions of homophobic straight cops when, for example, they are summoned to resolve a dispute between two gays. Consequently, some believe that, should they enter into a coupled relationship with a person of the same sex, events such as serious disputes, grave illnesses, injuries, accidents, or even the death of a lover could occur and bring the police to their doorsteps, thereby exposing their homosexuality.

In spite of these risks, many gay cops do choose both to remain in the closet at work and to actively pursue long-term relationships.

Coupled Living Arrangements

Despite many officers' expressed desire and need to establish long-lasting, stable relationships with lovers, the reality is that coupled living arrangements, for the great majority of them, have been relatively short. Indeed, few have survived for more than three years.

Observers of the gay community have noted that this apparent instability or inability to form long-lasting attachments seems to characterize the larger homosexual population. These researchers offer a variety of reasons to explain this lack of permanency. Bell and Weinberg, for example, citing other studies, point to the following factors: (1) society's prevalent antigay attitudes, which arouse anxieties in homosexuals, making it difficult for them to sustain enduring emotional commitments; (2) the culturally diverse nature of homosexual partnerships, which can create unresolvable tensions between two lovers; and (3) the broad marketplace for sociosexual contacts in the homosexual world. Barry Dank adds the absence of a "complete family" to this list. "Since homosexuals do not have children, their emotional relationships are more focused and, consequently, more fragile than those found in heterosexual marriages with children."[21]

Although the officers in this study did not link these particular factors to instability in their homosexual relationships, they did offer alternative explanations. A few indicated, for example, that because of the absence of social rules governing permanency among same-gender couples, a climate of infidelity and promiscuity thrives. The discovery or even fear of infidelity can, over time, readily promote jealousy and sexual possessiveness, which in turn can cause breakups. Other officers pointed to the unique nature of the police officer's job and work schedule as contributing factors in the instability and subsequent disintegration of their relationships. For example, the officer's revolving work chart does not conform to the conventional work week, so days off and weekends rarely coincide.

A lot of people, when they meet a cop, they'll say they like it, it turns them on, whatever. But they like it until they've been seeing you for a couple of months. Six months is like the threshold. Then they can't deal with the hours, the rotating shifts, no weekends off, making collars, and having to constantly cancel out of social engagements. The element of danger, too. They tell me they worry too much. So it's a combination of all these things.

I would add to this abbreviated list (though it has not been stated to me directly) the availability of sexual partners for the gay *police officer*. Even for the most family-oriented cop, there exists the temptation, created in part by this pool of potential partners, to cheat on one's lover. The mere fact that sexual partners are out there and available can create an atmosphere of distrust in the gay household, which can threaten the stability and centrality of a relationship.

Roles and Division of Labor in the Coupled Household

For those officers who have at one time or another entered into a stable homosexual relationship, the question arises as to who will assume what role and who will carry out which daily household chores. According to Alex Thio, among others, a common myth about coupled homosexuals is that each partner assumes one specific role. The reality, Thio claims, is quite different, in that "partners in homosexual relationships often resemble best friends, who, being equal, share and share alike so that *both* may cook, make money. . . "[22]

The interviews in this study tend to confirm these findings, at least to the extent that roles in the coupled household were either shared equally or divided in such a way that both partners felt comfortable with the arrangement. In no instance, at least among male officers, did I discover any sex-role distinctions in their relationships with other men.

Approximately half the male and female officers who had lived with a sexual partner said that there was an equal sharing of roles and duties in their household.

No roles whatsoever. When he's working really hard, I do the chores. When I'm tired, he does the cooking and cleaning. . . . We help each other.

What I've always had was a fifty-fifty deal. I definitely didn't want to be the bread-winner. I looked for someone who would complement me, work as a team.
All that [cleaning, cooking, etc.] should be a fifty-fifty thing. We didn't have any special stereotypical roles. . . . We both cleaned and cooked. The division of labor was just that—it was equal.

There are, of course, relationships in which one partner is ill-suited or unable, for one reason or another, to take on certain respon-sibilities in the household. One man did all the cooking because his lover, who had been previously married to a woman, had never ac-quired that skill. That lover's role in the relationship was to do the cleaning up after meals. Another man said that in his current relation-ship he does all the shopping and laundry because his lover *prefers* to do the cleaning, and a female reported an equal distribution of re-sponsibilities, except in one area. "It was pretty even. Whoever wanted to cook, shop, et cetera. The only thing was that she cleaned the bathroom because I just couldn't tolerate that. There were no rules."

In most of these partnerships there was, in addition to inter-changeable roles and responsibilities, an equal division of household expenses. There were some exceptions to these egalitarian arrange-ments, however. For instance, I found that in a few cases the pooling of funds and the organization of spending were handled exclusively by the officer. This contradiction was explained by the fact that the officer's lover had shown repeatedly that he or she was incapable of handling the couple's bills.

All the monies go together. But I handle the bills. He can't handle money. I handle the finances because he failed at it.

I'm running all the finances. She gives me all the money. My lover is irresponsible with some things. So I take care of the situation.

We would split things, but I was more on the ball with money. I was into keeping records. I pretty much controlled the finances, the household budget and things.

Another reason why the responsibility of managing the joint household expenses had been turned over to the officer in the coupled relationship is related, as a number of officers have suggested, to the cop's idealized image—that a cop is honest, aboveboard, and trustworthy. As one officer explained, "I manage the money, pay the bills. I make all the final decisions on purchasing things. [His lover] looks up to me a lot because, believe it or not, of my job. He trusts me because of this."

Interacting with the element of trust, from the point of view of the police officer, is the basic distrust that most cops have of people in general. "He chipped in his share, but I handled the expenses. There was a trust factor here. I want to be able to account for the money. It's a cop's cynicism. There was also trust on my lover's part, too. . . . The image of the cop as being honest, the last person who is going to rip you off."

Though the elements of power, authority, and dominance central to the officer's work role carry into some coupled relationships, for most these elements remain confined to the officer's work world. This is all the more interesting for the male officer, given the nature of his work role and the fact that he, like his lover, entered the relationship having been socialized into accepting dominant roles. For women in this study, this interchangeability of roles may represent a transitional stage in consciousness away from traditional roles and power arrangements in the household that have been shaped in part by the position of women in the labor force.

Nine
Coming
Out
to
Family

My mother doesn't really go out
of her way to be nice to
[his lovers] as she would with a girl.
But she has gotten closer
to them. Just in the way she says
hello, it's more sincere.

As the story of the homosexual cops' multiple worlds unfolds, it is increasingly evident that self-presentation takes on a central role in most of their social relationships. Whether they are navigating through their work world or interacting with straight police when off duty or with potential lovers, the dilemma of how to present themselves is invariably present. Even when interacting with or simply being in the presence of family members, they discover that they cannot escape having to deal with the question of identity management.[1] With family too their marginalized sexual status is often pivotal to their relationships.

Regardless of whether relations with family members are good or strained the gay officer invariably confronts the question of whether or not to reveal his or her homosexuality to them. The concern of most of the men and women in this study is, not unexpectedly, how family members will react when they either suspect or actually discover that their son or daughter is gay. This uncertainty of family reactions is what also separates the homosexual cop from most other stigmatized groups in society. Racial minorities, the handicapped, and the disfigured, to mention a few, generally do not suffer rejection and censure by family members because of their stigma. Gay cops may, however, should their supposedly deviant identity become public knowledge in the household.

The unpredictability of family members' reactions to disclosure of an individual's homosexuality, the anticipation that the reaction would not be sympathetic or supportive, or both were the dominant reasons offered by most of the forty-one officers for maintaining secrecy in the family household. Because the subject of homosexuality had seldom or never been raised in their parental household, some of these men and women had no direct indicators to predict the family's reaction. They were left with only the wider societal superstructure of mostly negative beliefs about homosexuality as a basis for anticipating family reactions.

We never discussed homosexuality around the house. I never had any inkling of how they felt, so I believe that my folks were like a lot of other parents who would condemn gays. But, I could be wrong. If I told them, they might say, "That's okay," or "Oh, my God." I'm not really sure how they would take it. That's what stops me from telling them.

For others who chose silence over openness, there was an expressed fear of being censured and rejected should they come out. This was the case even in those households in which relationships with family members were reported to be warm and loving. In fact, it was precisely the need to maintain this favorable relationship that kept some of them in the closet. One woman said she "knew how my family would react. I would be tabooed. My family's from the old country. They wouldn't be able to deal with it. Are you kidding me? No way [would she tell them]." Others in this group, certain that they would experience rejection, concealed their sexual orientation from family members in order to spare them anguish and embarrassment.

I know how she [her mother] would react. Crying would go on for days, weeks. She would blame herself. She wouldn't get over it [if she told her]. She'd be heartbroken.

My father would have a tough time dealing with it, comprehending it. It would be like hitting him over the head. My mother would be real hurt. That's why I don't tell her. I don't want to hurt her.

My parents would hit the ceiling. It would be like me coming home and saying, "Hey, Pop, guess what? I'm pregnant." It would be a terrible embarrassment.

Some of the male officers feared that a disclosure of their homosexuality would result in one of their parents, usually the father, blaming the mother for their son's perceived moral failing. One man who did confide his secret to his mother said that disclosure to his father would seriously disrupt an otherwise harmonious relationship between his parents.

I have not told him anything yet. . . . He's a very loving father with everybody, and he's especially proud of me. And my mother made me promise not to say anything to him because he would take it out on her. I want to tell him but I can't because of my mother. . . . Being gay, you have to hide so much.

A parent's poor health can also provide a guilt-ridden son or daughter with a justification for not revealing his or her homosexuality. Likewise, some cops felt that in the case of an aged parent there could also be health complications. For these officers, at this late stage in their parents' lives, there was no point in making matters worse by revealing their homosexuality. "My mother and father don't know. They moved to Puerto Rico some time ago and came back two years ago. I never told them. There's no sense telling them. They're in their mid-seventies."

Of course, not revealing their secret to family members means that the gay son or daughter must deceive them by constructing fronts similar to the ones they create at work. The masquerading that is an essential feature of closeted officers' work world now becomes an integral part of their family life. They must create fictional accounts of relationships with members of the opposite sex and reasonable explanations for not yet being married or going steady. They must never behave out of gender when in the company of family members. And, above all, they must be ever alert not to slip when referring to the sex of a lover. In short, they must maintain an appearance of heterosexuality at all times.

I made sure I didn't fit the so-called "bull-type"—short hair, no make up, that kind of thing. I wore dresses, skirts, heels, that kind of thing. More or less, I covered my tracks pretty well.

I take precautions with social gatherings at my house. When I have a party, a gay dinner party, I always invite gay female friends because it does look better.

The fully closeted gay must handle even commonplace occurrences such as receiving phone calls or mail from gay friends and lovers with care. (Of course, for some male closeted officers, phone calls from mostly men present little threat of exposure, as they work in a predominantly male world where an expectation may exist in the officer's household that callers would be other male cops.) The closeted cop who lives away from home, must also take precautions, when family members visit, that no "stigma symbols" are visible in the individual's apartment.[2]

In sum, the closeted cop is again thrust into a position of having to play the pretension game, only now the fear of being found out is magnified because in the more intimate family setting, one's social relationships and life-style are more visible and open to greater scrutiny by parents and siblings. For gay officers who choose secrecy both at work and at home there is no safe haven, as they find themselves backed into a corner where they must endure a life of lies and masquerading in both worlds. Though they may be able to relax somewhat in the company of other gays, even then, these officers, as we have seen, must grapple with the conflict of how to manage their occupational identities.

BEING OUT TENTATIVELY WITH FAMILY MEMBERS

The unwillingness of some subjects to openly and frankly acknowledge their homosexuality does not mean that family members do not suspect or even know of their true sexual orientation. Indeed, some parents and siblings may know of their son's or daughter's, brother's or sister's, homosexuality or have strong suspicions, yet for a variety of reasons choose to avoid a confrontation or even to voice those suspicions. Or, as is the case with *many* of the officers in this study who have not told their parents in so many words, there may exist a conspiracy of silence or mutual pretense in which the family knows of his or her sexual orientation but both tacitly agree to preserve a fiction about it.[3] For both, the officer's homosexuality is an open secret.

The various clues or indicators that family members piece together to help deduce that a police son or daughter is gay involve, for the most part, patterned deviations from a conventional life-style. That is, in virtually all instances it was not one but a combination of deviations that either aroused or confirmed their suspicion about their son's or daughter's true sexual orientation. For example, if over a period of time an individual's circle of friends and acquaintances seems to be restricted largely to members of the same sex, a signal is sent to some parents. They may then become more alert to other deviations. Such was the case with a number of officers who, while living at home, never openly expressed an interest in dating members of the opposite sex and who seemed to receive phone calls only from same-sex friends. One man said his mother "knew I wasn't dating girls. And she mentioned that I don't get calls from any girls. She would say, 'John called, Pete called, Fred called. Where's the Mary call?' Maybe she doesn't want to confront the situation." In another family, suspicion was aroused as the officer's circle of friends and phone calls to his house began to change drastically over a relatively short period of time. "I had a lot of girls calling me over the years before I came out. Then I went from five girls calling a day to none calling me to four guys calling me every day."

In most families, the question of marriage and grandchildren is inevitably raised by parents, and the individual's response can further strengthen parental suspicions.

They ask me and I tell them I'm never getting married. Kids? I don't know. Marriage, never. Once in a while they would ask me about marriage, and I would say that I didn't think so. Now, at family gatherings, I would say when I got there, "No, I'm not married. No, I'm not planning it." I would give excuses to get it out of the way. But people are not stupid.

A son's or daughter's unconventional appearance, style of dress, mannerisms, or even choice of vacation spots (such as known homosexual resort areas like Fire Island) can, when combined with other apparent departures from heterosexual behavioral patterns, lead parents to deduce homosexuality, though they may choose not to voice their suspicions.

They know, but they don't. You see what I mean? I never came out and said anything. I know they know but they don't want to talk about it. How do they

know? My vacations at Fire Island and Provincetown, my appearance, my clothes,
preferences for jeans [not dresses or skirts], the fact that I said I was never
going to get married and that I wasn't looking for a man.

While many of these same deviations eventually do, in time, become apparent to a gay officer's work mates, family members often
become the first to link them. Unlike the officer's colleagues, family
members have a longer time to observe and note these more subtle
changes in behavioral patterns, changes that may not be collectively
discernible at work. Moreover, because of the gay officer's closeness
to many family members, it is easier for them, in most instances, to
monitor the suspicious behavior. It is also important to note that
some officers actually make little or no attempt to hide major deviations from their parents or siblings. Though none confided as much
to me, it might be surmised from this lowering of one's guard that
these officers were expressing their need for authenticity at home.

DIVULGING OR ACKNOWLEDGING ONE'S HOMOSEXUALITY

When the officers in this study did either reveal or admit their homosexuality, the acknowledgment was usually made to the mother
or siblings; rarely was the father told by either a male or female
officer.[4] This is, as they explained, because mothers generally are
thought to be more forgiving, more tolerant, and thus more accepting of sexual diversity in their children. Both the men and the women
felt that fathers, on the other hand, were inclined to be less forbear-
ing and more rigid, tending to reject any indicators or even direct
evidence of homosexuality in the family. In some cases, the father's
unrelenting avoidance or occasional mocking of the subject of homosexuality was cited as a reason for not confiding in him.[5]

A few of the men and women in this study stated that they acknowledged their homosexuality to family members because they
shared an especially close relationship with them. Because of this
social bond they took a chance and gambled on their family's continued love and support. Others admitted that they were forced to finally admit their secret because family members had come to find
out through other means, usually from third parties such as other
cops or rejected lovers. "When I was eighteen I got involved with this

female. When it didn't work out she called my mother up and told her I was a lesbian."

Suspicions that a member of a family is gay can move parents or siblings to dig further into the secret personal life of the suspected member. Frequently, this quest for evidence to confirm or reject the suspicion involves a direct and blatant invasion of the person's privacy. In an ironic twist of events the police officer in this situation becomes the subject of an investigation, with the nonpolice family member assuming the role of investigator. Listening in on phone calls between the suspected son or daughter and his or her lover is not an uncommon technique of spying. Should any revealing information be gained through this eavesdropping, a full-scale investigation may then be launched, with the closeted gay officer finding himself or herself barraged with prying questions. One woman said this had happened to her "about five years ago. I had met my present lover. My mother was becoming suspicious of me. She was reading my mail, listening in on my phone calls, et cetera. She knew something was up. Then she started questioning me, giving me the third degree." At this point she decided it was time to come out. She revealed her lesbianism first to her sister, who, she thought, would serve as a buffer but who in fact informed their mother. "I told [her sister] I need your help handling Mommy. She was very hurt but supportive when I told her. I guess she must have gotten frightened. She didn't want the responsibility of knowing [she was a lesbian] by herself. . . . My mother finally came to me and said, 'I want you to tell me what you told your sister.'" As in the case of some criminal suspects who are confronted with overwhelming evidence of culpability, she felt she had no other recourse but to confess.

Another lesbian officer who found herself the subject of a family investigation reported that her mother, too, had confirmed suspicions of her homosexuality when she discovered incriminating evidence of an ongoing sexual relationship with a woman. Here too the evidence was uncovered as a result of the mother going through the subject's personal belongings. "My mother got into my dresser and found letters between the two of us. She confronted me. She said that she was not going to tell my father or anybody else."

In a third instance, a male officer's privacy was violated not by a parent or sibling, but by a sister-in-law who, through similar snooping, found revealing personal letters indicating he had a male lover. In this case the incriminating information was conveyed, not to his parents, but to the officer's brother and other in-laws.

GAY COPS

My brother found out last year. It turns out I gave my sister-in-law the key to my apartment because I had fish in there that needed to be fed while I was away. I didn't realize she was snoopy, but she snooped. She found some things. She told my brother. He confronted me and told me what my other sister-in-law read. I admitted it. That fucking cunt also told my aunts.

In an apparent moment of anger and, perhaps, of classic sibling rivalry, a lesbian sister of one male officer outed him to their mother and father. "My parents know now because I have a sister who is a lesbian. She's very open. . . . My mother was always nagging my sister. Then one day she said, 'Why don't you be like your brother? He's got a good job, et cetera.' And she said, 'He's a faggot, too.' That's the way she found out. She told my dad."

In one household the closeness of family members provided an occasion for the mother to discover the truth. In this case she felt comfortable enough to pay an unannounced visit to her son's apartment. The mother was aware that her son shared the apartment with a male roommate but unaware that the roommate was also his lover. It didn't take long, however, upon seeing only one bed in the apartment, for her to realize her son was gay. Like other powerful "stigma symbols," the sole two-person bed became indisputable evidence of her son's sexual inclinations, and she obtained an admission from him. "So she asked me if [his roommate] and I slept in the same bed. She knew, so I said yes. So now my mother knows."

Such overt incriminating actions on the part of the officer as being seen at a public demonstration in support of gay rights (particularly if it is televised), while not designed specifically to come out to family members, may nevertheless achieve that result. "They found out because GOAL was on TV one night and I was on the program. Someone saw me and told someone else who told my family."

When "stigma symbols" begin to accumulate and are believed to be known by other family members, the individual may come to feel a need to admit the homosexuality in order to relieve himself or herself of the continual pressure and guilt of having to deceive loved ones.

I told my mother. She knew I wasn't dating girls. She had some other suspicions too. One day she came to visit, and it was then that I told her. I said, "I have something to tell you." She goes, "What is it, _____?" She knew what I was going to say. She was bracing herself. And I told her. I said I was terribly sorry, but

I'm gay. I will always be gay. I have been gay and always will be. At that point a tremendous load was taken off my shoulders.

I was fed up with hiding the relationship. One Christmas I wanted to be with [his
lover] and we couldn't do it . . . . That's what I was tired of—not being able to
share him. So that day I couldn't be myself because I couldn't bring him to my
house and share him with the rest of my family. And that's not healthy. . . .
So I told my mother one day at my apartment. I just said, "There's something I
want to tell you." She said, "I thought so." She said she was not surprised, that she
suspected because I was thirty and not dating girls.

I know [her mother] knew but it wasn't spoken of. Only the sarcastic, indirect remarks occasionally. One night it put me over the edge. I came home at five in
the morning and I overheard her talking to my father. She said, "She's out with
that four-eyed bitch. When she got rid of that Guinea bitch I thought that was
it." It's almost six A.M. and I'm listening to my parents talk like that and I said
enough is enough. So the next evening my mother and I were sitting
downstairs watching TV. I said, "I got to tell you something. I heard what you said
last night." I told her that at this point in my life I just happen to really care
about and love somebody who happens to be a woman. She said, "I knew something was wrong."

As many of these comments demonstrate, there was little alarm or
even surprise on the part of most family members when an admission of homosexuality was made. This almost matter-of-fact reaction
suggests that the parents had surmised for some time that their son
or daughter was gay. When, however, "stigma symbols" began to
mount or became so obvious that no other plausible explanation
could account for the suspected individual's unconventional behavior
or life-style, and when these were coupled with the psychological
need to shed the pretense of heterosexual respectability, most of
these officers confirmed their homosexuality.

REACTIONS OF FAMILY MEMBERS TO DISCLOSURE

While there was no single discernible pattern of reaction or adjustment on the part of family members to disclosure, positive responses
clearly outweighed negative ones.[6] Some officers reported experienc-

ing only mild rejection or disapproval, while others reported extremely negative reactions on the part of family members. Still other family members chose, as I indicated earlier, to simply deny the individual's acknowledged failing. Most, however, responded to disclosure through demonstrations of accommodation, support, and, eventually, full acceptance. In a few cases, acceptance was preceded by an initial rejection or denial followed by passive accommodation.

What can be labeled as a comparatively mild negative reaction was evidenced in a few cases. A female officer, for example, talks of the disappointment her parents expressed upon her breakup with a male fiancé and her subsequent disclosure of homosexuality. "They genuinely wanted me to be married, and they were disappointed. They were upset. They liked my fiancé and had already helped us out with the wedding."

Disappointment was sometimes accompanied by attempts on the part of family members to arouse guilt in the individual by stressing the shame and embarrassment the immediate family would suffer should other family members or close friends find out. The same officer continued:

At first they were very angry and said I was shaming the family. After the wedding was called off and I stayed away for a while, things got a little better. But there will always be strong feelings of embarrassment and disappointment for them.

A male officer reports essentially the same reaction.

Mom, she took it like a cunt. Her main thing was she sent me to a Catholic school. What was she going to tell her friends. She was concerned only about image. That's her only hang-up, even today.

Another male officer, who never discussed his homosexuality with his father, describes his mother's and sister's negative reactions to disclosure, which can also be described as relatively mild.

My mother found out in a phone call she overheard. . . . She listened in on my call one day and surmised I was gay. She asked me about it. I sat down and said to her this is what I have chosen. She said, "I expected something different from you, but if that's what you choose, what can I say?" Her reaction was heartbreaking. Now she's somewhat normal, but not really accepting. . . . My older sister barely tolerates it. She's not very accepting.

While the individual's differentness may be accepted by knowing family members, that acceptance may hinge in large part on his or her willingness to maintain a heterosexual front when in the company of extended family members. "My mom didn't want [his lover] over for Thanksgiving dinner as a couple, only as a friend. We would have to pretend to be friends in front of the rest of the family."

A few family members' reactions could be characterized as severe and, perhaps, even threatening. These reactions, too, were accompanied by attempts to invoke guilt.

I got involved with a female, and when it didn't work out she called my mother up and told her. When I got home the shit hit the fan. She told me now I know why you left _____. You don't like men. She said that God would punish me, that this was not normal. I said, "Mom, that's how I am." She said, "Well I don't ever want to hear about it again. . . . Believe it or not, since that day I have not mentioned it. . . . My mother also told my sister, so I had to hear it from her too. "You're spoiling the family. God, how are we going to live this down? Why did you have to be the weird one in the family?" I said, "You're acting like I got a disease." She said, "It is a disease. It's not normal. It's against moral standards." That was ten years ago.

One male officer was the target of personally devastating remarks from both his father and his brother. "My father immediately told my stepmother that I should die, that I should be dead. . . . It was a major blow to me. . . . My older brother took me aside and went on for hours accusing me of everything in the book. He said that if he had his way he would kill everybody like me."

Some officers who confessed their sexual preferences to siblings were told in no uncertain terms to keep away from their nieces and nephews, as if the children could become contaminated or even converted by their presence. "When my sister found out she pulled the kids away from me. She told me she didn't want them to be exposed to me. She said to them, 'I don't want you nowhere near your aunt. One in the family is enough.'" Another cop was indirectly threatened with personal violence by an older brother, who "was not happy with it. He said to my other brother that when he sees me he will kick my ass good."

Partial and even total denial that a member of the family could be gay constituted another response pattern to disclosure or awareness. In these few cases family members began to behave toward the officer as if his or her homosexuality simply did not exist.

GAY COPS

My brother won't even discuss it with me. . . . He's so busy trying to live the American dream. He'd make a perfect cop. He knows what he knows and that's all he knows and that's all he wants to know. You can't tell him anything.

My mother would never discuss my situation. She pretended that she didn't know, that she didn't want to know. She couldn't handle it when she found out. So I never talked about it.

As evidenced in the above quote, a common form of denial is to disavow the fact of homosexuality in the family. In another case a mother persisted in refusing to acknowledge her son's male lover by his real name; she always used a *female* name when referring to him. Another reportedly distraught mother encased herself in a fictional, heterosexual reality whenever she talked to her son about his personal life.

My mother never mentioned it when she found out from my sister. I tried to bring it up, but she wouldn't talk about it. She just kept telling me about other things. . . . She will never accept it. She keeps asking me when I am going to get married and have a kid and all that bullshit.

Another mother laid the blame for her son's homosexuality on his lover.

[His lover], they met him, but they didn't know at first that he was my lover. As soon as my mother found out, she started hating him. She blamed it on him, that he was the one that made me gay. They never talked to each other after that.

Some of the officers insisted that they were not being rejected, but only their sexual orientation and accompanying life-style. This apparent incongruity was evidenced by the fact that in only *two* instances did the officer actually experience banishment or exclusion from the family upon disclosure.

Rejection of the gay cop's sexual orientation only was also demonstrated in the repeated attempts by some family members to help the fallen officer recover from the perceived disease or condition of homosexuality. In some cases, family members attempted to assure them that their present condition was not permanent, that they would eventually grow out of it. This response was often followed by compassionate attempts to persuade the stricken man or woman to seek professional counseling. Psychiatric therapy was generally suggested as a last resort, when it became apparent that the homosexual condition was not merely a fleeting phase.

My sister always took the "phase" theory that this was something that was going to pass. When it didn't, she suggested medical help.

In the beginning my sisters were great because they thought I would change. . . . As time went on one of my sisters told me that it [homosexuality] was making her sick and that she didn't want to know what I was doing. Then, when I was still not dating girls, they all started to say that maybe I should get some help. They would say, "We think you need help. We'll find you a good psychiatrist. We'll all take turns paying for your sessions."

For the homosexual officer who is secure and comfortable with his or her sexual diversity, references to the individual's life-style as "sick," "sinful," "immoral," or "criminal" by family members can seriously strain relationships within the household. The mother of one subject, unable to come to terms with her son's homosexuality, severely damaged their relationship by merely insisting that he seek professional help for his "problem."

Later, after I told her, I found out that she had sincere reservations about me being gay. . . . She said she was extremely disappointed, that it was learned behavior, and that I had a serious psychological problem. She insisted that I get therapy. My mother looked at me like I was a social misfit. It was devastating to me. It seriously affected our relationship. That was four years ago, and we don't talk as much as we used to. Because now she's picturing what her son is like in bed with another man doing all these things to each other.

It is not unusual, when parents are the first to learn of a son's or daughter's homosexuality, for them to attempt to hide this potentially discreditable information from other family members, at the same time exhorting the gay member to seek professional help. Should this therapy strategy fail, as it usually does, parents frequently attempt to enlist help from the son's or daughter's siblings. One officer's "father said, 'We could get some help for you.' I answered that I didn't need any help. He didn't say anything directly to me after that but then my brothers found out and they got on my case to get help. I found out that my father asked them to speak to me." Another cop had an identical experience. "On my parents' request my older brother spoke to me. He really didn't say much except that I should go for counseling. That's exactly what my father said."

Another approach by distraught family members is to urge the gay individual to resume or begin cross-sex dating. As a last-ditch effort to return the person to so-called normalcy, some family members have even set up unsolicited heterosexual liaisons for the gay family member. "My sister really wants me to get help. . . . And she's always setting me up with women she knows."

A popular misconception is that a man turns to homosexuality because he has never had intimate contact with women who know how to arouse and please men sexually. Consequently, the following reaction from a brother is not uncommon: "Another brother said that all I needed was a good blow job from a woman. That should change me. So he tried to hook me up with some prostitutes he knew."

In each of these reports there is evidence of an attempt by a family member to deny the individual his or her right to establish an identity, while at the same time imposing the family member's own beliefs and moral standards on that individual.

Over time if these attempts by family members to normalize the individual's behavior fail, they may be abandoned in favor of total rejection (in some cases banishment from the family entirely) or some form of accommodation. The tainted individual may be treated as is any other close family member with a permanent disability or physical shortcoming. This form of accommodation is then often followed by gradual acceptance of the individual's perceived personal failing. The following comments illustrate the transition from mild rejection to accommodation, and from accommodation to gradual acceptance.

I told my mother one day while we were heading downtown to the vet with our cat. I had planned this for a long time when I could be alone with her. . . . I remember giving her a lot of tissues, which she immediately threw at me saying, "I don't need these." She said she kinda knew. She suspected because of my relationship with _____. She said that she hoped I would get over this and go back to girls. That's all she said. . . . Since then [two years ago] she still cries on her own. But, she's gotten much better when we bring it up. Her eyes still get wet, and she will never totally accept it. But she loves me anyway.

Their first reaction was shock, of course. "It can't be," they both said. "Don't you want children?" Then they asked me why I was gay. I told them I was

sorry. . . . They pretended to ignore it for some time. But they stuck by me all
that time. They did not ignore me. They did not treat me bad at all. . . . Since then
they have come a long way toward accepting [her homosexuality].

My mom first said, "Oh, what, are you one of them?" But then she became very accepting. My father, he never denied my gayness. Both have gone to gay places
and events with me.

As I noted in the beginning of this chapter, the personal decision
to keep one's sexual orientation secret from family members hinges,
in large part, on the uncertainty of knowing how they will react, or on
the belief that their reaction will be decidedly unfavorable. Given the
atmosphere of loathing and contempt that continues to permeate society's views of homosexuality, and given the closeted gay officer's
observations of homophobic work mates, it is not surprising that
many of the gay men and women in this study anticipate similar rejection by their own family members. Yet, what a significant number
of them who had the courage to come out to family members found
was something quite different. To their surprise, both initial and enduring acceptance with no strings attached were the norm. In none
of these cases was there any attempt to seek professional help for the
homosexual son or daughter, or any effort to devalue the individual
or alter his or her life-style. The sole concern expressed by these
parents was the continued health and happiness of their son or
daughter. This reaction is typified in the following comments from
both male and female subjects.

They both know now. My mom said, "I always knew you liked girls." Her only concern was with AIDS. . . . I have a great relationship with them. I talk to them
every day.

Mom has been great about this. We talked about it. We were very open with each
other. She actually opened the conversation. She took me out to lunch. . . .
She said that if I ever needed any help or support, she would always be there. . . .
My relation with both my parents is still great.

My father's reaction was similar to my mother's. He said if this was the way I chose
to live my life, he could accept it. I visit with my parents a lot, especially my mom.

Siblings, too, in many instances, have demonstrated initial acceptance of the officer's homosexuality followed by pledges of continued

support. "I told my older brother first. His reaction was, well, you're still my brother and I still love you, and I will always be behind you."

In some instances officers believed the unexpected positive reaction to disclosure to be related to the closeness they always had with their siblings. In other cases, they thought acceptance was connected to the fact that they were not the first in the immediate or extended family to acknowledge their homosexuality. After one family member had disclosed his or her deviant sexual self, it gave other family members the time to come to grips with another son's or daughter's declared differentness. "My sister is a lesbian. She came out a few years ago. My parents and brothers and sisters [eight in all] had plenty of time to adjust to her coming out. They learned a lot about her life-style then. So it was just easier for me to come out, and everybody's been great to us."

Knowledge that another extended family member is gay may also serve to reduce or even eliminate potential shame and embarrassment on the part of some parents. In these cases, family members do not feel alone; they can and do share their problem with other extended family members who may be able to inspire a positive adjustment. Knowledge of the existence of another gay family member may also facilitate the coming-out process. "Both of my aunt's sons are gay. This made it easier for me to come out to my family. They have reacted very well to me, and I think it's because they are not alone. Having other gays in the family makes it easier for everyone concerned."

When reactions to disclosure of homosexuality are mixed in a family, as is sometimes the case, those reactions that can be labeled as most supportive are likely to come from siblings who have themselves experienced blemished pasts.

I have three brothers, and only my youngest has been on my side. He has a handicap. He's totally accepted my life-style, where the others haven't.

One of my brothers had been in jail. He used to do weird things. And he was the only one who came to my side. He basically said, "Fuck what they say. Fuck everybody else. You do what makes you comfortable."

Perhaps the most clear-cut evidence that family members have come to accept and support the homosexual cop's unconventional life-style is their demonstration of acceptance of and affection toward an officer's lover. In almost every instance in which family members expressed acceptance of the individual's homosexuality, there was a concomitant acceptance of the lover as well—in short, treatment of lovers as if their sex-sameness was irrelevant. What appeared to matter most in these cases was whether the lover was making the officer happy. When the son or daughter expressed happiness and seemed to be building a permanent, stable relationship with his or her lover, parental acceptance was affirmed. When family members saw trouble brewing in the relationship or saw prolonged signs of incompatibility, acceptance of the lover was abandoned, as it would be in most households.

They both hated [a former lover]. My father knew he wasn't making me happy. The same with my mother. _____ is fine with my dad. His attitude is he's making you happy.

They adored my last lover. They looked at her like, yes, this is the one. This is the one [their daughter's] going to be with for the rest of her life. She was treated real well. I'm very lucky.

For these parents, their offspring's compatibility with his or her lover combined with their own resigned acceptance that homosexuality is an integral and permanent feature of their son's or daughter's life outweighed the stigma attached to gay life-styles.

A further indicator of acceptance is the willingness of family members to extend invitations to their gay son's or daughter's lovers to attend important family get-togethers, or to spend holidays at their home. "In the beginning, they simply liked him. . . . It took a while, however, for them to really accept him. Now they treat him as a family member. He's always invited to family events." Lovers who are accepted by family members may also be invited to join the family on extended trips or vacations. "They are very supportive toward [his lover]. Me and _____ have even gone away with my parents where we would even sleep together. . . . My aunt, she fixed up the bed in the attic for [him] and me."

What is noteworthy about such demonstrations of acceptance is that they suggest that some family members not only have come to accept the fact that their offspring is different in a significant way from other sons and daughters but have been able to rid themselves of any shame and embarrassment attached to having raised a child that is, in fact, different from most others.

When parental acceptance of a son's or daughter's homosexuality was followed by rejection of a particular lover, the rejection did not spring from the lover's sexual orientation but from his or her ethnic or racial background. "The first one I brought here, they didn't like her at all. She was Hispanic, only because of that. . . . My mother was very hostile toward her because she was Hispanic. My recent lover, they adore her. She's white, Italian, older." One possible explanation for parental rejection of a son's or daughter's lover who is ethnically or racially different is that the knowledge on the part of other family members and perhaps close friends as well that one of them has taken up with a lover who possesses such failings may bring further discredit upon the family. It is one thing, as these parents may see it, to possess a stigma that is immutable, as in the case of a homosexual. It is quite another to now add insult to injury; that is, to further discredit the family by entering an intimate and visible relationship with someone who possesses, in the parents' eyes, what Goffman has called a "tribal" stigma.[7] Parents who find themselves in this situation may readily perceive this action on the part of their homosexual son or daughter as evidence of disrespect and disloyalty toward the family, because the choice of lover, unlike sexual orientation, is something he or she *does* have control over. Rejection in these cases may flow from the combination of stigmas that may prove too powerful for a family to defend itself against.

It is evident from the data presented in chapter 8 that gay cops, and especially officers who are attempting to keep their sexual orientation secret at work, cannot escape the problems attached to their dual identity by simply donning civilian clothes and leaving the precinct. While off duty in their social world, they must deal with many of the same identity management problems that they should have been able to leave behind in the workplace. Whether they are out cruising the more risky settings for quick, anonymous sex, walking with a homosexual friend or lover in a gay section of the city, or seeking companionship or sex in a more conventional setting, they must be constantly vigilant not to be seen and recognized as a cop by officers they know or by cops who might expose their secret to the department. They must be especially careful to avoid situations that attract police attention or incidents in which they must take police action. Although they do have choices about how to handle such occasions, each is fraught with risks—exposure, blackmail, suspension from the force, or damaged self-esteem. How they handle these potentially perilous situations depends to a great extent on the seriousness of the incident and whether or not they are out to their colleagues at work. Clearly, for most closeted gay cops, the most pressing problem is protecting their hidden sexual identity from exposure. When off duty they must also deal with departmental expectations and legal mandates that require them to take official action should a crime occur in their presence. However, as we have seen, that course of action, whether it involves making an arrest or simply reporting the incident truthfully to the authorities, could seriously jeopardize their moral standing in the department. Given the continued climate of homophobia in the department and hostility directed toward gay civilians, it is not surprising that most closeted officers opt to protect their secret sexual identity from exposure at work, even at the risk of incurring severe departmental or criminal penalties. Yet, gay officers' problems of self-presentation do not end here. When out cruising the more conventional gay settings, they must choose an appropriate occupational identity to present to others, especially potential lovers. Should they choose to present themselves authentically as cops, while they may experience greater opportunities for sexual adventurism, they may also experience greater risk of exposure at work. Moreover, should their purpose for cruising be to ultimately find a permanent mate, disclosure of their occupation could prove to be a barrier. Even when they find a more permanent partner, the nature of their job along with the negative stereotypes attached to policing could serve to hinder the growth of a long-term relationship. The fact that they are now known to be cops, but not known to be gay at work, could provide the fuel for exposure, blackmail, or other forms of personal victimization should the relationship sour and they be thought at fault. Even in the presumed safety of the family setting gay cops must confront the challenge of whether or not to tell other family members of their homosexuality like anyone else in any other profession. As in their work world, the uncertainty of their reactions only serves to magnify the problem in their eyes. Most gay cops choose secrecy over disclosure in both settings.

I want to stress once again one of my principal findings in this study: that individual choices of self-presentation to significant others in gay officers' multiple worlds are solidly linked to self-perception, to the officers' needs and expectations of how these others in their lives will react to the knowledge that they are homosexual.

Ten

Summary: The Challenge of Coming Out

n this study I have explored the dilemmas facing homosexuals who have chosen law enforcement as a career. In so doing, I have raised issues of sexuality in the workplace that concern heterosexuals as well as gays. In a society free of homophobia, being a cop and a homosexual should create no special problems and no need for a study such as this. But as we know, this is not the case. Gays across the country encounter negative attitudes and continued social restrictions. Being a police officer does not necessarily alter that situation. If anything, the job intensifies the homosexual's sense of inferiority and social exclusion. Indeed, many feel betrayed and rejected by their colleagues who, in various ways, have conveyed the message that gays cannot uphold the moral standards and work role expectations of policing;[1] others sense that they are pitied or at best tolerated by work mates who do not understand their differences and make it clear that they feel uncomfortable around them. Only a relative few feel they have come to be known as loyal members of the police family and accepted for who they are.

In an important way the situation of the gay officer parallels that of other minority newcomers to policing; they have all chosen to enter a profession that historically has been dominated by white, male heterosexuals. They pose the same challenges and encounter many of the same forms of resistance and threats to their psychological well-being that these other groups do (for instance, women and blacks). This is especially true for the majority of gays who work under the guise of heterosexuality, for it is precisely their attempts to manage or cope with a discreditable identity on a day-to-day basis that have played havoc with their professional and personal lives.

The problems gay cops face in managing a perceived deviant sexual identity at work and a problematic occupational identity in their social lives has formed the central concern of this research. In analyzing the problems of identity management, I have tried to portray gay officers, whether closeted or open about their sexual and occupational identity, as both actors and acted upon; as persons who size up situations and act according to the impressions they receive. This approach has necessarily raised a number of sociologically relevant questions concerning the meaning of homosexuality and other forms of socially imputed deviance in the workplace. Of specific concern to this study was how stigmas come to be built up, sustained, and conveyed to others in the work setting; how they can be transformed, modified, or neutralized; and how interactional processes, cultural prescriptions, and structural elements, both within and outside the organizational setting, contribute to these meanings. My strategy throughout this research has been to let my respondents tell most of the story. While I make no claim to statistical representativeness for my sample, the forty-one interviews along with field observations, media accounts, and my own experiences in policing have allowed me to identify common perceptions, problems, and management strategies that people with discreditable traits, like homosexuals, are likely to experience. I hope that the data and interpretations prove useful for general academic purposes, but especially for those interested in gaining further insight into problems of stigma and identity management.

I began this study by examining the private and professional lives of gay men and women, most of whom entered law enforcement in the 1980s. In actuality, though, the history of gays in policing dates back much further. There is little question that homosexuals held positions in police departments across the country well before people like Charlie Cochrane came out publicly and gays began forming fraternal police organizations of their own (as of early 1993, at least *ten* U.S. cities had gay police organizations that were either chapters of GOAL or similar in structure to GOAL—Los Angeles; San Fran-

cisco; Denver; Seattle; San Diego; Chicago; Springfield, Massachu-
setts; Marlboro, Maryland; and Portland and Eugene, Oregon—
along with affiliates in London and Amsterdam). Historically, however, we know little or nothing about these police officers and the
problems they faced except that as self-labeled deviants they dared
not expose themselves publicly. Given that society has only recently
become more sensitive to and accepting of the rights of homosexuals, one can only imagine the pain and anguish these men and
women suffered from having to spend their working days pretending
to be something they were not, and their off-duty nights worrying
that the on-duty police would discover them.

STRATEGIES AND STRAINS

Gay officers began experiencing stigma management problems with
their decision to enter the macho, masculine world of policing. Even
before their entrance into policing, these men and women were
aware of the beliefs of wider society toward homosexuals and accepted the possibility that these feelings would continue and perhaps
even intensify in the police world.[2] Whatever these prospective officers believed about homosexuality personally, they contemplated a
police career with enough understanding of society's attitudes to be
aware of the moral contours of the department regarding homosexuality. Few believed that they could escape the labeling process and
the classic stereotype of the homosexual should their secret be
discovered or revealed at work. Yet despite this seemingly unified
picture of hostility and the potential problems facing them as homosexuals, they still chose policing over other careers.

The motivations of homosexual men and women for selecting law
enforcement were not dissimilar to those of heterosexual groups
who entered policing over the past few decades (see chapter 3). Earlier research in this area indicates that both intrinsic (excitement,
adventure, community service) and extrinsic (salary, job security,
fringe benefits) factors often combined to make police work more
attractive than other careers.[3] Although the reasons for choosing law
enforcement were as varied for the women in this study as they were
for the men, women seemed far more security conscious, citing income, job tenure, and personal safety as primary factors affecting

their career choices. The reality that as women they were more vulnerable to certain crimes and that they would probably never marry (at least in a conventional sense) and have a male spouse to provide additional economic security may have steered them toward policing.

But from the outset of their policing careers the situation of gays departed substantially from that of other newcomer groups to law enforcement. Gays had the option of cloaking their marginalized status in the workplace, a choice not available to heterosexual women and racial minorities. And, as the study has revealed, it is precisely their discreditable status as homosexuals that was of greatest concern to most gays who chose to handle any workplace problems by concealing their differentness from others. This was, in fact, the strategy that was to be adopted even by those who claimed to have had a positive gay identity before becoming cops.

For most gay officers entering policing, earlier fears and concerns about the potential for persecution in the workplace were confirmed. The police world's seemingly endless demonstrations of contempt for homosexuals began to square with the impressions they had received from other sources while they were civilians. Gay men and women found in this new environment a work culture infused with beliefs and codes of behavior that often militated against their own interests as homosexuals as well as those of the wider gay community. In this new setting they also began to experience tremendous pressure to conform to these apparently shared views and to quietly compromise their personal integrity if they were to gain acceptance. In the precinct as well as on patrol they found themselves in settings that provided fertile ground for acquiring and strengthening homophobic attitudes and for communicating antigay sentiments. Locker rooms, bathrooms, and other private spaces in the precinct furnished both the fixtures and incentives for covert expressions of disapproval of homosexual life-styles. But not all expressions of aversion toward gays were covert. The successful pretense of heterosexuality carried out by most gays who entered law enforcement allowed for open expressions of homosexual bias in both the station houses and streets—expressions that these men and women had to deal with in silence, lest they draw the label closet queen or fag lover upon themselves. The terrifying fear of being labeled a freak and excluded from the police fraternity strengthened their resolve to keep their homosexual identity secret. If they had not already done so, most had to devise new skills of impression management or information control to convey to their heterosexual colleagues the message that they were just like them.

Stigma management strategies adopted by gay cops are in many ways similar to those used by other discreditable individuals whose self-esteem, social rank, and even legal rights would be threatened by disclosure. Specifically, such strategies involved the avoidance of symbols that could call attention to the individual's stigma or result in guilt by association. For the hard of hearing, for example, this some-times meant avoiding others who were actually deaf; those with im-paired vision or who suffered mild physical disabilities often avoided public contact with the blind or those who were more severely dis-abled. For the closeted gay cop, as well as for other secret homosex-uals, this meant, among other things, publicly shunning known or strongly suspected gay officers who could link them to the stigma.[4] Stigma management also entailed the use of disidentifiers, such as wearing a wedding band at work and, for men, engaging in stag talk and acting more masculine.[5] In short, gay cops, like others with hid-den moral blemishes, had to mentally assume the role of the het-erosexual (normal) in all matters of interaction with unsuspecting straights (normals)—an orientation not unfamiliar to the govern-ment spy or undercover cop.

The strains of secrecy—the frustration, shame, guilt, and ego-dis-tortion that flow from having to turn a deaf ear when openly hostile remarks are made about homosexuals, or when wrongful and some-times even criminal actions are taken against gays—are not unique to homosexual cops. They pervade the work settings and social lives of most homosexuals (and other discreditable persons) who have chosen concealment over disclosure. Yet I am inclined to believe, as a result of the interviews in this study and my experiences in polic-ing, that the strains of managing a discreditable identity are far more intense for gay cops than for homosexuals in most other conven-tional occupations. I can offer a number of interconnected reasons for this observation. First, policing, unlike most other professions, has a system of informal rules and expectations that serves to protect cops from the internal (departmental) and external (street) hazards of the job. Those who cannot or will not comply with these rules and expectations are often stripped of their membership in the police family and denied information and feedback vital to success in the department's informal structure. Moreover, in traditional police set-tings there exists a strong sense of resistance to change in the system among rank-and-file officers. Gays represent an element of extreme change in the structure of policing. Variably perceived by society as neurotic, emotionally handicapped, sexually confused, promiscuous, and incapable of forming bonded relationships, they are thought to lack the social and emotional requirements to carry out certain work role expectations. Moreover, because they are newcomers to policing their loyalties to fellow officers may be questioned, as was the case with blacks and women when they first entered law enforcement.[6] To dominant groups in policing, gay cops represent a threat not only to the prevailing cultural order but to the romanticized image of the job itself.

Second, in policing, as in any formal organization, an informal structure of rank-and-file officers exists whose perceived role is not only to define behavior that is a threat to the prevailing cultural order but to weed out and punish offenders. This group of police officers can be roughly divided into moral leaders and followers. The moral leaders, who, most of the officers in this study agree, constitute approximately 5 percent of any police command, see their function in the department as defining what is morally appropriate conduct and labeling those who fail to share or live up to their standards as morally reprehensible. Most, I have found in my twenty-three years with the NYPD, are very much in tune with the Durkheimian thought that society is, above all else, a moral community that demands consensus on certain moral issues. By speaking out against homosexuals, the moral leaders may feel that they are protecting the integrity and reputation of the department and, as well, society's moral order. Their continued rejection of gays (as well as other discreditable groups such as blacks and women) may also be viewed from a utilitarian position—the political utility of rejection as a way to control discreditable groups so as to maintain the status quo and maintain their own dominant position in the hierarchy of policing. In this sense the moral leaders in policing, as in any occupational or social setting, benefit both socially and psychologically from the devaluation of homosexuals and others. Moral leaders whose perceptions of homosexuals often form a central element of their belief structures pose a special threat to homosexual cops, because it is virtually impossible to convince them to alter their views. To do so would require them "to dismantle the mental and emotional structures that cradle their concepts of self."[7]

The followers, on the other hand, constitute a second and perhaps more pernicious group not only because they are in the majority but because they so strongly seek acceptance into the police family themselves. Followers, too, speak out boldly and publicly against homosexuals. Yet their actions may be prompted not necessarily by personal beliefs in the inferiority of gays, as some of the officers in this study have indicated, but by pressures to conform to what they perceive as a shared belief system. Whether or not these individuals actually believe their words to be true or their actions justified, fearing rejection and social isolation in the precinct they follow in knee-jerk fashion the moral leaders in condemning and excluding homosexuals. Judging from the interviews and my own casual conversations with gay cops it appears that most followers have had few, if any, occasions to work closely with homosexuals in their commands. Indeed, some followers seem to go out of their way to avoid contact with known or even suspected gays within the ranks, fearing perhaps that they themselves will be labeled as homosexuals or fag lovers. Consequently, their evaluation of the homosexual officer's individual worth, barring other favorable information, is heavily weighted by the prevailing stereotypes in society and by the actions of the moral leaders. Yet it is precisely their isolation from gays in the workplace (along with the reluctance of most homosexual cops to publicly reveal themselves) that has reinforced existing stereotypic generalizations that are, in large part, the cause of most gay officers' stress and secretiveness in the first place.[8]

Finally, because of the intense bonding, camaraderie, and sense of isolation from society at large, relationships among cops often carried over into their social lives. Yet this extension of relationships created additional strains and burdens on closeted gay officers, who now found that they had to work harder at maintaining a false identity to avoid unintentionally exposing their true sexual orientation.[9] For example, when off duty and in the company of heterosexual police who were both friends and co-workers, gay cops often brought others of the opposite sex who knew of their homosexuality into their conspiracy of secrecy either as purported lovers or as escorts at social events.

Given the pressure on rank-and-file members to conform to a perceived shared belief system, it is no wonder that most of the closeted men and women I spoke with felt surrounded by a hostile and extremely homophobic work force. Even though they are protected by law, for them to declare publicly their true sexual preferences, they argued, would almost certainly mean their banishment from the police family and loss of essential group support, leaving them largely unprotected from the dangers of policing. Fearing that a declaration of their sexual preference might destroy their careers and possibly even subject their loved ones to ridicule and abuse, most of these cops opted to continue on a course that would sustain their false identities as heterosexuals. This, paradoxically, meant distancing themselves socially from their heterosexual colleagues and supervisors as they came to terms with the strains of life in the closet.

While most homosexual cops chose to restrict their private lives and primary relations to other gays and to remain in the closet at work, others sought relief from the burden of personal dishonesty and self-abnegation through increased exposure as homosexuals (see chapter 6). This shift in behavior marked a pivotal point in the careers of these men and women and a significant step toward reconciling the fact of their gayness with their work world. Although much has been written about the stages or sequences through which individuals pass as they move from self-recognition as homosexuals to public disclosure, relatively little is known about the passage from secrecy to full visibility in the workplace.[10] The findings in this study indicate that this process, like the coming-out process in the gay social world, typically occurs in a succession of steps; that it is tied to a large degree to the individual's experiences and changing perceptions of self and others; that it generally involves as a first step a testing of the waters with one or more close work associates; and finally, that it can be for the gay officer both terrifying and inspiring.

Gays who have begun to reveal themselves in this fashion have more often than not already rejected the imputation that they are evil, sinful, inferior, different from, or worse than others at work. They have come out to their partners because they need to share their secret with others they trust and to convince these others that they are none of the foregoing. Yet the study also shows that some homosexual officers, still fearing the uncertainty of reactions even from close work associates, chose more circumspect or less direct paths to disclosure. One route was simply to avoid the more psychologically stressful and demanding aspects of heterosexual masquerading, without actually acknowledging their sexual differentness, even if asked by suspicious colleagues. Another choice was to drop the facade of heterosexuality entirely; they no longer avoided "stigma symbols" and stopped using disidentifiers. For others the intentional dropping of revealing clues in the workplace served as an appropriate strategy to gain greater visibility as homosexuals. Whatever form the process of coming out took, however, it required for many of these men and women countless rehearsals of strategies, each posed around the individual's unique needs, relationships, and work environment, as well as countless rehearsals of possible reactions from imaginary work associates and bosses.[11] Yet the further the gay cop moved out of the closet, the greater his or her capacity for resistance to returning to secrecy. For most who reached the tentatively out stage, as their freedom from self-distortion increased and as they began to gain self-respect and control over their social identities, a new sense of moral righteousness emerged. The gay officer coming out in this way found that the time had come to reorganize his or her social relationships and behavior at work around a new social identity.

Moving further toward the threshold of full disclosure, with its increased uncertainties as to how most other cops in the precinct would react, demanded an even greater degree of courage and commitment to be free of self-distortion. The decision to fully unmask a discreditable identity in a perceptively hostile work environment had to be strengthened not only by a sense of moral propriety and a shedding of any residual guilt and shame that may have accompanied years of personal dishonesty, but by a belief that acceptance eventually would be forthcoming in the workplace.

Central to the question of disclosure for many gay officers was the perceived conflict between their reputation as cops and their identity as homosexuals. Could their work-related reputations effectively neutralize this discreditable aspect of self? The findings clearly show that a stigma such as homosexuality does not invariably undermine a person's positive qualities and overall identity, as some social scientists have suggested in the past (see chapters 6 and 7).[12] Rather, they demonstrated that just the opposite effect can take place—an individual's positive qualities and behavior can neutralize or even replace a negative master status in designating his or her overall worth in the eyes of heterosexual co-workers. Thus, even though homosexuality and other personal qualities may be broadly defined as undesirable (or even perverse) in the (police) workplace, on an individual level such discreditable traits can be rendered irrelevant.[13] This process of redefining or of rendering irrelevant what society considers abnormal and thus highly relevant can occur, as this study reflects, when other highly valued, work-related qualities possessed by the individual become known and assume priority over the denigrated ones.

It was in this context that I considered the relationship between certain structural factors (such as assignment), strategies of stigma management, and reactions to stigma in the workplace. Interestingly, I found assignment (that is, street work versus office work) to be related to stigma management strategies and co-worker reactions through the intervening variable of reputation, suggesting that officers assigned to high-action duties (patrol, anticrime details, and criminal investigations) were more easily able to acquire the reputation of good cop than were officers assigned to low-action duty such as office work. These high-action assignments enabled gay officers to validate their reputations as good cops both in their eyes and in the eyes of others, which in turn allowed them to pursue a course of greater openness at work. Their belief was that their reputation as good cops was like money in the bank in that it would outweigh their stigmatized sexual identity and become the status that would designate their overall worth. For most, disclosure did pay off; their deviant status as homosexuals was no longer seen as consequential or as a handicap by most of their partners and work associates. These findings further suggest that it is not just a situation of cooperative interdependence in the workplace that may change the meaning of stigma, but the kind of interdependence and assignments that allow the stigmatized to be perceived as one of us rather than one of them. The corresponding findings in my earlier study of black-white relations in the NYPD offer further evidence of this.[14]

In mapping out directions for future investigations into the mean ings of deviance in the workplace, it might be fruitful to focus on different work settings to see which types of stigma are capable of being neutralized, subordinated, or replaced by other personal identities, and under what conditions. While this approach is important generally, it is especially relevant to studies involving individuals possessing multiple stigmas (such as black lesbians), as these individuals may have to deal with their colleagues' and superiors' antipathy not only toward gays but toward blacks and women as well.

Given the findings in this study, I suspect that research of this type will show that both meanings and consequences of stigma will depend on all or some combination of the following: (1) the nature and structure of the work setting—such factors as the degree to which individuals feel pressured to orient their behavior around their perceptions of others' beliefs, the need for cooperative interdependence among workers, and the organization of the workplace; (2) the perceived seriousness of the deviant attributes (homosexuality or alcohol abuse may be judged by one's co-workers as a social failing of relatively low seriousness compared to child molestation or hardcore drug abuse) or its perceived threat to individual members of the work group (the risk of social contamination an individual assumes in befriending a co-worker who is a known homosexual versus a colleague who is physically disabled); (3) the deviant's other social identities or known personal qualities—especially work-related qualities—and whether they are perceived to be of high or low value to the organization and its members; (4) the conditions of deviancy— *discovery* (how and when it came to be known), *responsibility* or *blameworthiness* (whether the individual is personally responsible for the devalued condition or social identity), *permanence* (whether the stigma is permanent or can be corrected, treated, eliminated, or normalized), and *visibility* (how visible its manifestations are). Regarding visibility, for example, gay male cops who are out in their commands and seeking acceptance may feel that even though they no longer have to hide who they are, they also cannot be too militant in their actions, flamboyant, or offensively obvious at work. In short, they may feel that they must behave as "gentlemen deviants."[15]

While this study has focused on the meaning and consequences of homosexuality in the police world, future research might inquire into the reactions of work associates to a *hero* firefighter who is known to be one or more of the following—a homosexual, an alcoholic, a wife beater, a pedophile, a drug user, or an AIDS carrier—or to a *highly skilled* corporate attorney, business executive, construction worker, or teacher who is known or suspected of being any of the above. Investigations into these areas should begin with the recognition that stigmas are social constructs, infused with cultural meaning.[16] Consequently, a fully developed model of stigma management in the workplace should incorporate relevant social and historical events (such as the spread of AIDS or legislation banning discrimination) into an interactionist approach that focuses on both the stigmatizers and the stigmatized.

OCCUPATIONAL IDENTITY AND THE GAY OFFICER'S SOCIAL WORLD

The pressure to conform to heterosexual norms and the absence of homosexual alternatives in the workplace made it all but impossible for gays and straights to become involved socially with each other on a comfortable and regular basis. As a result, most gay cops tended to confine their social relationships to similarly stigmatized persons from whom they derived among other things needed support and opportunities to meet new sexual partners. Yet the problem of possessing a doubly deviant identity did not end in the workplace for many gay cops. In their social life they were aware that if they were to be even marginally integrated into the homosexual community and gay life-style, they would have to continue to manage not only a discreditable sexual identity but an occupational identity that had multiple and often contradictory meanings in the gay world.

In 1963 Erving Goffman wrote of the divided world of the deviant: the "out-of-bounds" places where persons of the individual's kind are forbidden to be, and where exposure means expulsion; the "civil" places where they are carefully and sometimes painfully treated; and the "back" places where they stand exposed and need not try to conceal their stigma. The gay officer's social world, however, is not so neatly divided. Each setting—whether it be a "gay ghetto" such as Greenwich Village; a gay bar, social club, or community center; or a known public cruising ground—posed a set of corresponding problems that required the skillful managing of the officer's sexual or occupational identity or both in order to avoid victimization and exposure at work. These problems stem in large part from the unique nature of policing and the distribution of the police work force. Unlike other occupations in which workers are largely confined to a particular work area during the day or night, as in a hospital, school, office building, or construction site, police officers are scattered throughout the city twenty-four hours a day, seven days a week. For the closeted officer socializing in predominantly gay areas, this presented a constant risk of being seen and recognized by other colleagues working that area. Whether this risk was small or substantial (and that depended in part on the time the officer had in the department and the number of commands in which he or she worked), many closeted cops came to experience what Matza has aptly labeled a "fear of transparency," a self-consciousness that police on patrol, who associate certain places or "interactional territories" with particular stigmatized groups, would recognize the individual for what he or she was—a homosexual.[17] To cope with this problem, some gay cops adopted evasive cat-and-mouse strategies. Ducking down, hiding their faces, turning away, wearing sunglasses at night, and attempting to surreptitiously enter and leave known gay establishments when police vehicles approached became routine features of their off-duty social lives. It is, interestingly, an irony that these men and women have come to fear most not the criminal element in the street (although that is also a concern) but their own colleagues who routinely patrol the areas they frequent. This irony is perhaps most poignantly captured in the comment of one officer who confessed that, when he was in known gay areas of the city, he often found himself behaving like a "common criminal" hiding from the police.

While socializing in gay bars and clubs may release gay cops from the burden of having to maintain secrecy about their sexual orientation, it has not released them from maintaining secrecy about their occupational identity. Letting on to civilian gays that they are cops exposed them to the risk of disclosure at work should an incident occur or a serious problem arise in the bar that required police intervention. Cops are expected to act decisively in these situations. Failure on an officer's part to do so could result in complaints being lodged against him or her should individuals in the bar, knowing the person to be a cop, report the officer's inactions to the department. It is precisely because of the risks attached to being known as a cop that gay officers often chose, when out socializing in these potentially troublesome settings, to keep their police identity hidden from all but their close friends.

For closeted officers *cruising* these settings, the problems of managing their occupational identity became even more complex. Gay cops of both genders tend to rate their sexual appeal high because of the sexual imagery attached to their profession by some in the homosexual community (see chapter 8). Many have even come to view themselves, in comparison to gays in other occupations, as the ultimate catch. Because there are no qualifying attributes attached to their identity as cops, as there are in their work world (for example "good" cop), their occupation alone and what it stands for erotically becomes their primary identity. For the individual out cruising, simply being a cop could enhance his or her value as a sexual partner.

That is, unquestionably, the up side for homosexual officers who pursue sexual one-night stands. For those seeking a more permanent relationship, premature disclosure of their police identity could actually interfere with that objective. Conspiring to disrupt a developing relationship should the officer's occupational identity be revealed too soon may be the belief shared by some civilian homosexuals that gays simply shouldn't be cops, the fear that they could actually end up suffering physical abuse should they become involved with a cop, and their distrust of police in general. The officer's shared sexual orientation and social bond with other homosexuals may do little or nothing to offset these negative assessments.[18] Even in newly formed relationships, this study showed, there was the risk that the officer's acknowledged line of work could become a disruptive element should the idealized image and romantic mystique attached to policing fade. In extreme cases in which irreconcilable problems developed between officers and their lovers, the officers could find themselves facing extortion or the dreaded phone call to their command exposing their secret sexual identity. In either case, whether out socializing or searching for a sexual partner, premature occupational disclosure could leave the officer feeling betrayed and vulnerable. As with women who, at times, have been denied full human status and responded to in depersonalized, categorical terms, homosexual officers may find that they are being responded to as instances of the category cop with no other noteworthy status or identity.[19]

The cynicism toward strangers that often results from feelings of vulnerability and experiences of betrayal has led some gay cops to formulate strategies that helped them uncover the true intentions of individuals they met for the first time in bars and clubs and were attracted to. In relating to strangers, many gay cops drew upon the skills and resources acquired during their occupational training. As any seasoned police officer might do when checking out a criminal suspect, for example, they asked revealing questions aimed at uncovering potential danger signs. Appearances, which often lead to inferences of moral character, were also of concern to gay cops out cruising. Thus it was not an uncommon practice for these men and women, when engaging a prospective sexual partner in conversation, to carefully observe and take note of the person's general appearance. To protect themselves from harm, some even went so far as to routinely inquire into the individual's background by searching through departmental records of known criminals. Many, however, conceded that they relied largely on their gut feelings or instinct to recognize and distinguish between those who were sincere and honest and those who might be a potential threat to their safety. Even in situations in which gay officers initially felt comfortable with a prospective sexual partner, the eventual decision as to where they would go to have sex had to be weighed against the backdrop of risks attached to one place as opposed to another.

One might suppose that many of these concerns about strangers could be offset by the officer's license to carry a firearm off duty. However, for many cruising gay cops, their weapon became just one more potential source of trouble in their social lives (see chapter 8). Not only could the gun be taken and used against the officer if it were not adequately protected, but the mere theft of the weapon (or, for that matter, other serialized police items such as the shield or ID) necessitated an immediate official report to the department indicating the *circumstances* of the loss. Indeed, one could argue, the theft of serialized police property exposes closeted cops to a double-bind situation in which they must quickly weigh doing the right thing (filing a truthful report to the police) against the possible sanctions (public exposure and humiliation) that could befall them for exercising this choice. Doing the wrong thing (filing a false or misleading report) may protect their secret sexual identity for the moment but exposes them later to a gamut of departmental sanctions, including the disclosure of their sexual identity should their account of the incident be discovered during a follow-up investigation to be false or misleading. The risk of having an identifiable gun stolen while engaging in a sexual liaison with a stranger could, of course, be eliminated by leaving the weapon (and shield and ID) safely stored in the officer's command. This choice, however, leads to a trade-off situation in which the risk of theft or use of the weapon against the officer has to be balanced against its protective value when picking up or having sex with individuals whose true motives for being with the officer may be unknown. In fact, most of the cops I spoke with admitted that during their rounds of cruising bars and clubs, the question of their own safety and thus what to do with their weapon (and other valuables) invariably surfaced. These men and women attempted to resolve the dilemma by devising elaborate and sometimes even extreme plans to safeguard their valuables, protect themselves and others from harm, and secure their weapon in such a way that it was both hidden and accessible when they were contemplating sex in either their own or a stranger's apartment, or in a neutral setting such as a motel.

As this study has suggested, the risks of both victimization and exposure at work are greatly magnified for the homosexual officer who cruises the city's less conventional settings such as the parks and waterfront blocks (known in New York City's Lower West Side as the Dock Strip). Unlike the gay bar and social club scene, in which regular patrons often get to know each other, and in which there is usually time to inquire or even check into a prospective sexual partner's background, the social organization and function of these more clandestine locales with their norms of limited interaction that is not sexual greatly restrict the exchange and confirmation of such biographical information.[20] Cruising these far riskier settings for recreational sex raises once again the question of how gay cops ought to handle their occupational identity—officers must weigh the potential risks against the advantages of revealing their line of work to prospective sexual partners. Could disclosure, for example, reduce or even eliminate the risk of criminal victimization? Could it enhance the sexual encounter because of the erotic imagery attached to the officer's occupation? And lastly, could disclosure become a limiting or disruptive element in a sexual arrangement because of the stranger's fear and distrust of cops? On another level, should officers carry their weapon (and police ID) on their person or even in the car when cruising these areas? Does the protective value of the weapon outweigh the risk that it could be stolen during a robbery, or, worse, that the gun could be turned on the officer? If a decision is made to bring the weapon along, where should it be kept during a sexual encounter—under the front seat, in the glove compartment, in the trunk of the car? Which of these places affords both maximum protection against theft or use and accessibility in the event of trouble? How should officers handle an unexpected set up by a stranger's friends, or a sudden intrusion by police on patrol? How should they respond if stopped and questioned by the police? Should they own up to being police officers or attempt to conceal this information? What are the possible consequences of disclosure to the police, versus hiding their police identity from them?

If officers become targets or actual victims of a crime while cruising these areas, critical decisions have to be made concerning the handling of the situation. If they take direct action, that is, make an arrest, they must consider the strong probability that they will face revealing questions concerning their presence in a known homosexual cruising area that could subject them to ridicule, harassment, and even exposure as a faggot in their command. They also have to consider the risks attached to filing a false or misleading report. An important finding in this study is that the fear of exposure as a homosexual at work was so great among most of the closeted men and women I interviewed that the only viable option open to them was to falsify the circumstances of the incident, even though that meant risking suspension or, if the officer was on probation, termination from the job. To get around the problems of victimization, many of these police officers claimed that they now confined their cruising mostly to the more conventional gay bars, clubs, and community centers.

For other homosexual cops, cruising for sex has become an activity of the past, replaced by a search for a more stable, permanent relationship in which sex is just one essential feature. Like gays in other walks of life, most of these men and women have at one time or another experienced such a relationship, were actively pursuing one, or were currently engaged in what they hoped was going to be an enduring arrangement.[21]

Along with the obvious advantages of providing romance, security, emotional bonding, a sense of family, and, perhaps most importantly, a decreased risk of contracting AIDS, there is a liability to coupled living arrangements. As in any relationship, homosexual or otherwise, possessiveness and jealousy can surface and create in the household an atmosphere of hostility, which can trigger disputes violent enough to bring the police to the doorstep. While disputes can be disruptive to any relationship, they are especially troublesome to gay officers who are closeted at work, for it is *their* colleagues who are generally called to intervene and who may be informed by officers' lovers that they are cops. Moreover, there is always the risk that, should the relationship deteriorate to the point that the officer decides or threatens to terminate it, the lover may respond in kind by calling the officer's command and exposing the homosexual relationship or at least threatening to do so. In personally troubled times, gay cops who are not out publicly at work may well find themselves, as some in this study have reported, trapped in a sort of hostage situation with their live-in partners. Fearing blackmail and unwanted exposure in their commands, they may feel compelled to remain in an unhappy relationship. Even in untroubled times, a relationship with another gay poses the risk of exposure for a closeted officer. As in all arrangements in which couples live together, there occur unpredictable incidents such as crimes, accidents, serious injuries, illnesses, or deaths that police are called upon to deal with and that thus raise the threat of exposure for the officer.

Of particular interest to researchers has been the stability of relatively longstanding homosexual relationships in which partners make, at least initially, an emotional investment in each other. Investigations into the permanency of these relationships show that few survive ten years, with most lasting from three to five years. In this study, the average time gay cops remained in such a relationship was three years, with most lasting less than two. In summarizing other researchers' findings along with their own, Bell and Weinberg point to society's antihomosexual attitudes, among other reasons, for the lack of stability that seems to characterize so many homosexual partnerships. To these findings I would add the occupational dimension, the nature of the officer's job, which (1) can restrict normal socializing patterns; (2) increases the risk of death or serious injury to the officer, impacting on the perceived permanence of the relationships; and (3) increases the pool of available sexual partners in the officer's social world, thus creating a perception or even climate of infidelity in the household—either of which has been found to seriously disrupt relationships. In sum, the cop's line of work can add to the instability of the homosexual partnership, not gays' reputed emotional immaturity or maladjustment that supposedly makes them unable to form lasting attachments.[22]

In the gay officer's interaction and relationships with family members, meanings attached to his or her homosexual identity create difficulties too. Gay cops in this study, for example, could not automatically assume acceptance and support from family members who found out or suspected that they were gay, as could persons who suffered from physical disabilities or who possessed certain tribal stigmas, such as racial minorities. This unpredictability of family members' reactions to disclosure or discovery often resulted in actions designed to keep the officers' sexual orientation and private lives secret from them. As in their work world, heterosexual role playing took on a special importance. The avoidance of "stigma symbols" and the use of disidentifiers and other devices that would protect them from being seen as deviant all became part of homosexual cops' interactional repertoire. Because of the need to protect their sexual preferences and life-style choices from exposure, most gay cops in this study reported that they lived independently from their families. Clearly, one important reason for this arrangement, as Weinberg and Williams point out in their study of male homosexuals, is that it diminished parental surveillance.[23] Yet even when living away from home, the gay officer had to take precautions to insure that potential "stigma symbols," such as photos of gay friends and lovers, could be quickly hidden from view in the event of an unexpected visit from an unsuspecting family member.

For a substantial portion of these men and women, attempts to keep their homosexuality a secret occupied a central place in their relationships with family members, their chief concern being never to relinquish control over information about self. This finding seems to contradict the argument raised by some writers that many, if not most, homosexuals are able to compartmentalize their social lives with minimal strain and draw only periodically upon the skills needed to maintain a convincing heterosexual front.[24]

At work, most gay cops in this study have learned to successfully keep their personal lives private and hide their social stigmas from most, if not all, of their colleagues. The work world of the closeted officer was just that, a world in which work and personal matters could be compartmentalized. Maintaining secrecy over extended periods of time with family members was, however, much more difficult. Simply by being near, parents and siblings could observe and monitor much of what went on in the household.[25] Changes in behavior patterns (such as shifting from dating members of the opposite sex to not dating at all), for example, were more easily recognizable by family members than by work associates, as were continuities in certain patterns (such as the officer's expressed rejection of conventional marriage and child rearing). Moreover, certain disidentifiers or covers, such as a wedding band, that could be worn at work to help sustain a heterosexual front could not be used around knowing family members.

While these and other behavioral changes and consistencies often gave rise to strong suspicions on the part of family members about the individual's true sexual orientation, in most instances the subject was never brought up in the household. Rather, all parties seemed to engage in a mutual pretense in which discussions of sensitive or revealing topics such as marriage and other things that called for recognition of the officer's suspected homosexuality were carefully avoided.[26]

For some cops, the stated rationale for maintaining secrecy (often in the face of growing evidence of homosexuality) was not only shame but the sincere desire to spare parents any unnecessary unhappiness. For others, it was the concern that family members might react inhumanely; that they would not countenance the homosexuality and, out of fear of contamination, cut off their children's contact with the shunned gay relative. For still others, secrecy was grounded in the belief that certain family members would suppress their love, tenderness, and affection, irretrievably crippling the relationship.[27]

When officers admitted their homosexuality, it was usually because they shared an exceptionally strong bond with a particular family member or because incontrovertible evidence of homosexuality was uncovered and led to an unavoidable confrontation. In other cases of disclosure, the officer felt that he or she simply could no longer participate in the conspiracy of silence. The psychological stress and anguish experienced over lying to loved ones was becoming too high a price to pay. Under conditions of secrecy, normal interaction in the household became tense and strained by the very strategies adopted to reduce it.[28] Moreover, continued secrecy and denial were reinforcing the notion of unacceptability and self-alienation and sustaining barriers between the officer and others in the family from whom he or she might receive support.

Instances of discovered or disclosed homosexuality led to various reactions from family members, which ranged from acceptance and support at one end to isolation, treatment, or punishment at the other (see chapter 9).[29] In trying to account for the negative reactions, the social stigma and embarrassment that family members felt *they* would be subjected to should a member's homosexuality be discovered come into play. Yet the causes of these reactions as well as the reactions themselves cannot be viewed apart from the cultural context of the modern family. The family is not an isolated unit, but a product of society with all its social and political manifestations. Anti-homosexual bias has, in this sense, been built into the modern family through misinformation spread by the medical profession, clergy, and other interest groups, as well as through the mechanisms of law, censorship, and taboo.[30]

In sum, this study shows that the meanings attached to certain stigmas such as homosexuality can shift as the possessor of the stigma moves from one social context to another. At work, in the police world, and within the family setting, the gay officer's sexual orientation may be severely stigmatized, while in his social world of friends and lovers, it has no such negative meaning. Moreover, because it is a social construct and connotes a relationship between individuals, stigma can have multiple meanings within the same social context. In the gay officer's work world, for example, the strong sense of cooperative interdependence between gay officers and their close work associates can render an officer's homosexuality inconsequential, while in the officer's family circle, where cooperative interdependence is more diffused or even nonexistent, the individual's social failing is of consequence to some. Even in the context of the gay officer's social world of friends and lovers, where homosexual stigma is irrelevant, other social identities can take on importance. The individual's identity as a cop may, for example, be viewed as pleasing to some, as distressing to others, and both pleasing and distressing for still others. The meaning of stigma is thus tied to social context and situated in the prevailing cultural order of society.

SOCIAL AND POLITICAL IMPLICATIONS

The benefits of coming out, or at least increasing one's visibility as a homosexual, seem to reveal themselves throughout this study. Yet many, if not most, gay cops are pessimistic about what full public disclosure will bring. They tend to exaggerate the discomfort and social harm that would befall them should their secret sexual identity become known in their work world. However, this study has shown that while disclosure initially may be embarrassing or distressing, in the long run it leads to both acceptance and integration into the police world for most gay cops. It can be argued that these and other benefits of coming out extend not only to the individual but to the larger gay and straight police population as well as to the wider homosexual community. On a personal level the openly gay officer no longer has to experience the guilt and shame that results from having to stand silently by while gays are abused by the police. In fact, the mere presence of openly gay cops on patrol and in the station house serves to deter most open displays of homophobia. The response to discrimination in the workplace shifts even more powerfully when *gay ranking officers* come out. As Charlie Cochrane once

put it, in a strange twist of events, when gay bosses make their homosexuality known in their commands, it is the bigots who must then
retreat to the closet.[31] In short, coming out publicly enables gay cops
to confront social myths and biases, to counteract shame and guilt,
and to disarm hostile elements in the department and in society at
large.

Paradoxically, the decision to remain closeted helps reinforce the
negative stereotypical images of gays in the workplace by obstruct-
ing information that could enlighten heterosexual cops. Coming out
can, over time, help reverse or even eliminate those stereotypes,
which in turn would provide a strong incentive for other cops contemplating disclosure.[32] Moreover, gay cops who remain in the closet
allow elements in the police department to defend the false and misleading position that there are only a handful of gays in policing.
This, in turn, strengthens the sexual ideology prevalent in police
work and in society at large, making it more difficult for other gay
cops to come out and challenge that ideology. In this sense ideology
makers and defenders in the department (the moral leaders) gain
strength and support from gay cops who choose to remain largely
invisible. Disclosure, on the other hand, not only explodes this myth
of the handful but defies the stereotypes that are sustained by secrecy and silence.

Given these and other obvious benefits to coming out, why do
such a relative few homosexual cops take that step? A spring 1992
conversation with the executive director of GOAL suggests that, of
the two hundred or so members of the organization who are with city
police agencies (transit, housing, and the NYPD), roughly 50 percent
are out publicly in their commands. While that figure is a substantial
increase over the past two years in the number of openly gay cops, it
nevertheless represents less than 5 percent of the approximately
three thousand gays in city police agencies (based on the conventional estimate that one in ten is homosexual).[33] The comments of the
men and women in this study provide only partial and tentative answers for the low rate of disclosure. They indicate that, for the most
part, gays who continue to choose secrecy over disclosure do so because they are gripped by a fear of the unknown—the uncertainty of
what they would face should their true sexual orientation be known
in the workplace. Yet the findings in this study suggest, as have
others, that those fears are either exaggerated or unfounded.[34]

Perhaps the reason for most homosexual cops' determination to
remain in the closet lies not only in their fear of rejection but in their

concern that coming out will compel them to become politically active. Perhaps they have learned from homosexuals in policing and other walks of life that coming out marks the beginning of a political stage in one's career, a time to actively question social norms and relationships and challenge organizational policies and procedures that discriminate against gays. And many gay cops may be reluctant to become involved in a cause that appears to be in direct opposition to the dominant sexual ideology in this country. Furthermore, political consciousness is expressly discouraged in occupations such as policing that, by and large, represent and support the dominant ideologies in this country, sexual and otherwise.

There is yet another side to the issue of disclosure—that is, that homosexuals in policing may not see increased visibility as a panacea for their problems at work. In the past, minority groups such as blacks and women, whose identities could not be denied, did not necessarily experience reductions in racism and sexism as their numbers in police departments grew. Consequently, some tried to rationalize their disenfranchisement rather than use it as a stepping-off point toward positive identity development. Similarly, many homosexual cops whose visibility could not be easily detected have succumbed to a number of injurious ways of denying their true identity and disenfranchisement in society. And this denial of identity and resistance to developing a political consciousness has contributed to the difficulty of coming out. Before an oppressed people can free themselves from oppression, they must first know and admit to themselves that they are oppressed. They must search for political and historical events that have led to their oppression and learn the full meaning of their relationships with their oppressors. As a stigmatized group, homosexual cops must understand that the oppressor or stigmatizer has established a position of false superiority over them and needs to maintain the concept that homosexuals (and certain other discreditable groups) are fundamentally inferior in order to sustain that position. Coming out in the police world, as anywhere else, is a process that involves destigmatization. It is a process that enables gays and other stigmatized individuals to shift the balance of power away from the oppressor through strength in numbers.[35] In the final analysis, it is a process that allows members of these groups to accept themselves and enables others to accept them for what they are.

Entering the World of the Gay Officer

A number of problems face the social scientist interested in studying deviantized minority groups such as gay police. The first problem is gaining access to the group one wishes to study.[1] The second is deciding upon the most effective research approach. The third is locating subjects for the study and securing their ongoing cooperation. This section addresses these and other methodological problems and issues I confronted during the course of this project.

Soon after Charlie Cochrane informed the public of his homosexuality I attempted to contact him. After leaving a number of messages at his command, I received a call from Cochrane. His initial reaction to my interest in gay officers was understandably guarded. I later found out that immediately after his comments were aired on TV, Cochrane had been deluged with harassing phone calls at work and at home. Many seemed to be from other cops. I tried to assure him that the purpose of my call was purely academic. After I answered a few personal questions about myself, such as where I worked, he agreed to meet me at a local restaurant. The first few minutes of that meeting were somewhat tense, but then our conversation became more relaxed and cordial. I explained that I was completing a book on the occupational world of black cops, hoping this disclosure would convey my compassion for marginalized groups in law enforcement. I told him that as a future project, I would be interested in exploring the world of the gay officer. Cochrane was receptive but explained that, at that moment, none of the gay officers he knew were far enough out of the closet to be willing to talk with me. In short, he offered no assurance that he could help me locate gay cops for a study.

In the years that followed, I kept in touch with Charlie mostly by phone. In April 1982, he and a retired police sergeant from New Jersey formed New York's first gay police fraternal organization. They named it *GOAL*, the Gay Officers Action League. Charlie kept me abreast of GOAL's progress as it moved from a semisecret organization to one that gained increasing publicity and support from the NYPD. In the

GAY COPS

spring of 1987, I again approached Charlie with the idea of conducting research on gay police. He suggested that although most GOAL members were still in the closet, there was now a good chance that he could persuade some of them to talk to me. Charlie offered to set up a meeting in early September 1987 to introduce me to several GOAL board members. This gave me time to familiarize myself with the literature on homosexuality and to formulate tentative research questions. The meeting took place in a private apartment and lasted about two hours. Four members of the executive board of GOAL attended. I spoke about my academic career, discussed my current assignment as a lieutenant in the NYPD, and explained my interest in gay cops. The remainder of the meeting was spent fielding questions about this proposed research and my study of black police. In the end, the board members said one would get back to me within a few days with an answer to my request. Based on the cordial atmosphere, I felt confident that my presentation went over well and was hopeful that I would be granted access to other GOAL members as well as permission to study this emerging organization. Little did I realize at the time that this initial encounter was to be only the first in a series of meetings with various members of GOAL in which I would repeatedly have to sell not only my proposal for this study but myself as a credible and trustworthy researcher. The next day I received a call from Mike, one of the senior board members who had been at the meeting. He agreed that my presentation did go over well but said that I would have to make a more formal presentation to the entire board.

A month later I met with six board members and several regular members. Again I told them about my earlier research and fielded more questions concerning my proposal to study gay police. As with the last meeting, I left feeling comfortable with my presentation and both relieved and surprised that I had not encountered any overt resistance to the project. Two days later I received a call from Mike, who once again assured me that the board was receptive to my general proposal. However, he added, they all felt it was appropriate and necessary that the president of GOAL present my research ideas to the general membership at the next monthly meeting in November. It had now been nearly six months since I contacted Charlie about doing this study.

Over lunch a few days after the November meeting, Mike told me that the general membership had raised *new* questions about my proposal that neither he nor the board were able to answer. He asked me to make one more presentation at the forthcoming December meeting. Mike also made a startling suggestion. It was that I consider becoming a member of GOAL myself. He stated that my heterosexuality was irrelevant as long as my interest in the organization was sincere. He added that my joining GOAL might be a way for me to win the trust and support of the membership. I accepted this unexpected invitation with some reservations. My main concern was not that others in GOAL might misinterpret my membership as an indication that I was gay, but that some gay cops might perceive my joining the organization as a devious way of gaining research access. Mike did not appear concerned, and I agreed that he should submit my name for membership at the December meeting.

I was at that meeting when a pro forma screening committee was set up. After some formal questions were raised about my police career and personal background, I was officially voted in as a member of GOAL. I was then permitted to address the general membership and outline once again my research intentions. This presentation seemed to be going well until almost halfway through, when suddenly several members stood up and began voicing objections to the study. One of the members, who was apparently hearing about my proposal for the first time, expressed considerable resentment toward the project and explained that GOAL already "got burned once" by a reporter. Another officer angrily denounced even my presence at the meeting, adding that she was fed up with "being studied by outsiders." A third member matter-of-factly voiced his suspicions about who I was and what I *really* wanted of GOAL.[2]

Hearing these negative comments and later fielding more hostile questions from the group, I began to wonder whether this project was at all feasible. Was I only experiencing the tip of the iceberg as far as their fears, suspicions, and understandably self-protective natures were concerned? As I was to find out a few weeks later, the reservations expressed at this meeting had prompted several closeted members of GOAL to seriously consider terminating their membership should I be granted permission to pursue my research through their organization. Fortunately, these negative sentiments were not publicly aired. If they had been, I doubt that I would have been granted access to the organization.

Because a few GOAL members had opposed my proposal, the board decided to vote on whether to officially accept my research proposal. The vote was a disappointing seven to seven split with three abstentions. Based on previous meetings and conversations with Mike, I had expected to be accepted as a member and proceed with my research, which by now had been delayed nearly nine months.

Before this seemingly disastrous December meeting ended, Mike stood up and suggested that the skeptics in the group should read my book on black police to see how I had handled sensitive and controversial issues in the past. I gladly agreed to leave several copies of the book in Mike's office for any of those interested. The board then decided to postpone the vote regarding my proposal until the January meeting. I drove home that evening feeling both discouraged and frustrated and, for the first time, seriously contemplating abandoning the project altogether.

Each month's general meeting presented the possibility of the arrival of members who would oppose my proposal. I expressed this concern to Mike, who continued to be supportive, urging me to hang in. He followed through on a promise to speak with several of the more rebellious members and persuaded them to change their minds about my project. At the January meeting a second vote to accept my proposal was taken. The result was twelve in favor, none against. Finally, after more than ten months, I gained official approval from the membership to commence the study. However, my problems were not over. I was soon informed that the board would not exert any pressure whatsoever to encourage individual members to be interviewed. Armed only with formal access and the right to attend GOAL meetings, I was solely responsible for convincing individual cops to participate in the study.

Finding cooperative subjects presented an immediate problem; GOAL had provided me only with access to the organization. Fortunately Mike and a few key members introduced me to a handful of gay cops, some of whom were members of the organization. From that point, early in 1988 through late 1989, this network of gay men and women expanded and allowed me to interview a variety of New York City's gay officers.

Maintaining Access: Building Rapport and Trust

My success in getting gay cops to participate in such a sensitive and potentially risky research venture hinged, in part, on my continued attendance at GOAL meetings and related social functions. Through this continuity of contact, I was able to establish an ongoing dialogue and rapport with many of the members.

The importance of being *honest* with potential subjects concerning one's interests and objectives cannot be too strongly emphasized.[3] Besides informing the general membership on many occasions that I was interested in their world and especially in the *problems* of the gay officer as an academic pursuit, I candidly acknowledged that should the study eventually be published, it could help further my academic career. I later learned from several sources that most members of GOAL appreciated not only my expressed concern with the problems experienced by gay cops but also my frankness in admitting my self-interest.

As my participation in GOAL activities grew, and as I got to know members on a more social basis, my interest in the organization and compassion for the problems of its individual members grew. I was now regularly attending meetings and social functions (approximately bimonthly) and consequently feeling more at ease when buttonholed by a wary prospective subject with questions aimed at evaluating my motives and trustworthiness. Eventually, through continued exposure to this new setting I even became comfortable enough to speak up at meetings when I had an opinion on a particular subject, usually a problem confronting the organization. I always tried to make it clear, however, that I was expressing opinions *as a member of GOAL* rather than as a researcher.

Of *paramount* concern to many of the cops I met, and especially to those whose sexual orientation was still a well-guarded secret in their workplace, was how I would guarantee their anonymity. My answer was twofold: first, I assured these wary subjects that I would never, under any circumstances, divulge their names to members of the department because of the importance I as a researcher attached to this ethical standard. I further explained that, were I to reveal personal information concerning my subjects and it somehow got back to them, it would in all probability spell the end of my research. This seemed to many of the cops the more compelling argument. For instance, when someone raised the question of anonymity at a GOAL meeting in the spring of 1988, I presented a hypothetical situation: I asked the apprehensive member to consider what might happen if one of my research subjects who had been passing on the job as heterosexual were to suddenly discover that his or her true sexual identity had been exposed to co-workers. At whom would this betrayed person most likely point an accusing finger? My audience was pretty much in agreement that I would be the most likely suspect and that this would seriously jeopardize my ability to obtain any future subjects. In fact, I added, it would probably terminate the project. I later admitted to the members that this fortuitous exposure of a subject's sexual orientation, through no fault of my own, was one of *my* biggest fears, for I felt I would always be suspect. In my concluding remarks to the group I explained that I had already invested considerable time, effort, and expense in what I believed to be an important study. Therefore, it was in my best interest as well as theirs to protect the anonymity of my subjects at all costs. In honoring these promises I proposed to change or camouflage their names, assignments, time on the job, descriptions of events, and other identifiers without compromising the integrity of the research.

In addition to offering verbal assurances that I shared their concerns about anonymity, I took several additional steps to ease their fears of unwanted exposure. In the early stages of the research, I never asked the last names of GOAL members. I also decided not to reveal the nature of the research project to my police colleagues. My concern here was that heterosexual cops might accidentally see me with a subject, perhaps interviewing him or her in a restaurant or other public place, and then publicly label that officer a homosexual if they were to ever encounter him or her on the job.

Besides providing my subjects with assurances that I would never divulge their names to outsiders, I also entered into an unspoken agreement with some of them in which, when I could, I would attempt to assist them in resolving minor, on-the-job problems. This research bargain was readily accepted, as they all knew I was a police lieutenant with more than twenty years of service and had some connections in the department. The favors I provided were as diverse as acting as adviser to some of the gay officers who were unsure of which career path to take, to persuading a pharmacist friend to provide any member of GOAL who may fall victim to AIDS with the drug AZT at cost. Finally, the fact that I had shared membership in their work world for more than twenty years gave me a decided advantage in gaining their trust and confidence. Because of this connection to their world, my respondents did not perceive me or treat me as a total outsider. In their eyes I was someone who could both understand and appreciate what it meant to be a cop in New York City. In turn, they responded positively and often enthusiastically, honoring my seemingly never-ending requests for additional subjects.

Gaining the trust, confidence, and support of members of deviantized groups in society is no simple task. This undertaking can be further complicated when the potential subjects are overly cynical and suspicious of outsiders, as police most certainly are. My success in gaining access to GOAL and persuading both members and nonmembers to participate in this study can be attributed, I believe, in large part to the image I presented during my presentations to GOAL and to individual potential subjects. I took pains not to come off as a journalistic snooper interested in exploiting their marginalized status in society. Rather, I strove constantly to present a reassuring image as a sociologist cop who was sincerely interested in understanding, through their thoughts and personal experiences, what it meant to be a homosexual in a traditionally defined, macho-masculine world of policing.

Data Base

I was not interested in measuring the world of the gay officer. My concern instead was in finding out what this world looked like and explaining the ways these cops come to understand, account for, respond to, and manage their day-to-day situations. For this reason I chose partially structured interviews oriented toward the perspective of the gay officer as my primary research tool.[4]

The interviews, forty-one in all, lasted from four to ten hours, depending on whether they were taped or hand recorded. Most took several sessions to complete. The question of whether to hand record or to tape the interviews arose almost at the very onset of the project. Initially, I did not plan on taping our conversations for fear that even though most of the questions were of a nonsensitive nature, our discussions could result in my asking for information that the subject felt uncomfortable revealing on tape. Or if the subject did speak candidly on tape, he or she might later have serious reservations about having done so. Anxious that I not lose any valuable material, I chose to hand record the first six interviews. As the interviews progressed, however, I realized that I was not only wasting precious time but losing some important nuances of meaning in the rapid flow of normal conversation. At one point I asked my subjects if I could tape record their comments. To my surprise, almost all of them agreed. Although in most instances no verbal assurances on my part seemed necessary, I explained to every subject that upon completion of the transcribing process I would erase the tape so there would be no permanent *audible* record of our conversation.

Most of the interviews took place in neutral settings: either in a restaurant, bar, private auto, college campus, or public park, or at the New York City Gay and Lesbian Center. Others were held either at my apartment or, if the subject suggested it, at his or her residence. Overall, the interviewing sessions went well. Most of my subjects actually appeared anxious to talk with me; some even expressed this feeling during the course of the interview.

The observations of gay men and women in this study took place in a variety of settings. I made most of the observations at GOAL meetings, and some at parties, dinners, dances, gay parades, and other social functions sponsored by the organization. This wide scope enabled me to learn more about the world of the gay cop, while verifying data from the interviews and other sources.

A final data source upon which I drew heavily consisted of written materials: newspaper and magazine articles, NYPD memos, correspondence between GOAL board members and the New York City Police Department, GOAL memos, monthly GOAL newsletters dating back to 1984, and academic studies describing the gay world. These sources provided a wealth of documented information that enabled me to both supplement and cross-check data gained from my interviews and observations.

The Heterosexual Researcher in a Homosexual Setting: Researcher Anxieties

The Question of Misrepresentation of Self As a heterosexual researcher attending exclusively gay police meetings and social functions I was confronted, almost from the outset, with a unique problem; namely, how to present myself when meeting gay cops for the first time. Since GOAL was still in the process of growing and therefore constantly recruiting new members, there was a steady stream of fresh faces at each meeting I attended. Some were members who only occasionally attended these monthly meetings, others were there for the first time to find out what GOAL was all about, and still others were candidates for membership attending their second or third meeting. To many of these new faces, seeing me from across the room for the first time, I must have appeared as just another gay member of GOAL, and therefore one who could be somewhat safely approached and engaged in conversation. Herein lies the question of misrepresentation of self. The fact that I was not homosexual could not be visibly detected by gays who might spontaneously approach me in what they perceived to be a safe setting and quite casually divulge, in their own introductions, potentially harmful biographical information. For example, toward the end of one GOAL meeting in late spring of 1988 a gay cop considering membership came up to me and introduced himself by his first and last name. This officer could only assume that I was just like any other GOAL member—a kindred spirit. After he and I had a brief chat, primarily about the job, I decided to leave so that I could write up the notes I had taken during the meeting. On the way home I remember experiencing some uneasiness about this seemingly innocuous encounter. After mulling over our conversation, I realized that he knew little about me and was completely unaware of my research. I, on the other hand, now knew his name, the precinct where he worked, and the critical fact that he was gay. This bit of information falling into the wrong hands could have had damaging consequences for the officer, for he, as I later discovered, was very much in the closet at work and had only recently mustered up the courage to come out to some of GOAL's members. What disturbed me most about our initial encounter was that he had put himself at risk without even knowing that he had done so. Over the next few days I grappled with the question of whether I should have immediately informed him that I was not gay and then told him of my research. And if so, when and how could I have done this without creating a clumsy, unnatural, and perhaps even offensive encounter? My options were to tell him either at the beginning of our talk, at the end of it, or not at all. By identifying myself and my research interests as soon as we began talking, I would have provided him with a number of alternatives: he could have chosen to speak with me freely, to speak guardedly—not revealing his name and command—or to end the conversation. As I strongly believe that gay cops have the right to decide for themselves whether or not they want to divulge biographical information to an outsider, this would appear to be the most ethical posture. On a more practical level, however, try to imagine meeting a gay cop for the first time at a homosexual gathering and, before he has a chance to state his name, interrupting him to announce both your heterosexuality and your research intentions almost in the same breath. Pulling this kind of introduction off with enough finesse so as not to create a clumsy and potentially embarrassing situation would be nearly impossible. Though this approach would certainly cover me on both fronts, it would, at the very least, be intimidating and make those who continued conversing with me extremely uncomfortable. The second option, not revealing my sexual identity or purpose for attending the meeting until later in the conversation, carries with it the risk that the person speaking with me may have already, unwittingly, divulged personal information that he or she might then regret. Furthermore, this person might feel betrayed by the organization because it let an outsider into this safe inner chamber. The final option, not to say anything at all concerning my research interests or sexual orientation unless directly asked, constitutes, I suspect, a form of misrepresentation. To avoid the problem of possible misrepresentation again, I decided on the following approach: as it was a somewhat established practice at the beginning of each GOAL meeting to offer those present a chance to stand up and introduce themselves, I would take this opportunity to briefly present my research interests. On a few occasions I arranged for a board member, usually the president of GOAL, to do this for me. However, I felt that making a declaration of not being gay might alienate new members and create an uncomfortable atmosphere. After giving this much thought I finally decided to confine my comments to the description of my research project and not to mention my heterosexuality.

While I found this strategy helped avoid the problem of unintentional self-misrepresentation at GOAL meetings, it was of little use at less formal gatherings such as dinners or cocktail parties. At these more casual affairs it was not unusual to find myself engaged in a conversation with someone to whom I had yet to be formally introduced. Though *all* of these gay cops were out socially—that is, within their own homosexual circles—*most* were still quite closeted at work. Clearly, at these social affairs it was both inappropriate and, at times, virtually impossible for me to be formally introduced as a researcher to everyone present.

In this more informal atmosphere, the possibility of a closeted gay officer unwittingly revealing personal information to me was only one facet of the problem of misrepresentation. Cops meeting me for the first time in such an inner circle setting would, quite naturally, feel free to talk not only about themselves, but possibly about other gay members of the police department—members who may not be out enough to attend GOAL meetings—assuming, without prior introduction, that I was gay and consequently someone in whom they could safely confide. The problem here is that officers whose names were mentioned to me might never have chosen to divulge this information to a straight member of the department, especially one who was a ranking officer, whether he was doing research or not. Any gay officer meeting me for the first time and choosing to reveal information to me about someone else would have no way of knowing of my heterosexual identity or of my research intentions unless he or she had been informed beforehand.

This problem surfaced at a dinner party during a spontaneous conversation with a guest to whom I had not been formally introduced. Without exchanging names we casually began to discuss the party, with him readily commenting on the attractiveness and sexual appeal of some of the men present. His casual openness made it clear to me that he assumed I was gay as well. Then, still without having introduced himself, he asked my name and a few moments later asked where I worked. I gave him only my first name, as some closeted gays are inclined to do, and told him that I was a lieutenant and the unit to which I was assigned. Before I had a chance to reveal any more about myself, he casually dropped the names of two officers in *my own* command who he strongly implied were gay. Certainly, I thought, precisely this type of confidential information would never have been so casually divulged to a heterosexual member of the department, whose motive for being at this party might have been suspect. Later in the conversation when I eventually told this officer who I was and explained my research, he displayed no visible reaction to having provided me with potentially damaging information, not only about a brother officer but a member of my command as well. I left the party soon after this conversation, making a mental note to question him at a later date about his feelings at that moment when he realized that he had leaked the names of those still closeted officers. I was concerned that, besides his possible feelings of embarrassment at this indiscreet disclosure, he might also harbor some resentment toward me for not having immediately clarified my status and purpose, as well as resentment toward GOAL for allowing an outsider entry into a social setting in which members and guests were led to believe they were free to express themselves openly. When this type of supposedly protected setting is penetrated by an outsider who has not been identified as such to everyone present, it can have potentially serious consequences for both members and researcher alike.

A Chance Encounter with a Co-Worker It had occurred to me early on in the research that it was possible that I might come upon a closeted member of my own command at a GOAL meeting or social function. Based on the reports by Kinsey, it is estimated that roughly 10 percent of society is homosexually oriented. Knowing this, it would not have come as any surprise if a portion of the 115 cops and supervisors assigned to my command turned out to be homosexual. The question was how I would (or *should*) react if I suddenly encountered one of these officers at a gay function; and, perhaps more importantly, how would the unsuspecting officer react upon seeing me—his or her commanding officer—there. Also, how would we both react in the work situation?

At a GOAL meeting in the late spring of 1988, I was seated in the front row of the meeting room listening to two cops debate the merits of admitting honorary members into the organization when I heard the back door open and turned to see a young officer quietly walk in. It was the first time I had seen this officer at a GOAL meeting but I knew him well. He was a member of my own command. This officer, whom I will call Kevin (not his real name), recognized me and took a seat directly behind me. We briefly exchanged cordial, whispered greetings as he reached out to shake my hand. The appearance of one of my own men did not really surprise me, but I must admit that, even after associating with gay cops for almost a year, I had no previous indication that this officer was gay. So as not to make either one of us feel uncomfortable, I greeted him as matter-of-factly as I could and quickly turned my attention back to the discussion. However, my thoughts were on the officer seated behind me. I kept wondering what he might be thinking and feeling about my unexpected presence at the meeting. Did he, for example, make the obvious assumption that because I was there I, too, was gay? I doubted that he had been informed of my research because he appeared genuinely startled when he first saw me. I felt I had no alternative but to disclose to him, before he left that evening, my purpose for attending the GOAL meeting. While I sat there contemplating the choice of words I would use in my disclosure to Kevin, the officer seated next to me stood up and, in an attempt to resolve the on-going debate on the pros and cons of honorary membership, cited me as an example of just such a member, specifically pointing out that although I *was not gay*, the membership had accepted me because of my research interests. Kevin was now fully aware that he had unwittingly revealed his homosexual identity not only to a heterosexual co-worker, but to his commanding officer as well. I would have given anything to have witnessed and noted his first reaction, but under the circumstances it would have been uncomfortable for both of us for me to turn around. The moment the meeting ended I got up and headed straight for one of the board members with whom I was particularly friendly to ask if he would agree to speak to Kevin about me, thereby, I hoped, allaying any number of fears that he may now have been experiencing. But Kevin had another tack in mind. He had gotten up when I did and, before I reached the board member, tapped me on the shoulder. I turned around to see a very grim-faced Kevin. In a deadly serious voice he confided, "You know, I wish I were dead." I quickly ushered him off to the side where we could talk a little more privately and immediately tried to assure him that I had no intention of divulging his sexual identity to anyone, especially his fellow officers in my command. In attempting to allay the fears that were written all over his face I reiterated the two most salient points I had stressed to GOAL members at earlier meetings: that I personally attached the utmost importance to maintaining high, ethical standards (that is, respecting the anonymity of all those connected with my study), and that I could never reveal his identity to others because that act of betrayal would have the counterproductive result of damaging my credibility with those gay cops whose support was critical in order for me to complete the study. The disclosure of his sexual identity to others, I concluded, would mean a loss for both of us. I then took him over to one of my most supportive members, and, after a few minutes of hearing that member speak enthusiastically about me, Kevin seemed to relax and appear considerably less threatened. What follows is Kevin's account of that encounter related to me several months later once he had become one of my respondents. In his own words, he details his feelings from the moment he entered the room and first saw me sitting there.

I scanned the room as I always do with the anticipation that the wrong person might be there, and lo and behold it came through. Someone was there—you. I immediately said, "Holy shit, I know this guy. It's Steve Leinen, Lieutenant Leinen." I said, "Oh, shit. Lieutenant Leinen's gay. I hope I'm right." Then I said to myself, "What's he thinking, seeing me here?" I was thinking that we were both in the same position. I was completely blown away. "He must be gay," I kept saying. "That's why he's here." I felt he must be feeling the same tension I'm feel-ing. Then [another GOAL member] mentions to the group that Steve's the only straight at the meeting. My immediate reaction—I felt faint. Blood rushed to my head. My heart dropped into my stomach. I think if I had been standing I would have fainted. I felt so embarrassed. I said to myself, "Forget it, it's all over. It's all out now." Then I got angry and said to myself, "What the fuck is he doing here? This place is supposed to be safe. They are letting anyone walk in here." I was so angry. I mentioned this to a guy sitting next to me, and he agreed that this guy [Leinen] did not belong there. He was very angry. I spoke to some other guys during the meeting and asked, "What the fuck is this guy doing here?"

Kevin's reflections underscore a number of key problems related to conducting this sort of research. The sudden presence of an unknown outsider in a guarded social setting, one thought to be exclusively for homosexuals (1) has the potential of triggering feelings of anger, distrust, and betrayal by the organization that permitted the outsider entry; (2) can create, for closeted men and women, the fear that the carefully guarded secret of their identities is unimportant to the organization; and (3) can seriously jeopardize the completion of the research itself. Had this officer com-plained to members of GOAL about the intrusion of an outsider, and those members complained to the board, my access to the group might have ended. Even though the board had formally granted me access to GOAL, under those strained circum-stances, it is conceivable that the board would have had to retract its support for my project, given that the alternative might be a loss of some of its members. For-tunately for me, this never occurred. The more meetings I attended, the more activ-ities I participated in, the more support and encouragement I received for the project. Members who once objected to the research gradually began to rally to my side, although understandably some degree of guarded concern did persist through-out the research.

I add a final note of caution for researchers considering similarly sensitive proj-ects. When an interview has been arranged by a third party (in my case usually a GOAL member who either knew of my research or had previously been interviewed by me), that interview should never be approached with the assumption that the prospective subject has been fully briefed as to the nature of the research. Nor should the researcher automatically assume that the subject has been filled in on the researcher's sexual orientation.

When I first began this project I approached my homosexual subjects with the quite natural assumption that they were as much aware of my sexual orientation as I was of theirs. I also assumed that they were aware that the interview was to be part of the data I would be using for a dissertation. These assumptions proved to be not only erroneous at times but awkward and embarrassing for both myself and the inter-viewee. Twice, for example, while ordering drinks or dinner before the formal in-terviewing stage, I was asked by one of these new subjects about the purpose of the interview. Was it for an article I was writing? Was I simply gratifying my own personal curiosity? Or was it for some other reason? When I explained that I was conducting an in-depth study of the world of the gay police officer for my dissertation, I was greeted with varying degrees of surprise and disappointment.

On three other occasions, besides saying little about my research intentions, the third parties who had set up the interviews failed to inform the new subjects that I was *not* a homosexual. Based upon my interest in meeting and questioning gay cops about their work and social worlds and my nondescript demeanor and self-presentation, these new subjects understandably assumed that I was gay too. In one of these instances the question of my own sexuality was raised by the subject during a break in the interview, an exchange I instigated. When I began to sense his misunderstanding I immediately started to send signals to him that I was straight. Specifically, in conjunction with his comments about gay lovers and some of the gay bars he frequented, I casually responded that I was living with a woman. By using the term *woman* I was sending a far stronger heterosexual message than if I just said I was married, which could have left open the strong possibility of a dual identity. This casual mention of a relationship with a *female* was immediately greeted with the somewhat stunned response, "You're straight! God, I didn't know that!" A similar reaction attended the disclosure of my heterosexuality in another interview. In both cases I hastily apologized and accepted the blame for any misunderstanding or confusion, explaining that I had taken it for granted that the third party had informed them. Fortunately, the revelation of my sexual orientation neither offended any of these subjects nor did it, as far as I could ascertain, interfere with the candor of their responses in the remainder of the interviews. In a third instance, though the interview proceeded comfortably and the subject's responses were quite open from beginning to end, I began to get a gut feeling that once again the individual was mistakenly accepting me as another gay. At a GOAL meeting sometime later, my suspicions were confirmed when this man approached me and said that after I had interviewed him a couple of my earlier respondents had told him that I was straight. In this instance I felt not only embarrassed but to some degree deceptive for not having put all my cards on the table at the outset of the interview, or at least enlightened him when I first began to sense his misunderstanding.

Something positive did emerge, however, from these occasions of unintentional misrepresentation. I learned firsthand, albeit in a very limited sense, what it feels like to find oneself hiding in the shadow of pretense with its associated burden of unjustified guilt. It gave me a poignant and unexpected insight into what it must be like for those truly closeted men and women in policing who daily walk a narrow line, constantly masquerading as something they are not.

The Question of AIDS Transmission and Other Concerns The escalating AIDS, or health, crisis, as many gays now refer to it, has made both straights and gays more aware of and concerned about protecting themselves from this deadly disease. At the same time, unfounded fears based on misinformation can cause heterosexuals to take extreme precautions when interacting with persons in high-risk groups. These include IV drug abusers, prostitutes, homosexual males, and the sex partners of each of these groups. On two occasions, early in the research, my fear of contracting

AIDS surfaced, causing me to take certain precautions that, at the time, I considered necessary. The first occurred at a Christmas affair sponsored by GOAL where I found myself seated at a table with ten gay men. As this was a dinner party among friends, there was some sharing of food and drink. What surprised me most was their communal exchange of glasses, spoons, forks, for it appeared to me they were placing themselves at risk should anyone of them unknowingly be carrying the AIDS virus. The fact that over the past few years several members of GOAL have died from AIDS-related diseases fueled my concern, but as I was not participating in the sharing of food and drink I did not think I was at risk. Toward the end of dinner, however, I was asked to leave the table for a moment to be introduced to a new member of GOAL. I remember, as I got up, casually placing my vodka and tonic near where I was sitting. I did not give anything so trivial a thought until a short time later when I returned to the table and found that I could not be certain which glass was mine. For the first time, I noticed that the drinks on the table were similar in appearance to mine. Fearful that I might put myself at risk by choosing the wrong glass, I decided to go to the bar for a fresh drink. This time I made a point of ordering a vodka and orange, a drink that could easily be distinguished from the other clear-colored beverages should I have to leave mine unattended once again. This marking of my drink also gave me some assurance that none of the other people at the table would pick up *my* glass by mistake.

A similar situation occurred several months later while I was interviewing a member of GOAL. We were seated at a table in a restaurant when, after dinner, I got up and went to the bar to order another round of Bloody Marys. I handed the bartender the two empty glasses and went off to chat with the owner. When I returned to the bar, the drinks were waiting for me. But when I asked the bartender which glass was mine, he couldn't remember. As I carried both drinks to the table, I found myself reflecting back on the Christmas party that past winter where a similar glass mix-up caused me considerable concern. Certainly, had this evening's mix-up occurred several months earlier, I probably would have insisted upon two fresh glasses rather than risk drinking from my subject's glass. However, since that Christmas party I have read much of the literature on AIDS written by leading medical authorities and now realize that my fear of contracting this disease by simply sharing a drinking glass was unfounded. I also believe that as I became more familiar with the homosexual world and as my number of gay contacts grew, my anxieties about contracting this disease through casual social contact diminished.

Profile
of
Officers

The 41 subjects in this study represent a range of biographical backgrounds and positions within law enforcement agencies. It is impossible at this time, however, to generate representative statements concerning the backgrounds of the larger population of gay police in New York City, as the extent and characteristics of this group are virtually unknown. Consequently, the following demographic data are derived solely from the group of men and women who chose to speak with me.

Demographic Characteristics

Age —The largest group of subjects (20) fall between the ages of 25 and 30. Four are younger than 25, and 17 are over 30. These figures are consistent with the general age breakdown of the NYPD in which approximately 11,000 of 26,000, or 42 percent of the cops, are under age 31.[1] Based upon these comparisons I was able to achieve a fairly representative age sample of the larger population of New York City police officers for the study.

Gender, Race, and Ethnic Background —Of the 41 officers interviewed, only 13 were women (as of 1992, 10.3 percent of the membership of the department is female).[2] I did not intend to end up with this relatively small number. Initially, I thought about limiting the study to gay males, fearing that the inclusion of lesbians might complicate the analysis by creating an additional set of gender-related problems, but after some time in the field I was persuaded to include women as well. Some not-so-gentle coaxing on the part of a few of the more knowledgeable male members of GOAL was instrumental in bringing me to the decision that women should be part of the study. It was the view of these men, and one I now share, that because gay women constitute a yet unknown but presumably sizable segment of the homosexual police population in New York City, the lesbian view ought to be added even if gender-related problems surfaced. Once convinced of the need to include their views in the study, I attempted to reach out through my male contacts to lesbian officers. Unfortunately, I experienced some difficulty locating women who were willing to speak to me on the record. As the final figures show, I was only somewhat successful. In retrospect, it is my impression that many lesbian cops do not feel comfortable speaking freely with a heterosexual male about their sexual orientation as it relates to their occupational and especially their personal world. I base this assumption purely on personal intuition buttressed by the comments of two female interviewees. Yet I must also mention that a number of the gay policewomen I interviewed at great length did appear comfortable and at ease talking with me.

As for race and ethnicity, the majority (27) of the respondents were white. Seven were Hispanic and 7 were black. Of the women interviewed, 3 were Hispanic, 1 was black, and 9 were white. Among the ethnic whites, 12 were of Italian extraction, and 15 were of Irish and/or German mix. As approximately 25 percent of all cops in the NYPD are either black or Hispanic, the 14 minority subjects in this study is slightly over-representative of the department's minority population. That, of course, is not meant to imply that racial minorities are over-represented in the New York City gay police population. The above ethnic/racial breakdown merely reflects the chance combination of those officers who made themselves available to be interviewed.

Education —Roughly 4 out of 5 subjects had college backgrounds. This is an interesting finding when set against recent New York City Department of Personnel figures, which show that the percentage of college-educated officers in the NYPD as a whole is only 60 percent. Among the 34 subjects who had pursued a college education, 21 had graduated. Thirteen had not completed their degree programs. At the time of the interviews, however, 9 of the 13 said they were still attending classes and hoped to attain their degrees within the next year or so. Among the 21 who had finished their studies, 3 had degrees in psychology, 7 in criminal justice, 2 each in communications, accounting, and English, and 1 each in police administration and forensic psychology. Of the 3 officers interviewed who possessed graduate degrees there was 1 each in criminal justice, psychology, and education.

Marital Status and Living Arrangements —Only 4 of my respondents had ever been married, and 3 were still living with their wives or husbands at the time of the interview (2 of these officers had children). The fourth was separated from his wife and children.

Most of these men and women lived in private houses. Three resided outside the New York City area—1 in New Jersey and 2 on Long Island. At the time we spoke, 16 were living alone, while 13 shared living space with either a lover or gay roommate. The remaining 12 lived with their parents. Interestingly, of that group, only 2 lived in a household where the father was present. Three had totally separate living arrangements within their parents' home (private entrance, kitchen, bathroom) while 9 chose to share living quarters with their mothers. In two of these cases the fathers were deceased. In most instances, however, where a living father was either separated or divorced from the subject's mother, the officer elected to live with the mother. This finding is consistent with and perhaps related to the nearly unanimous decision on the part of gay male cops whom I interviewed to attempt to conceal their homosexuality from their fathers. The finding that roughly 30 percent of the subjects in this study were currently living with their parents is also consistent with the apparent trend among New York City employed young men and women, both homosexual and heterosexual, to remain in the parental household long after the age in which young men and women are expected to establish their own residences. The decline in available, moderately priced housing in New York City over the past decade is a strong factor and clearly impacted on the decision of many of these men and women to continue living at home.

Working Identities

Just as there are stages in becoming a homosexual (that is, with coming to grips with the fact that one prefers both social and sexual relationships with other homosexuals), there are stages or phases through which gay cops pass in terms of how much information about their homosexuality they release to others in the workplace. At the time of the interviews for this study, fourteen of my subjects were totally closeted. Fifteen were in or moving through the tentatively out stage in their police careers; that is, they had either confided their homosexuality to a partner, were under strong suspicion of being gay due to their reluctance or inability to maintain any longer the pretense of heterosexuality at work, or were suspected of being homosexual as a result of self-initiated clues they had been dropping at work. Twelve of my respondents were completely out.[3] Since the formal interviews ended in 1989, four of the officers that were closeted have disclosed their homosexuality to a close partner (or partners) and four of the tentatively out cops had moved on to the final stage.

Current Positions and Assignments

Among my respondents all but two were working for law enforcement agencies within New York City. These two officers were assigned to small-town departments just a few miles outside the city, in New Jersey. Of those working within New York City, two were with the Department of Corrections, one was with the Housing Authority Police Department, seven were assigned to the Transit Authority Police Department, and the remainder worked for the NYPD.

As for rank, six were sergeants, one was a lieutenant, and one had achieved the position of deputy warden with the Corrections Department, a rank equivalent in status to lieutenant in the NYPD. Though I have been assured by members of GOAL that they know of gays who hold higher ranking positions in these law enforcement agencies, I was unable to include any in this study because these officers refused to meet with me. I can only speculate on the reasons for their reluctance, but I suspect that because they anticipated climbing even higher in their department's rank structure they did not want to jeopardize these future positions by revealing their homosexuality to a stranger, even if they had been assured by other gay cops that this stranger was someone who could be trusted.[4] As advancement above the rank of captain is not determined by objective scoring procedures (as is the case with lower-level civil service positions), their concerns about being passed over for promotions because of discovered homosexuality can be understood.

Appointments to these positions (for instance, deputy inspector, full inspector, deputy chief) are made by the police commissioner's promotional review board with his approval. It is common knowledge among ranking personnel in the NYPD that the commissioner's review board need not provide a promotional candidate occupying a position of captain or above with a *reason* for passing him or her over. Caution, I have been assured, is the key word among those homosexual bosses who aspire to higher positions in New York City's police agencies. As one ranking officer told me,

They can't fuck with me now. But they can when I make captain. I could easily wind up spending the next ten years waiting to make D.I. [deputy inspector] and never really finding out what's holding things up. They can fuck with you all they want then. . . . That's why, personally, I'm still in the closet. And that's why I'm gonna stay there unless I don't ever make captain. Then I won't give a fuck what they do.

As for individual job designations, 11 of the nonranking officers interviewed were assigned to special plainclothes units, while 4 performed detective investigative functions. The remainder were uniformed officers assigned to precincts or other police commands. Among the 12 men and women who were, at the time of the interviews, publicly out of the closet in their respective commands, 7 either held ranking positions or were assigned to more prestigious plainclothes units. This breakdown suggests that openly gay officers are *not* confined to bottom-level patrol assignments or placed in other units where they are hidden from public view. Nor are openly gay officers in the NYPD denied promotions up through the rank of captain simply because of their sexual orientation.

Notes

I. Introduction: "Gay and Proud of It"

1   For excerpts of the speech, see *New York Native*, December 7–21, 1981.
2   See also, Alex Thio, *Deviant Behavior* (New York: Harper & Row, 1988), p. 225; Alan Bell and Martin Weinberg, *Homosexualities: A Study of Diversity among Men and Women* (New York: Simon & Schuster, 1978), p. 230.
3   Donna Minkowitz, "Uncaged Heat," *Village Voice*, January 15, 1991; see also Kenneth Plummer, *Sexual Stigma: An Interactionist Account* (London: Routledge & Kegan Paul, 1975).
4   Michael Goodwin, "A Tough Month in the New Life of a Policeman," *New York Times*, December 5, 1981.
5   On the Bay Area, Bell and Weinberg, *Homosexualities*, pp. 64–66. Martin Weinberg and Colin Williams, *Male Homosexuals: Their Problems and Adaptations* (New York: Penguin, 1974), p. 127. On false biographies and selective disclosure, see Plummer, *Sexual Stigma*; Stanford Lyman and Marvin Scott, *A Sociology of the Absurd* (New York: Appleton-Century-Crofts, 1970); Saul Feldman, *Deciphering Deviance* (Boston: Little, Brown, 1978). On specific cover-up strategies, see J. Carrier, "Family Attitudes and Mexican American Male Homosexuality," *Urban Life* 50 (October 1976): 359–375; Barbara Ponse, "Secrecy in the Lesbian World," *Urban Life* 50 (October 1976): 313–338; Weinberg and Williams, *Male Homosexuals*; Richard Zoglin, "The Homosexual Executive," in Martin Levine (ed.), *Gay Men: The Sociology of Male Homosexuality* (New York: Harper & Row, 1979), pp. 68–77.
6   Joseph Schneider and Peter Conrad, *Having Epilepsy: The Experience and Control of Illness* (Philadelphia: Temple University Press, 1983), pp. 158–162. Zoglin, "Homosexual Executive," p. 72.
7   Laud Humphreys, *Tea Room Trade: Impersonal Sex in Public Places* (New York: Aldine, 1970), p. 44.

2. Recruiting Gay Cops

1   Nicholas Alex, *Black in Blue: A Study of the Negro Policeman* (New York: Appleton-Century-Crofts, 1969), pp. 26–31.
2   *GOAL Gazette*, July 1990.
3   On the IACP stance, see "Gay Police," *New Jersey Record*, August 12, 1979; see also Erdwin Pfuhl, Jr., *The Deviance Process* (New York: Van Nostrand, 1980), p. 224. Angrissani is quoted in "San Francisco Recruiting Gay Police Officers," *New Jersey Record*, April 10, 1979.
4   Cynthia R. Fagen quotes Caruso in "Cops Will Fight Hiring of Gays," *New York Post*, October 10, 1984. The PBA quote appeared in the *Chief-Leader*, November 2, 1984 (reprinted in the *GOAL Gazette*, November 1984).
5   Larry Celona and Ruth Landa quote the Shomrim and Emerald society speakers in "Cop Units Hit Gay Recruitment," *Daily News*, May 19, 1987. On the COPS booklet, *GOAL Gazette*, September 1989; for a discussion of COPS see *New York Newsday*, November 21, 1990.
6   Mary Ann Giordano, "I Am Proud of Being Gay: Cop Asks Passage of Rights Bill," *Daily News*, November 21, 1981.

7   See "San Francisco Recruiting," *New Jersey Record*, April 10, 1979; and "Gays to Teach at Police Academy," *New Jersey Record*, February 17, 1982.

8   Eugene Levitt and Albert Klassen, "Public Attitudes toward Sexual Behaviors: The Latest Investigation of the Institute for Sex Research," in Weinberg and Williams, *Male Homosexuals*.

9   On Dallas and Chicago, *GOAL Gazette*, July 1990; Steven Petrow, "True Blues; Gay and Lesbian Cops Battle the Closet," *Advocate*, January 29, 1991. On New Jersey, Jeff Simmons, "In N.J., Uniforms Dare Not Come Out of the Closet," *New Jersey Record*, July 29, 1987, and "Why Cops Stay in the Closet," *New Jersey Monthly*, August 1992.

10 Giordano, in "Proud of Being Gay," quotes Koch. On recruiting gays, Patricia Wen, "Gay Police—New York's Experience Is Called Largely Positive," *Boston Globe*, March 24, 1987; Giordano. For the ten cities, Wen, "L.A. Cops Recruiting at Gay Festival," *New York Post*, June 20, 1991; *GOAL Gazette*, October 1986. On other cities' policies, Linda Wheeler, "Two Cops Who Fight Crime and Prejudice," *New Jersey Record*, March 2, 1983; *GOAL Gazette*, November 1988.

11 See "NYPD Recruiting Lesbians and Gays," *Village Voice*, May 20, 1987. On no admittedly gay officers, Wen, "Gay Police."

12 *GOAL Gazette*, October 1986 and February 1991 on Atlanta, September 1989 on Philadelphia. On Los Angeles, see "L.A. Cops Recruiting." On San Francisco, see Petrow, "True Blues," and "Gay Police."

13 Fagen, in "Cops Will Fight," quotes the EEOU head; Celona and Landa, in "Cop Units," quote the assistant commissioner. The GOAL quote appears in a memo sent to the police commissioner from GOAL in May of 1987 commending the NYPD on its efforts to reach out into the gay community for candidates.

14 *GOAL Gazette*, November 1984; Cynthia R. Fagen, "Gay Cop Blasts PBA Boss," *New York Post*, October 11, 1984.

15 See *GOAL Gazette*, especially the November 1989 issue.

3. Taking on a Doubly Deviant Identity

1   Charlie Cochrane is quoted in Robert Massa, "One of New York's Finest," *Village Voice*, December 1, 1981.

2   See Plummer, *Sexual Stigma*, pp. 135–153.

3   William Dubay, *Gay Identity: The Self under Ban* (Jefferson, N.C.: McFarland, 1987), chap. 3.

4   Massa, "New York's Finest."

5   Stephen Leinen, *Black Police, White Society* (New York: New York University Press, 1984).

6   See George Kirkham and Laurin Wollan, *Introduction to Law Enforcement* (New York: Harper & Row, 1980), pp. 332–364; Richard Lundman, "Police Patrol Work: A Comparative Perspective," in Richard Lundman (ed.), *Police Behavior: A Sociological Perspective* (New York: Oxford University Press, 1980).

7   Joe Nicholson, "Police Dept. Woos Gays in New Hiring Drive," *New York Post*, October 9, 1984.

4. What It Means to Be Gay and a Cop

1   See Susan Ehrlich Martin, *Breaking and Entering: Police Women on Patrol* (Los Angeles: University of California Press, 1980).

2   Ibid.; see also Alex, *Black in Blue*.

3   Schneider and Conrad, *Having Epilepsy*, pp. 71–72.
4   See Zoglin, "The Homosexual Executive"; Weinberg and Williams, *Male Homosexuals*, pp. 207, 258.
5   Massa, "New York's Finest"; Sharon Rosenthal, "Charlie Cochrane Takes His Stand—He's the First New York City Cop to Announce That He's Gay," *Daily News*, December 16, 1981; Fagen, "Cops Will Fight."
6   Mike McAlary quotes the ex-cop in "This Irishman Had a Gay Old Time," *Daily News*, June 30, 1989. The other two quotes appear in Wen, "Gay Police."
7   The article to which this officer was referring, printed in the *Boston Globe*, March 24, 1987, was later sent to me.
8   *GOAL Gazette*, November 1988.
9   Petrow, "True Blues."
10 *GOAL Gazette*, June 1988.
11 Petrow, "True Blues."
12 Ibid.
13 Wen, "Gay Police."
14 On the myth, see Thio, *Deviant Behavior*, p. 225.
15 See, for a discussion of the conflict between gender norms and occupation, Anthony Astrachan, *How Men Feel: Their Response to Women's Demands for Equality and Power* (New York: Anchor, 1988); Martin, *Breaking and Entering*.
16 See also the discussion by Martin (*Breaking and Entering*, p. 75) concerning the interaction between race and gender as it affects the expectations of black female police officers.
17 See Plummer, *Sexual Stigma*.

5. Staying in the Closet

1   Simmons, "In N.J."
2   Kinsey is quoted in Guy Hocquenghem, . . . *Homosexual Desire* . . . (London: Allison & Busby, 1978). Erving Goffman, *Stigma: Notes on the Management of Spoiled Identity* (Englewood Cliffs, N.J.: Prentice-Hall, 1963), p. 42.
3   See also Plummer, *Sexual Stigma*, p. 96.
4   See Pfuhl, *The Deviance Process*, pp. 249–250; Zoglin, "The Homosexual Executive."
5   Leinen, *Black Police, White Society*.
6   Rosenthal, "Charlie Cochran."
7   Denise Barricklow, "Lesbian Cops vs. Closet and Peers," *NYQ*, March 22, 1992.
8   Ibid.
9   Michelangelo Signorile, "True Blue," *Out Week*, December 10, 1989.
10 Simmons, "Why Cops Stay in."
11 Donatella Lorch, "Openly Gay in Blue: Officers Tread Warily," *New York Times Metro*, July 13, 1992.
12 On stigma symbols, Goffman, *Stigma*. See also Pfuhl, *The Deviance Process*, pp. 250, 252; Zoglin, *The Homosexual Executive*; Plummer, *Sexual Stigma*; Stuart Hills, *Demystifying Social Deviance* (New York: McGraw-Hill, 1980); Jerry Simmons, *Deviants* (California: Glendessary, 1969); John Reid, "The Best Little Boy in the World Has a Secret," in Erich Goode and Richard Troiden (eds.), *Sexual Deviance and Sexual Deviants* (New York: Morrow, 1974).
13 Plummer, *Sexual Stigma*, p. 193.
14 Martin, *Breaking and Entering*, p. 97; Clifton Bryant, *Sexual Deviancy in Social Context* (New York: New Viewpoints, 1977), p. 4.
15 Barricklow, "Lesbian Cops."
16 Goffman, *Stigma*.

17   Arnold Bierenbaum and Edward Sagarin, *Norms and Human Behavior* (New York: Praeger, 1976), p. 135.

18   See Humphreys, *Tea Room Trade*, pp. 84–87.

19   Martin Hoffman, *The Gay World* (New York: Bantam, 1968), pp. 167–184; Evelyn Hooker, "The Homosexual Community," and Nancy Achilles, "The Development of the Homosexual Bar as an Institution," both in John Gagnon and William Simon (eds.), *Sexual Deviance* (New York: Harper & Row, 1967).

6. Coming Out Tentatively at Work

1   See Everett C. Hughes, "Dilemmas and Contradictions of Status," *American Journal of Sociology* 50 (March 1945): 353–359; Howard S. Becker, *Outsiders: Studies in the Sociology of Deviance* (New York: Free Press, 1963); Signorile, "True Blue."

2   See also Johnathan Rubinstein, *City Police* (New York: Farrar, Straus & Giroux, 1973), pp. 266–277.

3   On the good cop, see also Kirkham and Wollan, *Introduction to Law Enforcement*, pp. 357–363; Taylor Buckner, "Transformations of Reality in the Legal Process," in Thomas Luckmann (ed.), *Phenomenology and Sociology* (Middlesex, England: Penguin, 1978); Jennifer Hunt, "The Development of Rapport through the Negotiation of Gender in Fieldwork among Police," *Human Organization* 43 (1984); William Westley, "Secrecy and the police," in Arthur Niederhoffer and Abraham Blumberg (eds.), *The Ambivalent Force: Perspectives on the Police* (San Francisco: Rinehart Press, 1973), p. 131. Timothy Egan quotes the Portland chief in "Chief of Police Becomes the Target in an Oregon Anti-Gay Campaign," *New York Times*, October 4, 1992. On resulting rejection, see Martin, *Breaking and Entering*, pp. 85–88.

4   Bierenbaum and Sagarin, *Norms and Human Behavior*, p. 129.

5   Goffman, *Stigma*.

6   Quote by Charlie Cochrane in *GOAL Gazette*, October 1988.

7   Jim Mitteager, "NYPD's Gay Cops," *National Centurion*, February 1984.

7. Coming Out Publicly at Work

1   *GOAL Gazette*, June 1984.

2   George Weinberg, *Society and the Healthy Homosexual* (New York: Anchor, 1973), p. 124.

3   See also Wen, "Gay Police."

4   See Plummer, *Sexual Stigma*, p. 81.

5   See also Signorile, "True Blue."

6   See Jennifer Crocker and Neil Lutsky, "Stigma and the Dynamics of Social Cognition," in Stephen Ainlay et al. (eds.), *The Dilemma of Difference* (New York: Plenum, 1986), chap. 6.

7   See also Wen, "Gay Police," and Signorile, "True Blue."

8   See I. Katz, *Stigma: A Social Psychological Analysis* (New Jersey: Erlbaum, 1981).

9   See Alex, *Black in Blue*; Leinen, *Black Police, White Society*.

10   Nicholas Alex, *New York Cops Talk Back: A Study of a Beleaguered Minority* (New York: Wiley, 1976).

11   Bierenbaum and Sagarin, *Norms and Human Behavior*, pp. 108–109; the first quote is from Erving Goffman.

12   See Lorch, "Openly Gay in Blue."

13   Ibid.

14   See Crocker and Lutsky, "Stigma," p. 100.

15   I benefited immensely in these concluding statements from the comments of Christina
      Spellman, a colleague at New York University.

8. The Off-Duty World of Gay Cops

1   On camaraderie outside work, see Martin, *Breaking and Entering*, p. 85. On expectations
      of shared social activities, Kirkham and Wollan, *Introduction to Law Enforcement*, p. 361.

2   Rosenthal, "Charlie Cochrane."

3   See Leinen, *Black Police, White Society.*

4   Quoted in George Heymont, "California Style—New York Style," *Stallion*, September
      1984.

5   Wertheimer is quoted in "There's No Excuse for Bias Violence," *New York Post*, May 6,
      1988. See also Laud Humphreys, *Out of the Closets: The Sociology of Homosexual Libera-
      tion* (Englewood Cliffs, N.J.: Prentice-Hall, 1972), p. 25; Bell and Weinberg, *Homosex-
      ualities*, p. 188; Kirkham and Wollan, *Introduction to Law Enforcement*, p. 99.

6   Quoted in McCaffrey, *The Homosexual Dialectic*, pp. 66–67; see also Bell and Weinberg,
      Homosexualities, pp. 73–74; Dennis Altman, *Homosexual: Oppression and Liberation*
      (New York: Avon, 1971), pp. 24–25; Gary Marx, "Ironies of Social Control," *Social Prob-
      lems* 28 (February 1981), pp. 221–246.

7   This I found to be especially true of the uninitiated closeted cop who has only recently
      acknowledged his or her homosexuality to self and is a relative novice in the cruising
      scene.

8   See Donald Webster Cory, *The Homosexual in America: A Subjective Approach* (New
      York: Greenberg, 1951); Achilles, "Development of the Homosexual Bar"; Jack Hed-
      blom, "The Female Homosexual: Social and Attitudinal Dimensions," in McCaffrey, *The
      Homosexual Dialectic*; Evelyn Hooker, "The Homosexual Community," in Gagnon and
      Simon, *Sexual Deviance.*

9   Hoffman, *The Gay World*, p. 60; Weinberg and Williams, *Male Homosexuals*, p. 45. Bell
      and Weinberg, *Homosexualities*, p. 73.

10   Hoffman, *The Gay World*, p. 191.

11   Signorile, "True Blue."

12   See McCaffrey, *The Homosexual Dialectic*, p. 140, and Hedblom, "The Female Homosex-
      ual," p. 48.

13   See Signorile, "True Blue."

14   Ibid.

15   See *New York Post*, January 26, 1990.

16   On gay males, Humphreys, *Tea Room Trade*; Charles Silverstein, *Man to Man: Gay
      Couples in America* (New York: Morrow, 1981). Hedblom, "The Female Homosexual,"
      p. 42.

17   See also Peter Fisher, *The Gay Mystique* (New York: Stein & Day, 1972); Howard Brown,
      Familiar Faces, Hidden Lives: A Story of Homosexual Men in America Today (New York:
      Harcourt Brace Jovanovich, 1976); Hooker, "Male Homosexuals and Their World."

18   Quoted in Humphreys, *Out of the Closets*, p. 116. See also Weinberg and Williams, *Male
      Homosexuals*, p. 309; Hoffman, *The Gay World*, p. 187.

19   See also Hocquenghem, . . . *Homosexual Desire* . . . , p. 94; Goode and Troiden, *Sexual
      Deviance and Sexual Deviants.*

20   Hoffman, *The Gay World*, p. 153.

21   Bell and Weinberg, *Homosexualities*, p. 83. Barry Dank, "The Homosexual," in Goode
      and Troiden, *Sexual Deviance and Sexual Deviants*, p. 188. See also Hoffman, *The Gay
      World*, p. 42.

22   Thio, *Deviant Behavior*, p. 225; see also Bell and Weinberg, *Homosexualities*, p. 84; Dank,
      "The Homosexual," p. 187.

9. Coming Out to Family

1   See also Weinberg and Williams, *Male Homosexuals*, p. 338.
2   Goffman, *Stigma*.
3   Ibid.; Pfuhl, *The Deviance Process*, p. 253.
4   See similar findings in Bell and Weinberg, *Homosexualities*, pp. 62–65, and in Sue Kiefer Hammersmith, "A Sociological Approach to Counseling Homosexual Clients and their Families," *Journal of Homosexuality* 14 (1987): 173–190.
5   See also Merle Miller, "What it Means to Be Homosexual," *New York Times Magazine*, January 17, 1971.
6   See also Peter Wildeblood, *Against the Law* (New York: Penguin, 1957), p. 37.
7   Goffman, *Stigma*.

10. Summary: The Challenge of Coming Out

1   See Eli Coleman, "Developmental Stages of the Coming Out Process," *American Behavioral Scientist* 25 (March/April 1986): 222.
2   See Goffman, *Stigma*, p. 32.
3   See Martin, *Breaking and Entering*; Alex, *Black in Blue*; Alex, *New York Cops Talk Back*.
4   On stigma management, see especially Goffman, *Stigma*; Humphreys, *Out of the Closets*, chap. 8; Plummer, *Sexual Stigma*. On avoiding "stigma symbols," Pfuhl, *The Deviance Process*, p. 250. On the handicapped, see Frederick Gibbons, "Stigma and Interpersonal Relationships," in Ainlay et al., *The Dilemma of Difference*, p. 138. On shunning other gays, Zoglin, "The Homosexual Executive."
5   See Rodney Karr, "Homosexual Labeling and The Male Role," *Journal of Social Issues* 34 (1978): 73–83; ibid.
6   On ostracism, see Martin, *Breaking and Entering*, p. 205. On resistance to change, Alex, *New York Cops Talk Back*, chap. 3. On questionable loyalties, see Leinen, *Black Police, White Society*, Martin, and Alex.
7   The quote is from Larry Martin, "Stigma: A Social Learning Perspective," in Ainlay et al., *The Dilemma of Difference*, p. 153. On the utility of rejection, see Karr, "Homosexual Labeling," pp. 81–82; S. Taylor, "Adjustment to Threatening Events: A Theory of Cognitive Adaptation," *American Psychologist* 38 (1983): 1161–1173; Crocker and Lutsky, "Stigma"; Coleman, "Developmental Stages," chap. 11. On the benefits of devaluation, see Edwin Schur, *Labeling Women Deviant: Gender, Stigma, and Social Control* (New York: Random House, 1984), p. 237.
8   See Goffman, *Stigma*; Edward Sagarin, *Deviants and Deviance: An Introduction to the Study of Devalued People and Behavior* (New York: Praeger, 1975); B. A. Wright, *Physical Disability: A Psychological Approach* (New York: Harper & Row, 1983). On the influence of social stereotypes on followers, see Katz, *Stigma*; S. E. Taylor and S. T. Fiske, "Salience, Attention, and Attribution: Top-of-the-Head Phenomena," in L. Berkowitz (ed.), *Advances in Experimental Social Psychology* (New York: Academic Press, 1978), pp. 250–288. On isolation and ignorance as reinforcing of stereotypes, see Jennifer Crocker and Neil Lutsky, "Stigma."
9   On police bonding and so on, Arthur Niederhoffer, *Behind the Shield: The Police in Urban Society* (New York: Doubleday, 1969); Leinen, *Black Police, White Society*. On managing their identities, see Goffman, *Stigma*.
10 On the stages, see, for example, Barry Dank, "Coming Out in the Gay World," *Psychiatry* 34 (May 1971); Richard Troiden, "Becoming Homosexual: A Model of Gay Identity Acquisition," *Psychiatry* 42 (November 1979): 362–373; William Simon and John Gagnon, "The Lesbians: A Preliminary Overview," in Gagnon and Simon, *Sexual Deviance*; Plum-

mer, *Sexual Stigma*; Coleman, "Developmental Stages." See, for an exception that deals with stages in the workplace, Zoglin, "The Homosexual Executive."

11 See George Herbert Mead, *Mind, Self, and Society* (Chicago: University of Chicago Press, 1934); Schneider and Conrad, *Having Epilepsy*.

12 See, for example, Becker, *Outsiders*; Edwin Lemert, *Social Pathology* (New York: McGraw-Hill, 1951); R. M. Kanter, *Men and Women of the Corporation* (New York: Basic Books, 1979).

13 See Coleman, "Developmental Stages," pp. 220–221; E. Jones et al., *Social Stigma: The Psychology of Marked Relationships* (New York: Freeman, 1984); K. Rasinski et al., "Another Look at Sex Stereotypes and Social Adjustment," *Journal of Personality and Social Psychology* 49 (1985): 317–326; Fred Davis, "Deviance Disavowal: The Management of Strained Interaction by the Visibly Handicapped," *Social Problems* 9 (Fall 1961): 120–132.

14 On high-action vs. low-action duty, see also Hunt, "Development of Rapport." On change in perceived status, see also Davis, "Deviance Disavowal"; Leinen, *Black Police, White Society*.

15 On work pressures to conform, see Mark Stafford and Richard Scott, "Stigma, Deviance, and Social Control: Some Conceptual Issues," in Ainlay et al., *The Dilemma of Difference*. On blameworthiness, Jones et al., *Social Stigma*; Eliot Freidson, "Disability as Social Deviance," in Marvin Sussman (ed.), *Sociology and Rehabilitation* (Washington, D.C.: American Sociological Association, 1965). On gentlemanly deviance, Goffman, *Stigma*, pp. 110–111.

16 Plummer, *Sexual Stigma*, p. 102; Ainlay et al., *The Dilemma of Difference*, chap. 1; Gaylene Becker and Regina Arnold, "Stigma as a Social and Cultural Construct," in Ainlay et al., *The Dilemma of Difference*, chap. 3.

17 Goffman, *Stigma*, p. 81. Martin Levine, "Gay Ghetto," in Levine, *Gay Men*. David Matza, *Becoming Deviant* (Englewood Cliffs, N.J.: Prentice-Hall, 1969), p. 150.

18 See Signorile, "True Blue."

19 See Schur, *Labeling Women Deviant*, pp. 30, 238.

20 Edward Delph, *The Silent Community: Public Homosexual Encounters* (Beverly Hills, Calif.: Sage, 1978); Humphreys, *Tea Room Trade*.

21 See Weinberg and Williams, *Male Homosexuals*; James Spada, *The Spada Report* (New York: Signet, 1979), pp. 176–185; Karla Jay and Allen Young, *The Gay Report* (New York: Summit, 1977), pp. 339–354; Joseph Harry, *Gay Couples* (New York: Praeger, 1984), p. 102.

22 On the permanence of gay relationships and reasons therefor, Bell and Weinberg, *Homosexualities*, pp. 82–83, 102. On the job's effect on normal socializing, Kirkham and Wollan, *Introduction to Law Enforcement*, p. 373; Arthur Niederhoffer and Elaine Niederhoffer, "Policemen's Wives: The Blue Connection," in Niederhoffer and Blumberg, *The Ambivalent Force*. On the effects of possible infidelity, see Harry, *Gay Couples*; Rex Reece, "Coping with Couplehood," in Levine, *Gay Men*, pp. 211–221. On beliefs regarding gays' maladjustment, Bell and Weinberg, *Homosexualities*, p. 102.

23 Weinberg and Williams, *Male Homosexuals*, p. 338.

24 See, for example, Hills, *Demystifying Social Deviance*, p. 183.

25 See also Weinberg and Williams, *Male Homosexuals*.

26 See also Ponse, "Secrecy in the Lesbian World," pp. 323–326; Carrier, "Family Attitudes," p. 317.

27 On fear of contamination, see also Weinberg, *Society and the Healthy Homosexual*, pp. 93–108; Frederick Gibbons, "Stigma and Interpersonal Relationships," in Ainlay et al., *The Dilemma of Difference*, pp. 126–127. On fear of losing family love, see also Dubay, *Gay Identity*.

28 Pfuhl, *The Deviance Process*, p. 254.

29 See also Weinberg, *Society and the Healthy Homosexual*, pp. 91–119.

30 See Dubay, *Gay Identity*, chap. 5.

31 Fagen, "Cops Will Fight."

32 See Hills, *Demystifying Social Deviance*, p. 181.

33 Mike Santangelo, "Badge: Marching with New York's Gay Cops," *Daily News Magazine*, June 24, 1990.

34 See Zoglin, "The Homosexual Executive"; Weinberg and Williams, *Male Homosexuals*.

35 Much of this discussion was recorded in a conversation with Sam Ciccone, then executive director of GOAL.

Entering the World of the Gay Officer

1 See William Shaffir et al., *Fieldwork Experience: Qualitative Approaches to Social Research* (New York: St. Martin's, 1980), p. 23; John Lofland and Lyn Lofland, *Analyzing Social Settings: A Guide to Qualitative Observation and Analysis*, 2d ed. (Belmont, Calif.: Wadsworth, 1984), p. 25.

2 For a discussion of researcher as social critic or spy see John Van Maanen, "Epilogue: On Watching the Watchers," in Peter Manning and John Van Maanen (eds.), *Policing: A View from the Street* (Santa Monica, Calif.: Goodyear, 1978), p. 316; Martin, *Breaking and Entering*, p. 225.

3 See Lofland and Lofland, *Analyzing Social Settings*, p. 25; Shaffir et al., *Fieldwork Experience*, p. 23.

4 See John Van Maanen, "Reclaiming Qualitative Methods for Organizational Research," in John Van Maanen (ed.), *Qualitative Methodology* (Beverly Hills, Calif.: Sage, 1983); Hoffman, *The Gay World*, p. 8; Jack Douglas, *Creative Interviewing* (Beverly Hills, Calif.: Sage, 1985).

Profile of Officers

1 NYPD Personnel Bureau Report, 1990.

2 NYPD Personnel and Data Section, 1992.

3 See also *New York Newsday*, August 13, 1987.

4 See also Weinberg and Williams, *Male Homosexuals*, pp. 318-319.

Index

Acquired Immune Deficiency Syndrome
(AIDS), *4, 35, 189, 204*; gay cops' fears of,
56, 61, 160–163, 166, 210; and the homo-
phobia of cops, *58–59, 60, 82, 117*
Advocate, 36
AIDS, *see* Acquired Immune Deficiency Syn-
drome
Angrissani, Robert, *8*
Atlanta, Ga., *11, 12*

Bell, Alan, *133, 171, 211*
black cops, *7*; compared to gay cops, *2, 8,
14, 43, 109–110, 124*; lesbian, *117, 203*
Boston, Mass., *12*
Boston Lesbian and Gay Political Alliance,
12

Caruso, Phil, *8–9*
Central Rabbinical Congress, *10*
Chicago, Ill., *37, 196*
Chief-Leader (NYC), *8*
closeted gay cops: and career choice, *28–29,
30–31*; and coming out (*see* coming out);
and cruising (*see* cruising); and discrimination against gays by cops, *14–15, 37–
40, 43, 66, 197*; and family (*see* family);
harassment of, *41*; identity management
of, *47*; invisibility of, *3, 13–14, 47–48*; and
long-term relationships (*see* long-term relationships); motives for remaining, *2, 27–
28, 34, 45, 48–62, 154–155, 215–216*;
and occupational disclosure (*see* occupational disclosure); strategies used by, *5,
62–71, 83, 89, 91, 197–198, 212*; suspected by co-workers, *83–89*
Cochrane, Charlie, *1, 3, 17, 44*; on closeted
gay cops, *3*; coming out of, *2, 5, 94, 102,
103, 195*; fears about coming out of, *53*;
on gay ranking officers, *214–215*; social
world of, *123*
coming out, *xii*, and authority held by gay
cops, *87–88, 99–100, 105, 120, 214*; benefits of, *14, 15, 214–215, 216*; as burden to
informed straight partners, *81–82, 114–
115*; as a cop to gays (*see* occupational disclosure); to family (*see under* family); and
moral righteousness, *95, 100, 109–110,
111–112, 202*; motives for, *74–78, 95, 97–*

102; and political consciousness, *100–
102, 216*; publicly, *85–86, 89, 97, 120*; reactions of individuals to, *75, 76, 77, 81–
82, 89–96, 105–106, 202, 214*; reactions
of the precinct to, *2, 39, 105–109, 113–
116, 118–120, 200, 202, 214*; selectively,
*5, 71, 72–73, 79, 80–82, 85, 89, 97, 120,
201, 202*; stages of, *46–47, 72–73, 81,
201*; strategies used in, *72–73, 86–89,
102–105, 201–202*
Community of Police Societies (COPS), *9*
Conrad, Peter, *33*
cops (*see also* law enforcement): black (*see*
black cops); and the black community, *7,
19*; camaraderie among, *50, 64–65, 78,
105, 119–120, 121, 122, 198, 200, 214*;
crimes reported by, while off-duty, *125–
126, 147*; good cop status of, *78–81, 89,
93, 95–96, 114, 203*; leisure activities of,
122, 200, 205; media portrayal of, *19, 24,
26, 121, 134, 136*; peer pressure among,
119–120; treatment of gays, *7, 14–15, 24,
35–36, 37–40, 45, 66, 88, 119, 124, 193,
197*; viewed by gays (*see* gays: views on
cops); views on gays, *xi, 3, 8–9, 10, 48,
117–118, 119, 194, 196, 197, 199–200*
COPS, *see* Community of Police Societies
cruising: and AIDS, *160–163*; crimes witnessed by gay cops while, *105, 126–133,
147, 192–193, 206, 209–210*; in gay locales, *125, 133–134*; guns safeguarded
while, *155–157, 208–209*; in nonconventional locales, *124–133*; and occupational
disclosure (*see* occupational disclosure);
recognition by straight cops avoided
while, *67–71, 85, 159, 196, 205*; victimization avoided while, *148–163, 165, 205,
206, 207–210*

Daily News (NYC), *11*
Dallas, Tex., *11*
Dank, Barry, *171*
Detroit Police Department, *35*

family: coming out to, *180–183, 193, 211,
213*; homophobia in, *213*; and identity
management, *175, 193*; lovers' treatment
by, *190–192*; motives for secrecy from, *213*;

family (continued)
    reactions to coming out, *175, 176, 183–192, 193, 211, 213, 214*; secrecy maintained concerning gayness, *176–178, 193*; strategies to avoid disclosure to, *211–212*; suspicions of homosexuality in, *178–180, 212–213*

gay activism, *xi, 95, 109–112, 216*; and the conflict between police and the gay community, *7, 15*; gay cops hired as result of, *7–10, 11–15*
Gay and Lesbian Police Advisory Task Force, *12*
Gay and Lesbian Pride Festival, *12*
gay cops (*see also* lesbian cops): attractiveness to gays of, *134, 135–137, 138–139, 166, 172, 193, 206*; closeted (*see* closeted gay cops); coming out of the closet (*see* coming out); compared to other minorities, *14, 95, 109, 175, 194–195, 197, 198, 199, 207, 216* (*see also* black cops, compared to gay cops); and cruising (*see* crusing); and the development of sexual identity, *16–19*; and discrimination against gays, *14–15, 37–40, 43*; families of (*see* family); fears of aging of, *165–166*; as good cops, *47, 78–81, 91, 93–94, 95–96, 101, 105–109, 110, 113–114, 119, 124, 202–203, 214*; harassment of, *35, 40–44*; heterosexual relationships maintained by, *17, 18, 19, 76*; hired as result of gay activism, *7–10, 11–15*; history of, *195–196*; and homophobia in law enforcement, *27–31, 39–45, 47–49, 52–53, 109, 171, 189, 193, 194, 197*; and homosexual militancy, *95, 109–112, 216*; humor employed by, *112–113*; identity management of, *xi–xii, 1, 4, 5–6, 46–47, 71, 78, 120, 123–124, 163, 175, 192–193, 195, 198–201, 203, 213–214*; language used by, *121*; leisure activities of, *66, 122, 200, 205* (*see also* cruising); and long-term relationships (*see* long-term relationships); low profiles maintained regarding homosexuality of, *5, 110–112, 204*; masculinity and/or femininity of, *50, 67, 91*; media portrayal of, *34–37*; motivation for career choice of, *20–27, 30, 196*; numbers of, *14, 215*; and occupational disclosure (*see* occupational disclosure); perception-action linkage in world of, *78, 80, 193, 201*; social identities of, *xii, 123, 163, 192–193* (*see also* cruising; occupational disclosure); status

conflict of (*see* status conflict); straight cops' support of, *37, 114* (*see also* coming out, reactions to)
Gay Officers Action League (GOAL), *3, 43, 53, 181*; and coming out, *15, 215*; in Gay Pride Parades, *43–44, 103, 113*; nationwide, *195–196*; and the recruitment of gays, *9, 12, 13*; as source of status conflict for gay cops, *34–35*; straight cops' opinions of, *34, 37*
Gay Pride Parade, *40, 152*; coming out by marching in, *103–104, 106, 107–108, 113*; straight cops' reactions to, *34, 43–44*
gays (*see also* homosexuality): and activism (*see* gay activism); closeted, *4–5*; coming out, *5*; crimes reported by, in gay locales, *125*; crusing locales of, *125*; gay cops viewed by, *124* (*see also* gay cops: attractiveness to gays of); identity management by, *33*; and long-term relationships, *171, 172, 211*; masculinity and/or femininity of, *3*; media portrayal of, *33, 34, 117*; perceived by cops (*see* cops: views on gays); as police officers (*see* gay cops; lesbian cops); public perception of, *10–12, 41–42, 48, 49–50, 67, 94–95, 101, 117–118, 163, 172, 189, 194, 196, 199, 215*; sexual identity discovered by, *16*; views on cops, *7, 15, 24, 27, 124, 141–143, 146, 209*; violent crimes against, *157–158*; youth emphasized by, *165, 168*
GOAL, *see* Gay Officers Action League
GOAL Gazette, 35–36, 44, 114
Goffman, Erving, *46, 64, 90, 205*

Handler, Rabbi Hillel, *10*
Hedblom, Jack, *163–164*
Hoffman, Martin, *133*
homophobia: in the family, *213*; in law enforcement, *27–31, 35–36, 39–45, 47–49, 52–53, 102, 193, 194, 197, 199–200, 214*; sources of, *117–120*
homosexuality (*see also* gays): activist groups (*see* gay activism); discrimination against prohibited, *9, 11, 13, 22, 28, 29, 40*; laws and policies restricting, *xi, 11, 12*; in the workplace, *204*
homosexuals, *see* gays
Humphreys, Laud, *6, 132*

ICAP, *see* International Association of Chiefs of Police
Institute for Sex Research, *10–11*

International Association of Chiefs of Police (IACP), *8*

Irish Emerald Society, *9*

Jewish Shomrim Society, *9*

Kinsey, Alfred, *46*
Knights of Columbus, *10*
Koch, Ed, *11, 13, 29*

law enforcement (*see also* cops): as antithetical to homosexuality, *xi, 28*; change resisted in, *198–199, 216*; gay cops recruited by, *7–10, 11–15*; gays viewed in (*see* cops: views on gays); and military standards, *9*; moral and professional statuses bound together in, *33*; moral leaders and followers in, *199–200, 215*; unique nature of, *143–144, 205, 211*

lesbian cops, *145*; and AIDS, *161, 162*; attraction of gay women to, *135–136, 137, 138–139*; black, *117, 203*; and coming out, *50, 78, 114–116, 118*; and homophobic co-workers, *42–43*; motivation for career choice of, *21–22, 25, 196–197*; and occupational disclosure, *135–136, 137*; solidarity with gay male cops, *43*

long-term relationships: difficulty of, for gay cops, *168–171, 171–172, 193, 207, 210–211*; sought by gay cops, *139–140, 163–174, 193, 207, 210, 211*; labor divisions in gay cops', *172–174*; versus multiple partners, *167–168*

Los Angeles Police Department, *11, 12, 35, 36, 195*

Madison, Wis., *11*
Matza, David, *205–206*
Miami Beach, Fla., *36*
Minneapolis, Minn., *11*

New Jersey, *11*
New York City, N.Y.: antibias legislation in, *28, 29, 40, 132*; gays in, *133*
New York Police Department (NYPD): Catholic Holy Name Society of, *9*; gays in, *2, 3,* *8, 34*; and the recruitment of gay cops, *9, 11, 13*
NYPD, *see* New York Police Department

occupational disclosure, *134–135, 178, 195, 214*; motives for, *135–139, 206, 209*; motives for secrecy concerning, *139–148, 154–155, 193, 205, 206, 207, 209*
Office of Equal Employment Opportunity, *102*

Patrolman's Benevolent Association (PBA), opposition to recruitment of gay cops by, *8–9, 10, 32, 34*
PBA, *see* Patrolman's Benevolent Association
Philadelphia, Pa., *11, 12*
police, *see* cops
policing, *see* law enforcement
Portland, Ore., *11, 79, 196*

San Francisco, Calif., *195–196*; harassment of gay cops in, *36–37*; and the recruitment of gay cops, *11, 12*; strength of gay community in, *12–13*
Schneider, Joseph, *33*
Seattle, Wash., *11, 196*
Signorile, Michelangelo, *134*
Solomon, Mort, *12*
status conflict: defined, *32*; and the gay cop, *32–33, 123–124*; and gays, *33*; sources of, for gay cops, *33, 34–45*
stigma management, in the workplace, *203–204*

Texas, *11*
Thio, Alex, *172*
Transit Police Department, *20, 21*

Union of Orthodox Rabbis, *10*
United States Supreme Court, *12*

Weinberg, Martin, *133, 171, 211, 212*
Wertheimer, David, *125*
Williams, Colin, *212*
workplace, stigma management in, *203–204*

Zoglin, Richard, *5*

About the Author

Stephen Leinen was a lieutenant in the New York City Police Department and is now retired from the force after twenty-three years of service. He has a Ph.D. in sociology from NYU, teaches part-time at NYU and SUNY, and is the author of *Black Police, White Society*. He lives with his wife, Eleanor, in New York City.